About Island Press

ISLAND PRESS, a nonprofit organization, publishes, markets, and distributes the most advanced thinking on the conservation of our natural resources—books about soil, land, water, forests, wildlife, and hazardous and toxic wastes. These books are practical tools used by public officials, business and industry leaders, natural resource managers, and concerned citizens working to solve both local and global resource problems.

Founded in 1978, Island Press reorganized in 1984 to meet the increasing demand for substantive books on all resource-related issues. Island Press publishes and distributes under its own imprint and offers these services to other nonprofit organizations.

Support for Island Press is provided by The Geraldine R. Dodge Foundation, The Energy Foundation, The Charles Engelhard Foundation, The Ford Foundation, Glen Eagles Foundation, The George Gund Foundation, William and Flora Hewlett Foundation, The John D. and Catherine T. MacArthur Foundation, The Andrew W. Mellon Foundation, The Joyce Mertz-Gilmore Foundation, The New-Land Foundation, The J. N. Pew, Jr., Charitable Trust, Alida Rockefeller, The Rockefeller Brothers Fund, The Rockefeller Foundation, The Tides Foundation, and individual donors.

PAVING OVER THE PAST

PAVING OVER THE PAST

A History and Guide to Civil War Battlefield Preservation

Georgie Boge and Margie Holder Boge

Foreword by James M. McPherson

ISLAND PRESS

Washington, D.C. • *Covelo, California*

To Margaret Honie and Julia Holder

Library of Congress Cataloging-in-Publication Data

Boge, Georgie
Paving over the past : a history and guide to Civil War
Battlefield preservation / Georgie Boge and Margie Holder
Boge : foreword by James M. McPherson.
p.   cm.
Includes bibliographical references and index.
ISBN 1-55963-191-0 (hard : alk. paper).
ISBN 1-55963-192-9 (pbk. : alk. paper)
1. United States—History—Civil War, 1861–1865—
Battlefields—Conservation and
restoration.   2. Battlefields—United States—Conservation
and restoration.
I. Boge, Margie Holder,   II. Title.
E641.864   1993
973.7'3—dc20   93-12198
                                 CIP

Printed on recycled, acid-free paper

Manufactured in the United States of America

10   9   8   7   6   5   4   3   2   1

The land is holy where they fought,
And holy where they fell;
For by their blood that land was bought,
The land they loved so well.

The Soldier's Record of Jericho, 1868

Contents

Abbreviations

ABPP   American Battlefield Protection Program

ACHP   (President's) Advisory Council on Historic Preservation

APCWS   Association for the Preservation of Civil War Sites

CBA   Chantilly Battlefield Association

CCBF   Cedar Creek Battlefield Foundation

CWT   Civil War Trust

DOTA   Department of Transportation Act of 1966

GBMA   Gettysburg Battlefield Memorial Association

GIS   Geographic Information Systems

HPF   Historic Preservation Fund

LWCF   Land and Water Conservation Fund

NEPA   National Environmental Policy Act of 1969

NHPA   National Historic Preservation Act of 1966, as amended

NPS   National Park Service

SBC   Save the Battlefield Coalition

SHAF   Save Historic Antietam Foundation

SHARP   Save Historic Antietam with Responsible Policies

TDR   Transfer-of-Development Rights

Foreword

THE THIRD battle of Manassas in 1988 proved to be as important to the cause of battlefield preservation as either of its predecessors was to the course of the Civil War. The campaign of 1988 began when developer Til Hazel proposed to build a 1.2 million square foot shopping mall on land where General Robert E. Lee's headquarters had been located during the second battle of Manassas in 1862, and also on land where General James Longstreet's corps deployed for its victorious counterattack against the Union army. A coalition of historians, conservationists, and ordinary Americans—concerned about the destruction of a vital part of their heritage—mobilized to stop this paving over of the past. They won the "third" battle of Manassas when Congress enacted a bill to add this hallowed ground to the Manassas National Battlefield Park.

The victory had far-reaching consequences. It galvanized the community of Civil War buffs and historical preservationists. It spawned the Secretary of the Interior's Battlefield Protection Program, the congressional Civil War Sites Advisory Commission, the Civil War Trust, the Association for the Preservation of Civil War Sites, and a host of local battlefield protection organizations. The third battle of Manassas also inspired this book, which began as a senior thesis at Princeton University. *Paving Over the Past* tells the story of that battle in vivid prose, with more details about what happened and more analysis of why it happened than anything else in print. Georgie Boge interviewed every participant in the affair, including the indomitable Annie Snyder, who led the Save the Battlefield Coalition, Senator Dale Bumpers, who brilliantly piloted the bill to acquire the land through Congress, and Til Hazel himself.

But the book is far more than a history of the third battle of Manassas. *Paving Over the Past* is a comprehensive guide to the whole subject of battlefield preservation and provides a concise history of the creation of Civil War battlefield parks. The book also discusses several other important preservation controversies, most notably the complex maneuvers at Brandy Station Battlefield. Throughout, the authors offer a balanced analysis of all sides of these controversies at all levels of government, from local zoning boards to the U.S. government. They describe the numerous ways in which preservation can be accomplished, from fee-simple purchase of threatened sites to farmland tax credits. The most incisive and significant contribution of *Paving Over the Past*, however, is its demonstration that historical preservation can provide more economic benefits to a community than can residential, commercial, or industrial development of the same property. If this seems like heresy, read the book and you will become a convert.

But the most important reason for preservation of Civil War battlefields is not the economic benefits it reaps. On those lands occurred the most momentous events in American history—events that decisively altered the course of national development and shaped the future. We would be a radically different country today had those events not occurred. The Civil War resolved two fundamental, festering problems that had been left unresolved by the Revolution of 1776: whether the precarious experiment of a democratic republic federated in a union of states would survive and whether slavery would continue to mock the ideals of this boasted land of liberty. Union victory preserved the republic and purged it of slavery. But the cost was high—at least 620,000 lives were lost. The battlefields are a monument to the soldiers' supreme sacrifice. To deface the ground on which they fought is to dishonor their memory.

To pave over the past would also make it difficult to understand the battles themselves. An essential part of my research for *Battle Cry of Freedom* was my repeated visits to Civil War battlefields. The hundreds of hours I spent walking and bicycling over them added a crucial dimension to my understanding of what happened there, why it happened, and what it meant. In part, this was simply a matter of visualizing how geography and topography influenced the outcome of a battle—the pattern of fields and woods, hills and valleys, roads and rock outcroppings and rivers. I have taken many people on tours of Civil War battlefields. Most of them had read something about the battles before going there, but it was not until they actually saw the ground that real understanding dawned. Not until they had viewed the three-quarters of a mile of open fields over which Pickett's charge at Gettysburg took place and had walked the ground where those Confederate soldiers trod, had they truly understood why the assault failed. If they had been able to view and walk the attack route of Union troops against Missionary Ridge in Chattanooga, they would also have begun to understand why that seemingly hopeless attack succeeded. Alas, Missionary Ridge is nearly all built over, so we cannot comprehend the contours of that battle by walking the ground as it was in 1863. Battlefields in Nashville, Atlanta, Richmond, Winchester, and elsewhere have similarly disappeared under asphalt and concrete; others are in danger of the same fate.

Understanding the Civil War experience is more than a matter of grasping its topographical and tactical details. Standing on the battlefields, we can experience an emotional empathy with the men who fought there. With a little imagination we can hear the first rebel yell at Manassas, commune with the ghosts that haunt Shiloh, watch with horror as brush fires consume the wounded at the Wilderness, experience the terror of the raw recruits who came under fire for the first time at Perryville, share the anguish of the families of eight hundred unknown soldiers buried in a mass grave at Cold Harbor, or hear the hoarse yells of exhausted survivors of the 20th Maine as they launched a bayonet charge at Little Round Top. I know, because I have been there and have felt these things. And I have seen countless others experience the same emotions.

My most vivid memory of thirty years of teaching at Princeton is a tour of Gettysburg with students in 1987. One of the students had written her senior thesis on Joshua Lawrence Chamberlain, colonel of the 20th Maine at Little Round Top. When we reached the place where the regiment fought and Chamberlain won a medal of honor, the student shed tears of empathy from the emotional intensity of the moment—and so did I.

These kinds of experiences make it possible to appreciate what the Civil War meant for America. But such experiences are impossible at many battlefields, and may become impossible at still more. *Paving Over the Past* will help us prevent that tragedy. As Abraham Lincoln said of Gettysburg in 1863, so can we say of all Civil War battlefields in 1993: "The brave men . . . who struggled here, have consecrated it, far above our poor power to add or detract. The world will little note, nor long remember what we say here, but it can never forget what they did here." We cannot consecrate that ground, but we can desecrate it. To take note and long remember what Georgie and Margie Boge tell us in *Paving Over the Past* will help prevent that desecration. It is for us the living, therefore, to be here dedicated to this great task, so that the world will not forget what they did here.

James M. McPherson

Preface

NEARLY five years have elapsed since the fight to save Manassas thrust the issue of Civil War battlefield preservation into the national spotlight. During this short period, government commissions were appointed, private fund-raising drives inaugurated, and local preservation organizations founded with the single goal of saving the battlefields. Such activities convey the impression that all is well on the battlefield preservation front. A closer inspection reveals that battlefield destruction continues, paralleling the ebb and flow of the real-estate market.

In 1993, the recession poses a new threat to battlefield preservation. Activist property-rights organizations as well as some land developers blame Civil War battlefield preservation efforts for the precipitous drop in property values. The property-rights movement has already inspired the Virginia state legislature to rescind key provisions of its historic preservation program. Many battlefield preservationists fear other state, county, and city governments will follow suit.

The issue of Civil War battlefield preservation should not be construed as a growth-versus-conservation debate. It is really about long-term planning and cultural values. The rolling green fields of Antietam and the craggy heights at Gettysburg's Little Round Top are not just vistas for the pleasure of the park visitor; they are great repositories of American values. Fundamentally, Civil War battlefield preservation forces us to confront the forces that defined our nation. It raises questions relating to private property rights, national heritage, freedom of economic opportunity, and commemoration. Elected officials must determine when a nation's need to preserve its heritage outweighs an individual's private property rights. The choice is fraught with problems. Too often the lure of

short-term economic benefit or political gain has profaned the hallowed ground of Civil War battlefields. Still, this book should not be
viewed as a diatribe against land development or "progress." On the
contrary, it offers a creditable development program designed to
accommodate the needs of both historic preservation *and* economic
growth.

Our intention in analyzing past and present policies formulated to
protect Civil War battlefields is to show why current policies often
fail to guarantee the long-term preservation of Civil War battlefields
and other historic landscapes. Our case studies of endangered sites
introduce the key players and issues in the debate. We also explore
the political machinations of battlefield preservation, with an in-
depth review of the State of Virginia's policies. A detailed cost-
benefit assessment of battlefield preservation is then considered.

Our purpose in writing this book is threefold. First, we hope that
anyone with an interest in Civil War history, land-use planning,
environmental affairs, or historic preservation will find our information both disturbing and enlightening. Moreover, by raising awareness, we hope to generate public support to stem the waves of
destruction. Second, for those individuals who are keenly aware of
the plight of Civil War battlefields, we attempt to explain why many
government and private initiatives have failed to protect our historic
landscapes. Third, we offer a number of conservation models for
local and city planners so at least some progress can be made before
national leaders initiate a comprehensive Civil War battlefield preservation program.

Most of the things that we consider important in this era of American history—the fate of slavery, the structure of society in both North and South, the direction of the American economy, the destiny of competing nationalisms in North and South, the definition of freedom, the very survival of the United States—rested on the shoulders of those weary men in blue and gray who fought it out during four years of ferocity unmatched in the Western world between the Napoleonic Wars and World War I.

James M. McPherson
Battle Cry of Freedom

The Civil War is, for the American imagination, the great single event of our history. Without too much wrenching, it may, in fact, be said to be American history.

—Robert Penn Warren

 1

Civil War Battlefield Preservation: The Dilemma

FOR POTOMAC area residents July 16, 1988, will long be remembered as one of the hottest days of the century. On this day a host of Civil War enthusiasts gathered on a vacant parcel twenty-five miles southwest of Washington, D.C. They were there to generate support for the preservation of a portion of the Manassas battlefield. While a full-scale encampment was being staged by Union and Confederate reenactors, thousands of people milled about the grounds. Children darted around, jostled parents and interrupted conversations. Sundry information booths were hastily set up. Everywhere volunteers hawked T-shirts, bumper stickers, and Civil War memorabilia to raise money to save a 542-acre tract of the battlefield. Bagpipers, blue-grass musicians, and gospel groups provided entertainment. As the day wore on, the sun slowly arced westward, casting down its merciless rays.

When the organized program finally began, a reverent stillness settled through the heat. Across the field tramped scores of soldiers in a solemn parade reminiscent of Civil War days, appropriately called the March of Ghosts. The rally continued with a spirited round of speeches from the podium. Members of Congress joined forces on the hustings with NBC's Willard Scott, President Jimmy Carter's White House press secretary Jody Powell, and Jan Scruggs of the Vietnam Veterans' Memorial Fund. In the crowd stood *New York Times* columnist Tom Wicker, listening to a series of speeches about threatened Civil War sites. They struck a chord. Wicker wrote, "I once felt that the American people were innocent of their history. But I've never seen such an outpouring of support [to save Manassas from the bulldozer's blade] as I do here. . . ."[1]

Some observers tried to dismiss this gathering of five thousand individuals in 104° heat as an isolated local affair. It was not. The struggle to save part of the Manassas battlefield from becoming a shopping mall drew national attention. The media orchestrated a public-awareness campaign. *Time* magazine and CBS's "Sunday Morning" covered the Manassas preservation efforts. *USA Today* ran a front-page story citing the national implications of the rally. Mail poured into the headquarters of the Save the Battlefield Coalition (SBC) from every state of the Union as well as from Germany, England, and Japan.

Less than three months after the Manassas rally, a smaller but no less impassioned show of support occurred on the floor of the United States Senate. On Friday October 7, 1988, Senator Dale Bumpers (D-Arkansas) approached the chamber's well.[2] The hour was late. Legislators were anxious to return home for weekend campaign appearances. Elections were just weeks away. To Bumpers's astonishment a large contingent of senators remained on the floor for his decidedly Southern interpretation of the Second Battle of Manassas. With maps as props, the senator detailed battles and pointed out the William Center tract that might someday be lost to development:

> [Longstreet] sent out a couple of brigades to see what the strength of the Union was. . . . And he found out that the Union was there in strength. He pulled those brigades back and deployed all 30,000 of his men in woods. . . . You go down there right now and you will see where Longstreet had his men deployed behind all those trees down there. . . .
>
> Sixteen thousand men in about 48 hours either lost their lives or were wounded in this battle. It was perhaps the third bloodiest battle of the war. . . .

I told you about these hospitals. They are our Confederate troops buried on this property around the hospitals. . . . I believe strongly in our heritage and I think our children ought to know where these battlefields are and what was involved in them. I do not want to go out there 10 years from now with my grandson and tell him about the Second Battle of Manassas.

He says, "Well, Grandpa, wasn't General Lee in control of this war here? Didn't he command the Confederate troops?"

"Yes, he did."

"Well, where was he?"

"He [was] up there where that shopping mall is."

I can see a big granite monument inside that mall's hallway right now: "General Lee stood on this spot."

Senator Bumpers concluded his history lesson with a challenge to his colleagues: "If you really cherish our heritage as I do and you believe that history is very important for our children, you will vote for my amendment."[3] The nation's historic integrity was at stake.

History endows society with a sense of purpose and provides answers to the fundamental question of what defines a nation. This is no revelation to Americans: The insatiable drive to discover our heritage shows no signs of diminishing. In the past twenty years alone, the National Endowment for the Humanities reports, the number of historical organizations in the United States has doubled from five thousand to more than ten thousand.[4]

The desire to explore our past is no more clearly exemplified than in the popularity of Civil War history. One hundred and twenty-five years after General Robert E. Lee's surrender at Appomattox, thousands of reenactors still gather on the rolling hills of Fredericksburg and Gettysburg to relive the horrors of war. Dressed in authentically reproduced blue and gray uniforms, these living-history activists brandish weapons and march for miles in the biting cold of winter and the suffocating heat of summer to pay tribute to their fallen heroes. Other Civil War enthusiasts prefer less strenuous activity, content to remain at home poring over firsthand accounts of Johnny Reb and Billy Yank. They can choose from hundreds of new

books and pamphlets published each year or from the fifty thousand previously published works that analyze every aspect of the
war. More books have been written on the Civil War than on any
other event in American history. Roundtable associations, popular
and professional Civil War magazines, television documentaries,
and relic-collecting clubs provide countless opportunities for America's quarter million Civil War buffs to sate their fascination with
this fratricidal conflict. The number of recent books and films
achieving critical acclaim—among them James M. McPherson's *Battle Cry of Freedom,* Gore Vidal's *Lincoln,* the movie *Glory,* as well as
the PBS Civil War documentary produced by Ken Burns, which
attracted approximately 39 million viewers—vividly attests to the
widespread appeal of Civil War history.[5]

Edwin Bearss, chief historian of the National Park Service (NPS),
describes the popularity of Civil War history as cyclical. He argues
that an interest in Civil War history began in the 1890s when Union
and Confederate veterans sought to heal old wounds by holding
massive reunions at Civil War sites across the country. Popularity
surged again in the 1920s when the newly instituted five-day work
week provided ample leisure time for people to indulge in the study
of Civil War history. Henry Ford's automobile fueled this renewed
interest by enabling enthusiasts to explore once-inaccessible battlefields. Then America refreshed its memory during the Civil War
Centennial from 1961 to 1965. Today, as we have seen, fascination
with Civil War history has reached new heights and shows no signs
of dwindling.[6]

America's infatuation with Civil War history has several sources.
Unlike our more recent wars, the Civil War was not a depersonalized
conflict fought abroad. Rather, it was an internecine struggle, a
violent clash of values contested on American soil. It was also the
first major war that produced a thorough written legacy. Scholars
and lay historians alike enjoy relatively easy access to material contained in soldiers' diaries, government documents, personal letters,
and chronicles written by leading generals and enlisted men. On a
more personal level, many Americans can trace their lineage to at
least one Civil War veteran, familial ties that offer an emotional,

almost palpable link to the past. And because it was uniquely America's war, pitting brother against brother, all Americans regardless of family history derive a sense of what it means to be American through study of the Civil War.

What was its legacy? Four long years of suffering, destruction, and tragedy settled once and for all the question of whether or not a democratic republic could survive. The loose confederation of states created by the founding fathers between 1776 and 1783 was now strengthened with a sovereign federal government, while secession ceased to exist as a viable political option. Blessed with a government that had withstood the test of time, America became "a nation, only with the Civil War," wrote Robert Penn Warren.[7] The war also decided a number of social questions, most notably, of course, whether slavery could exist within a democratic republic. It did not, however, resolve the issue of race relations, as policymakers' ongoing attempts or lack thereof to address problems in this area make clear. Dr. John Boles, editor of the *Journal of Southern History*, attributes much of the new interest in the Civil War to the civil rights movement: "People wanted to know why in this land of the free we still had second-class citizens."[8] The war shaped America's social, economic, and political character in a number of other ways. It inspired passage of the Thirteenth, Fourteenth, and Fifteenth Amendments. It influenced women's domination in the fields of clerical work, teaching, and nursing. Modern phenomena like the income tax and the national banking system developed during the Civil War era.[9] And, more generally, as President Woodrow Wilson remarked in 1913, the Civil War "created in this country what had never existed before—a national consciousness. It was not the salvation of the Union, it was the rebirth of the Union."[10]

The Value of Civil War Battlefields

Civil War battlefields are essential for helping us comprehend the significance of this tumultuous conflict. Visitors are not drawn by

flashy neon signs, bargain tourist shops, or recreational opportunities but rather by curiosity and profound reverence for the
soldiers who fell in a war of clashing ideals. Battlefields enable
visitors to visualize conflicts in a way that shrines cannot. Stone
monuments etched with the names of lives spent and battles fought
belie the trauma of war. It is almost impossible to understand, for
example, the miserable failure of the Pickett-Pettigrew charge at
Gettysburg or the mastery of Jackson's campaign in the Shenandoah Valley without access to an unspoiled fraction of the site. Thus
battlefields are unparalleled teaching tools, far more effective than
textbooks in chronicling the drama of war. They enable students to
learn about the sacrifices borne by the likes of the Pelican Rifles
(Third Louisiana Infantry), the Fifty-fourth Massachusetts Regiment, and the Thirty-third Illinois Teachers' Regiment, and to picture how and why more than twenty-three thousand casualties
occurred in a single day at Antietam. The Antietam cornfield dramatically demonstrates what no written word could convey. Battlefields are also scholarly tools: Academics researching particular
campaigns encounter a lamentable dearth of evidence when battle
sites have been buried under residential or industrial projects.

Preservation is not justified solely on educational or academic
grounds. More importantly, Civil War battlefields are solemn monuments to human tragedy. More than 620,000 soldiers and an unknown number of civilians perished in the Civil War; altogether,
more Americans died in the Civil War than in all other American
wars combined. Battlefields puncture myths about the glory of war.
The land is consecrated in the blood of men who died fighting for
principles—not for land, or money, or personal advancement. Perhaps the greatest tribute to the sanctity of Civil War battlefields
was offered by President Abraham Lincoln in his Gettysburg Address: ". . . in a larger sense, we can not dedicate—we can not
consecrate—we can not hallow this ground. The brave men, living
and dead, who struggled here, have consecrated it, far above our
poor power to add or detract. The world will little note, nor long
remember what we say here, but it can never forget what they did
here."[11]

The Conflict: Preservation and Development

Unfortunately, the very places where visitors can learn about and connect with the past are seriously endangered by development pressures. Urban encroachment threatens to destroy Civil War battlefields formerly protected by rural countryside. Jerry Rogers, associate director of cultural resources at NPS, claims "there isn't a battlefield in the country that doesn't have to be watched on a daily basis."[12] Those battlefields receiving protection under the auspices of the NPS are still threatened by development on adjacent lands, viewsheds (landscape visible from the battlefield), and inholdings (private land within a park unit). And the boundaries of all national battlefield parks except Pea Ridge have been whittled away so they are far smaller than historians and master planners recommended at the time of establishment. Poorly defined boundaries at Gettysburg, for instance, encourage development on historically significant tracts supposedly owned by the federal government. Open space bordering preserved battlefields provides an ideal opportunity for builders to construct developments like the Battlefield Business Park near Manassas. Mike Johnson, chief ranger of the Fredericksburg-Spotsylvania County Battlefields National Military Park, cautions, "Most developers in the Fredericksburg area today recognize the park as an economic force . . . [that can] actually enhance their development."[13]

Battlefields that primarily rely on state or local protection usually receive less of it than those protected at the national level. State preservation efforts vary widely and are largely determined by political machinations and fiscal constraints. All too often, preservation responsibilities are delegated to local governments that are ill-equipped to protect significant historic resources. While cities and counties have the option of enacting preservation ordinances, few acknowledge the threat of impending development before it is too late. Many rural areas lack county master plans and zoning ordinances. Developers who flock to rural communities, attracted by cheap land and lax zoning regulations, occasionally begin construction on historically significant sites. According to Ian Spatz of the National Trust for Historic Preservation, "We don't have a way to save these places where [local] people with control over them don't care about saving them, whereas there is a large constituency across the United States that favors them. That is where the system has broken down."[14] Unprotected by national and state government regulations or by preservation-oriented nonprofit organizations, Civil War sites frequently fall victim to the financial needs of landowners and the political orientation of local boards of supervisors.

The Civil War was fought not in cities or in urban areas but in the countryside. Preservation advocates working in the nineteenth and early twentieth centuries never imagined that urban encroachment would eventually threaten the integrity of rural battlefields. They simply embarked on a program of placing commemorative markers on land they believed would always retain its agricultural character. Preservationists, developers, and government officials all agree that most unpreserved Civil War battlefields will vanish within a few years if the present pace of development continues unabated. Demographic data indicates that more Americans are moving to rural areas than ever before. This will certainly intensify developmental pressures already threatening significant Civil War sites. A comprehensive study completed by the Conservation Fund revealed that fifty-four Civil War battlefields require immediate protection; sixteen of them are totally unprotected.[15]

Already in Virginia, Chantilly (Ox Hill), large portions of First and Third Winchester, much of the Richmond-Petersburg earthworks, and essential portions of the Fredericksburg battlefield have disappeared under the bulldozer's blade. County rezoning has reached the final stages for a major industrial/residential complex at Brandy Station, the location of the largest cavalry engagement on the North American continent. Residential housing has gradually enveloped Cold Harbor, Spotsylvania, and the Wilderness. Elsewhere, battle sites at Nashville and Atlanta were lost to development more than forty years ago. A. Wilson Greene, executive director of the Association for the Preservation for Civil War Sites, (APCWS), recently

Conflicting skirmish lines, Steinwehr Avenue, Gettysburg, Pennsylvania, looking northwest. The area near the NPS's cyclorama and visitors center, Steinwehr Avenue/Business Route 15 (also known as the Emmitsburg Road), is still a "battle line" between historic preservation and incompatible development. In the foreground, the monument and flank markers of the memorial for companies G and I, Fourth Ohio Volunteers, mark the approximate position of those Buckeyes on the Yankee skirmish line late on 2 July 1863. They stand in stark contrast to today's fast-food establishments. (Elwood W. Christ)

conjectured that "by the turn of the century, almost the whole corridor [of real estate] between Gettysburg and Petersburg will be developed. So what we save in the next decade is what we're going to save from now on."[16]

This is not to say that development does not confer benefits upon a locality. Economic growth can bring jobs, tax revenues, and social amenities. Industrial development offers tax benefits without demanding costly residential services such as extensive police and fire protection or schools. Construction of parks, roads, sewer systems, and other municipal services under proffer agreements negotiated between zoning officials and developers provides benefits previously beyond a community's financial means. If people enter an area to shop in recently constructed stores or resettle as employees of newly established industries, communities reap additional economic benefits.

The value of development raises a fundamental question pertaining to private property rights. The Fifth Amendment to the U.S. Constitution confirms the right of private land ownership by prohibiting the taking of private property "for public use without just compensation." Nevertheless, for almost one hundred years the federal government has been vested with the power of eminent domain to acquire property of national significance. Case in point, Manassas. Although courts have generally recognized the right of government to protect certain resources for the public good, America's deeply ingrained tradition of private property rights can and does present a major barrier to the cause of historic preservation.

A Cooperative Planning Approach

Seemingly, the goals of historic preservation and land development are irreconcilable. Leo Marx, author of *The Machine in the Garden*, explains that the divide between our reverence for "unspoiled" nature and our enduring devotion to "progress" far surpasses any other rifts in the American national character.[17] But with intensive effort, a balance can be achieved without fundamentally compromising an area's economic growth or the nation's need to preserve its most significant historic resources. Preserved battlefields offer numerous opportunities for communities to establish lucrative tourism industries without the major service costs associated with permanent residents. Preservation is also an ideal complement to environmental as well as community goals. Public demands for the aesthetic benefits of "green space" may provide the necessary impetus for developers to preserve at least some Civil War battlefields. Preservation advocates readily acknowledge that it is impossible to preserve all ten thousand sites of Union and Confederate battles and skirmishes.[18] Therefore the task at hand is not one of choosing between preservation and development but rather one of formulating a policy of *planned* development.

Preservation of Civil War battlefields warrants an unprecedented level of cooperation among all levels of government and the private sector. The federal budget deficit and a political agenda averse to federal land acquisition have severely limited the potential for traditional approaches to protection. Similarly, funding constraints at the state and local levels have restricted preservation endeavors to only the most significant parcels of land. Given the current fiscal and political climate, cooperative ventures involving innovative zoning, easements (legal restrictions on property use), and government–private sector partnerships would be the most practical way to save America's battlefields. All such efforts must be premised on the fact that it is possible to reconcile the goals of resource protection and economic development through planned policy. Future generations may not have to grapple with the preservation dilemma. The choice will already have been made for them.

The Example of Civil War Battlefields

The conflict between battlefield preservation and development interests illustrates the types of problems confronting most of America's historical, cultural, and natural resources. Representatives of SBC at Manassas recognize the relevance of Civil War battlefield preservation to the national preservation agenda: "The emerging national coalition is predicated on the belief that what is at stake here goes well beyond Manassas. Throughout the land, Civil War and Revolutionary battlefields—as well as many other units of the National Park System—are threatened. . . . The fight to protect summons all."[19] Policy decisions regarding Civil War battlefields will significantly influence our nation's long-term approach to the protection of other historical, cultural, and natural resources. A rare opportunity exists for the creation of innovative preservation arrangements. Our response to the current preservation dilemma will determine the value we place as a country on historic, cultural, and natural as opposed to solely economic resources.

The fate of the preservation movement rests with the American people. Fortunately, as journalist Roger Mudd reports, "Most Americans have a love affair with their parks and their battlefields and their rivers and with knowing what America was like."[20] Until very recently, this custodial relationship toward resources peacefully coexisted with private property rights. Accustomed to a seemingly unlimited supply of land, people rejected the notion of governmental action to guarantee the survival of public assets. But in the wake of widespread development Americans have begun to reevaluate the idea of open space as nothing but land ripe for the taking. As Pulitzer Prize–winning author Wallace Stegner points out, "We need to remind ourselves constantly that the land resource itself is what must be served; that like liberty, democracy, all the freedoms guaranteed by the Constitution, like everything we truly value to the point where we might die for it, the heritage of our public lands is not a fact but a responsibility, an obligation, a task. A pleasure."[21]

The American public must now accept responsibility for protecting these land resources through concrete policy action. It *is* feasible to preserve historic, cultural, and natural resources without incurring major economic costs—if, that is, we stop characterizing the debate as one simply of preservation versus development.

A nation with no regards for its past will do little worth remembering in the future.

—Abraham Lincoln

 2

Early Preservation Efforts

AMERICA'S historic preservation movement began in the mid-1800s when disparate local groups organized to save individual buildings threatened by demolition or historically inappropriate renovation.[1] Most of the groups attempted to protect buildings where famous people had resided or historic events had occurred. Preservation of architectural treasures and historic sites other than buildings was not yet a consideration.[2] Mount Vernon serves as one of the best examples of early grassroots preservation. The owner of George Washington's famous home demanded more money than either the federal government or the Commonwealth of Virginia was willing to pay. Furthermore, prospective buyers proposed to convert the property into a hotel. The mansion had begun to deteriorate from neglect when finally Miss Ann Pamela Cunningham and a number of prominent Virginia women launched a successful fund-raising drive to purchase the home. More than a century later, the Mount Vernon Ladies' Association of the Union still owns and operates the home.

Despite growing public interest in the 1800s, state and local governments refrained from active participation in the preservation movement. Most government officials regarded historic preservation as a private-sector responsibility. Accordingly, governments only intervened to protect a historic site after intensive grassroots lobbying efforts. For example, the City of Philadelphia responded to numerous public demonstrations, petitions, and letters in support of preserving the old state capitol by purchasing the structure in 1816.[3] It was not until many years later, in 1872, that the federal government joined the preservation movement with the creation of the first national park at Yellowstone. Four years later, during the centennial commemoration of the Revolutionary War, Congress began to review several issues directly related to historic preservation. Between 1880 and 1886, legislators introduced eight separate bills concerning Revolutionary War battlefield preservation. None was enacted, but "these bills and the accompanying committee hearings raised important questions of national historic preservation policy in Congress for the first time."[4]

The Evolution from National Cemeteries

Between 1890 and 1899, federal government acquisition of five Civil War battlefields—Chickamauga and Chattanooga (Georgia and Tennessee), Antietam (Maryland), Shiloh (Tennessee), Gettysburg (Pennsylvania), and Vicksburg (Mississippi)—laid the cornerstone for national historic preservation policy.[5] The national cemetery system became a blueprint for a battlefield preservation program. During the Civil War several states and localities had established cemeteries in the wake of major battles. The Gettysburg Soldiers' National Cemetery, acquired and laid out days after the July 1863 battle, set the standard in form and landscaping for more than seventy soldier and sailor cemeteries established in the years after 1866. In 1867, after determining that the creation and protection of soldiers' cemeteries were a federal responsibility, Congress passed a general measure "to establish and to protect national cemeteries." Following President Andrew Johnson's approval of the measure, the War Department embarked on a program of establishing and developing cemeteries and acquiring certain cemeteries administered by local commissions.

Custer Battlefield National Cemetery was among those created by army decree, but its final boundary marked a significant departure from previous federal policy. Ten years after the cemetery's establishment, a large number of fallen soldiers still reposed in shallow, hastily dug field graves. Rather than pursuing a policy of excavating bodies, President Grover Cleveland signed an executive order that greatly expanded the cemetery's boundaries. Key areas of the battlefield site believed to contain skeletal remains were incorporated as part of the national cemetery. Hence the general authority granted to Congress for the creation of national cemeteries was expanded to preserve a battlefield. Congress eventually established national military parks or battlefield sites in the vicinities of eleven national cemeteries without retitling or abolishing the cemeteries.[6] For example, in 1870 Congress directed the secretary of war to accept and take charge of the Antietam National Cemetery at Sharpsburg, Maryland. Seven years later, Congress appropriated fifteen thousand dollars to pay the balance of indebtedness to the cemetery's board of trustees. The late 1880s saw Congress appropriating funds for the construction of a road from Antietam Station to the national cemetery. Federal funds were also forthcoming to survey, mark, and preserve the lines of battle at Antietam. Thus was born Antietam National Battlefield.

Fort Donelson, in northern Tennessee, offers another example. After the general legislation for national cemeteries passed in 1867, the War Department acquired fifteen acres of "burial" land near Dover, Tennessee, a site once occupied by a federal garrison. Insufficient funds hampered improvements at this cemetery, as reinterring the skeletal remains of soldiers became too expensive. Moreover, in those early days few visitors came to the cemetery to pay their respects. Somehow the cemetery survived, becoming the nucleus for Fort Donelson National Military Park, established in 1928. Other national cemeteries that evolved into parks or battlefield sites include Shiloh (1894), Gettysburg (1895), Vicksburg (1899), and Fredericksburg and Spotsylvania County Battlefields Memorial National Military Park (1927).[7]

Early National Military Parks

The establishment of Gettysburg National Cemetery preceded the creation of Gettysburg National Park. Veterans' groups regarded the preservation of battlefields as an integral part and symbolic gesture of national reunification. Fearing that the Civil War would be forgotten in the next generation, veterans pushed for the creation of the Gettysburg Battlefield Memorial Association (GBMA). Chartered on April 30, 1864, GBMA was one of the earliest historic preservation organizations in the country. In 1880, GBMA asked for assistance in undertaking and completing a survey of the battlefield. On June 6, 1881, President James A. Garfield, a Civil War veteran, signed into law a congressional bill calling for a survey of the battlefield. This study, conducted by John B. Bachelder, provided for the accurate marking and mapping of troop positions in the battlefield.[8]

In 1890, a bill to establish the park was rejected by the House Military Affairs Committee on grounds that certain areas of the battlefield were already owned by a private, state-chartered organization. It had received support from the Grand Army of the Republic, an organization established by Civil War veterans of the Union army and navy. The GBMA intensified the Grand Army of the Republic's activist role at Gettysburg by focusing nationwide attention on preservation activities and by enlisting support from almost every northern state. In 1887, Pennsylvania state legislators appropriated sufficient funds for the GBMA to make additional land purchases at Culp's Hill, Little Round Top, and East Cemetery Hill. By 1890 the GBMA had acquired "several hundred acres of land on the [Gettysburg] battlefield including the Wheatfield, land adjacent to Spangler's Spring, the Peach Orchard as well as the small, white-frame house Gen. Meade had used as his headquarters."[9] GBMA later opened miles of roads along the Union lines of battle and coordinated the erection of three hundred monuments by states and regiments.

In 1894, Congressman Daniel E. Sickles, a highly controversial former Union general, called for the establishment of a national military military park at Gettysburg.[10] It was largely due to his leadership of the Third Corps at Gettysburg, coupled with his political know-how, that Gettysburg was preserved. Undaunted by opposition to his proposals, Sickles introduced legislation authorizing the secretary of war to accept a deed of conveyance for all lands owned by GBMA, approximately 800 acres. Moreover, the secretary would gain authority to "acquire additional lands on the [Gettysburg] battlefield, not exceeding in area the parcels shown on a map prepared by Gen. Sickles, which were occupied by the infantry, cavalry and artillery on the first, second and third days of July 1863."[11] Congress inserted this provision as a means of securing Confederate representation in the national park. The Sickles bill passed both houses of Congress and was signed into law by President Grover Cleveland in January 1895. Over the next eight years government officials acquired certain privately owned and unmarked tracts once trod upon by the Army of Northern Virginia.

In 1893, two years before the establishment of the national military park, the Gettysburg Electric Railway Company announced plans to build a tourist line through the Little Round Top–Devil's Den area. Members of the GBMA expressed concern and urged Congress to enact protective legislation. Their recommendations were heeded, and on June 6, 1894, Congress passed a joint resolution proclaiming an "imminent danger" and noting "that portions of said battlefield may be irreparably defaced by the construction of a railway car over same."[12] The secretary of war later obtained authority to acquire the threatened land by purchase or condemnation. When the railway company refused to negotiate terms for the government purchase, the attorney general initiated condemnation proceedings. Claiming that the establishment of Gettysburg National Park was not a public purpose, the railway company disputed the legality of government condemnation for historic preservation.

The Supreme Court's decision in *United States v. Gettysburg Electric Railway Company* resolved two fundamental questions related to the future of national preservation policy: Does preservation of a historic battlefield site qualify as a public purpose, and if yes, does Congress have the authority to acquire relevant tracts of land through the power of eminent domain? Justice Rufus Wheeler Peckham announced the court's unanimous ruling on January 27, 1896:

> Can it be that the government is without power to preserve the land, and properly mark out the various sites upon which this struggle took place? Can it not erect the monuments provided for by these acts of Congress, or even take possession of the field of battle, in the name and for the benefit of all the citizens of the

country, for the present and for the future? Such a use seems necessarily not only a public use, but one so closely connected with the welfare of the republic itself as to be within the powers granted Congress by the Constitution for the purpose of protecting and preserving the whole country.[13]

Before the 1890s, the idea of federal acquisition of land for purposes of historic preservation was rarely considered. The Supreme Court's landmark decision in the *Gettysburg Electric Railway* case determined that preservation of historic resources was indeed a responsibility and a purpose of the U.S. government.

While the Gettysburg dispute was being fought in the courts, two national battlefield parks were established in the Civil War's western theater. The government created the nation's first national military park at Chickamauga and Chattanooga in 1890, then Shiloh National Military Park in 1894. In many ways these parks manifested a growing public sentiment of national unity. Immediately after the peace accord at Appomattox there had been almost no preservation activity in the South. Unlike their Northern counterparts, embittered residents of Southern communities possessed neither the financial means nor the personal sensibility necessary to effect a policy of preservation. Four long years of battle fought mainly on Confederate soil had destroyed the economic base of the South. Many Southerners believed preservation would merely serve as a reminder of the terrible losses suffered in life, property, and economic vitality. The passing of time mellowed these feelings. Twenty years after the war concerned citizens began to protest the absence of a national battlefield park commemorating the actions of both Southern and Northern soldiers. In 1889, one year after the Crawfish Springs reunion, a coalition of Confederate veterans, Union veterans, and local residents formed the Chickamauga Memorial Association in hopes of convincing Congress to create a truly national military park. At the time, the properties owned by the GBMA protected only Union positions and featured only Northern memorials. Less than a year later the House Committee on Military Affairs issued a report recommending the establishment of a national military park at Chickamauga and Chattanooga: "The preservation for national study of the lines of decisive battles, especially when the tactical movements were unusual both in numbers and military ability, and when the field embraced natural difficulties, may properly be regarded as a matter of national importance."[14]

Congress passed the final bill, which was signed into law by President Benjamin Harrison, on August 19, 1890. The act confirmed the House committee's ideals by stating that the purpose of a park is for "preserving and suitably marking [an area] for historical and professional military study." The criteria used by the committee to establish the military park became the standard against which all future park proposals would be reviewed.[15]

Legislation creating Shiloh National Military Park found its rationale not only in historic significance but also in geographical balance: "In order that the armies of the southwest which served in the Civil War like their comrades of the eastern armies of Gettysburg and those of the central west at Chickamauga may have the history of one of their memorable battles preserved on the ground where they fought. . . ."[16] In 1894, nine months after U.S. Representative David Henderson introduced legislation, President Cleveland signed a bill authorizing the creation of a 3,000-acre national military park at Shiloh. Another site, at Vicksburg, was the last major battlefield park created by Congress in the nineteenth century. Legislators initially questioned the logic of establishing one more battlefield in honor of the armies of the southwest. Widespread public support and three endorsements by the Grand Army of the Republic eventually convinced Congress to act.

Congress justified the preservation of Vicksburg by the site's historic significance. On February 21, 1899, President William McKinley signed enabling legislation that outlined Congress's purpose for preserving the area: "In order to commemorate the campaign, siege, and defense of Vicksburg, and to preserve the history of the battles and operations of the siege and defense on the ground where they were fought and carried on, the battlefield of Vicksburg. . . ."[17] Once again, a grassroots effort based on the historic significance of a site led to the preservation of a Civil War battlefield.

Significance of the Early Preservation Efforts

The ultimate success of these early initiatives rested on the effectiveness of a unique coalition. Favorable political and economic conditions in the aftermath of the Civil War provided an ideal background for veterans, railroad magnates, and the army to promote the cause of battlefield preservation. Veterans, many of whom by the late nineteenth century had achieved political and economic power, performed as adept lobbyists at the local, state, and federal levels. Their efforts were significantly bolstered by powerful railroad corporations. Unfurling the banner of patriotism, the railroads successfully disguised their true motives—the lucrative benefits of increased tourism. War Department officials formed the final component of this alliance in order to guarantee the protection of certain battlefields for on-site study.[18]

Overall, the Department of War profoundly influenced the size, design, and purpose of the first four national battlefield parks. Several bills passed by Congress expressly highlighted the practice of military tactics and strategy as one of the principal reasons for supporting the creation of military parks. Three of the four national military parks encompassed especially large tracts of land because of "military necessity." Military maneuvers requiring large tracts and involving both the army and national guard were conducted at Chickamauga. General acceptance of the "military necessity" clause can be discerned from the nomenclature utilized in the early 1890s as compared with that at the end of the decade.[19] Shiloh and Vicksburg were established as national military parks, while Gettysburg and Chickamauga and Chattanooga were originally designated only as national parks.

Historian Ronald F. Lee summarizes as follows the preservation policies established during the creation of the first four national military parks:

1. Federal acquisition of private land for historic preservation was accepted as a public good. Historic areas could be ob-

tained through donation, purchase, or eminent domain, if necessary.

2. Congress adopted a policy of preserving battlefields as they appeared at the time of the conflict.

3. The federal government formed three-man commissions operating under the general authority of the secretary of war to manage each military park. This policy signaled a tacit recognition that "specialized knowledge was required to ascertain, mark and preserve the main line of battle and the cultural features of the terrain." .

4. Financial responsibility for the preservation of these early battlefields was divided between federal and state governments.

The federal government purchased or acquired the land through donation, constructed access roads, delineated the major lines of battle, and exercised management authority over the parks. Each state government involved in a cooperative venture was expected to mark and commemorate the activities of its troops. Ronald Lee described the implication of these early policies: "The groundwork had now been fully laid for a phase of the historic preservation movement that was to go on for over seventy years, and still continues."[20]

History from 1900 to 1920

Historic preservation in the early decades of the twentieth century was characterized by a policy of centralization and reorganization. Initially, members of Congress introduced thirty-four bills to create twenty-three additional historic sites between 1901 and 1904. House Military Affairs Committee staff members calculated that passage of all thirty-four legislative items would require a federal outlay of $2 million. These bills extended beyond the realm of Civil War battlefield preservation and involved a number of other historic sites. Adding to the confusion associated with the overwhelming number of proposed bills, systematic management of the established national military parks had become virtually impossible. In the absence of stringent federal supervision, the numerous park commissions functioned as autonomous entities.[21] At this stage, Congress agreed it was time to enact a general historic preservation policy. Decision-making on a case-by-case basis was no longer a viable option.

Government procurement of the first four military parks had involved the acquisition of massive tracts of land which many legislators felt was unnecessary given their isolated locations. In addition, with the exception of Vicksburg these sites had been relatively expensive. Hoping to explore ways to achieve historic preservation without incurring such cost, the House Military Affairs Committee held a hearing on April 2, 1902. Testifying before the committee, Brigadier General Breckenridge Davis, himself a Civil War veteran and chairman of the Commission for Publication of the *Official Records of the War of the Rebellion*, fundamentally altered the course of battlefield preservation in the United States. His proposal, later known as the Antietam plan, guided the War Department's approach to battlefield preservation until the national military parks were transferred to the Department of the Interior in 1933.[22]

General Davis recommended that the government curb preservation costs by drastically restricting the amount of land purchased at each battlefield site. Instead of acquiring an entire battlefield, General Davis suggested that the government procure land along roadways and narrow tracts delineating the lines of battle, as it had at the Antietam National Battlefield Site established on August 30, 1890. Aside from the construction of several roads and the erection of a number of historic markers, the agricultural setting of the battlefield area would supposedly remain intact. According to General Davis, "If it is the purpose of Congress to perpetuate this field in the condition in which it was when the battle was fought, it should undertake to perpetuate an agricultural community. . . . That was its condition in 1862, and that is the condition in which it should be preserved."[23] Members of the House Military Affairs Committee were instantly attracted by the economic benefits of the new plan. Committee chairman Richard W. Parker of New Jersey issued a favorable report to Congress on May 14, 1902. Congress, however, assumed that the areas surrounding battlefields were isolated from the threat of urban encroachment and would always retain their agricultural character. This critical assumption sowed the seeds for future destruction of America's Civil War battlefields.

The next battlefield preservation task Congress tackled concerned the growing number of national military park commissions. One of the first pieces of legislation introduced on this subject called for a transfer of management authority for federally protected Civil War battlefields from relatively autonomous battlefield commissions to a centralized, five-member body. Later, after some members expressed concern over limiting the scope of legislation to Civil War battlefields alone, the chairman of the House Committee on Military Affairs introduced a new bill that granted a national military park commission "general power" over "battlefields, forts, cemeteries, or parts thereof, of the colonial, Revolutionary, Indian or Civil Wars of the United States, as may hereafter be acquired by the United States, and to establish military parks thereon."[24] Chairman Parker's bill also provided the commission with authority and funds for acquisition of historically significant tracts as long as each expenditure was limited to five thousand dollars. Even though the House Committee on Military Affairs favorably reported the bill to Congress on six separate occasions, vociferous opposition by individual battlefield commissioners thwarted any chances of passage.

The absence of a central commission, coupled with the onset of World War I, resulted in a lapse in battlefield preservation activity. Only five bills authorizing minimal land acquisitions received congressional approval between 1900 and 1925. In 1912 Congress finally transferred authority from individual battlefield park commissions to the secretary of war.[25] Four years later it created the NPS, an administrative body within the Department of the Interior. The National Park Service Organic Act of 1916 explicitly linked historic preservation with the purposes of national parks by stating that they exist "to conserve the scenery and the natural and historic objects, and the wildlife and to provide for the enjoyment of the same in such a manner and by such means as will leave them unimpaired for the enjoyment of future generations."[26] The 1916 act was eventually interpreted as offering two alternative means of historic preservation under the auspices of the NPS. Historic sites and structures within the park system itself, whether in natural, historic, or cultural areas, were automatically accorded protection. The NPS also provided limited protection for historic sites and structures located on other federal lands and on private property. Although the national military parks remained within the War Department's jurisdiction, the 1916 act provided the foundation for future transfer of authority to the NPS.

Executive branch activity during this period was limited to passage of the Antiquities Act of 1906. The act enabled the president to designate as national monuments "historical landmarks, historic and prehistoric structures, and other objects of historic or scientific interest" located on federal lands. John M. Fowler, deputy executive director of the president's Advisory Council on Historic Preservation (ACHP), explained that this transfer of authority from the legislative to the executive branch "eventually evolved into today's administrative system for the identification, evaluation and designation of a historic property."[27]

History from 1920 to 1933

In the postwar climate of the 1920s, automobiles and better roads spawned a renewed interest in historic preservation. In 1926 alone legislators introduced twenty-eight bills pertaining to historic preservation, fourteen of which called for the creation of new national military parks. Before any decisions were made on the pending legislation, Noble Johnson of Indiana, chairman of the House Military Affairs Committee, called for a general battlefield-site study. Congress had already approved two independent studies of the Fredericksburg (1924) and Petersburg (1925) battlefield sites. On June 11, 1926, following congressional approval of the Johnson committee recommendations, President Calvin Coolidge signed legislation directing the War Department to complete a general study of all

American battlefields. This was the first time Congress had mandated a major appraisal of its battlefield resources.

The War Department subsequently directed the Army War College to devise a classification scheme. Under the direction of Colonel Howard Landers, officials placed each battlefield into one of three major categories and, if applicable, a subcategory. Those sites placed in class I merited designation as national military parks. Gettysburg, Vicksburg, and Chickamauga and Chattanooga were the only Civil War battlefields selected to receive a class I ranking. Despite its congressionally mandated status as a national military park, Shiloh was not placed among the other class I battlefields. Most class II battlefields warranted recognition as national monuments; however, some of the sites were further subdivided into class IIa and IIb categories. Battlefields assigned to class IIa merited a series of markers or tablets indicating the location of battle lines, although not necessarily commemorative monuments. Class IIb battlefields would be identified by some type of monument, tablet, or marker.

Secretary of War Dwight Davis endorsed the Army War College's classification system and urged legislative action. In 1926 Congress passed an act directing the secretary of war to complete "studies and investigation and, where necessary, surveys of all battlefields within the continental limits of the U.S. . . . with a view to preparing a general plan and such detailed projects as may be required."[28] Until the secretary issued his report, the acquisition of additional land for military parks was prohibited. Finally, between 1926 and 1932 the War Department completed a comprehensive national survey of battlefields utilizing the threefold classification criteria developed by the Army War College.

On the basis of recommendations promulgated in the War Department's battlefield surveys, staff members of the House Committee on Military Affairs drafted a comprehensive bill describing each battlefield project and authorized appropriations for land acquisition and commemoration. Colonel Landers, director of the original Army War College survey, reported that implementation of the Omnibus Battlefield Preservation Bill (1926) would require an expenditure of $20 million, to be divided equally among the national military parks and various battle-site programs. Although the bill was reported to the floor with a favorable committee recommendation in 1930, it never passed. As a result Congress returned to a case-by-case acquisition policy. Overall, fourteen battlefield sites were added to federal holdings between 1926 and 1933.

History from 1933 to the Present

President Franklin D. Roosevelt inaugurated the next era in preservation history by signing the Historic Sites Act of August 1935. Finally, leaders in the federal government were willing to embrace historic preservation as an official policy. The act stated, "It is hereby declared that it is a national policy to preserve for public use historic sites, buildings and objects of national significance for the inspiration and benefit of the people of the United States."[29] It granted the Department of the Interior authority to acquire historic property, to engage in cooperative agreements as a method of protecting and preserving such property, and to provide educational and technical assistance for preservation activities. In addition, it mandated that the Department of the Interior conduct a national survey of historic sites and buildings. A number of sites and structures were studied, the documentation was reviewed by the NPS advisory board, and beginning in 1960 a number of properties were designated as national historic landmarks by the secretary of the interior. This listing recognized resources of national significance and laid the groundwork for the future National Register of Historic Places. Still, while the Historic Sites Act fostered the creation of an administrative infrastructure for preservation, its impact was limited because federal ownership was not promoted as the primary preservation tool. The act did not provide any funds for state or local preservation programs, nor did it require implementation of less expensive federal preservation techniques such as easements and cooperative management agreements.

Another one of President Roosevelt's major actions involved transferring, by executive order (in 1933), authority over national military parks, national battlefield sites, and national monuments from the War and Agriculture departments to the Department of the Interior. Horace Albright, one of the founders of NPS and its second director, wrote that the "transfer of the military sites would make the National Park Service a truly national bureau. . . ."[30] In reality, the transfer itself achieved more on paper than in operation. NPS officials continued to base decisions regarding acquisition of Civil War battlefields on the Army War College classification system and on politics. Also, use of federal funds for land acquisition did not apply to two Civil War battlefields, Manassas and Richmond, added to the system during Roosevelt's first two terms. The Kennesaw Mountain Battlefield in Georgia saw its land base greatly expanded under the auspices of the Emergency Land Conservation Program.

During this period, Congress recognized the need for public participation in the preservation of America's historic resources by founding the National Trust for Historic Preservation. The National Trust Act, signed on October 26, 1949, by President Harry S. Truman, advanced the national historic preservation policy first proclaimed in the Historic Sites Act of 1935. It also created an educational, nonprofit organization "to facilitate public participation in the preservation of sites, buildings, and objects of national significance or interest. . . ."[31] The National Trust was granted power to acquire, hold, and administer historic properties as well as to accept donations of money, securities, or property for the purposes of preservation.

Significant alterations in the national battlefield preservation policy occurred as the hundredth anniversary of the Civil War approached. In the mid-1950s, Congress abandoned the Army War College classification system. Political aims, rather than the professional recommendations of NPS personnel, now became the driving force behind most battlefield-acquisition proposals. In 1956 members of the Arkansas congressional delegation proposed legislation to make Pea Ridge a national military park. According to the classification system, Pea Ridge should have been commemorated with an acre of land and a monument. However, the political muscle of the Arkansas delegation prevailed, and on July 20, 1956, Congress enacted legislation authorizing the acceptance of a 5,000-acre donation from the State of Arkansas. Missouri was the next beneficiary of a national military park. Native son President Truman lobbied Congress to create Wilson's Creek National Battlefield Park on April 22, 1960, even though it was only a class II battlefield. In 1960 Horseshoe Bend National Military Park was similarly established as a result of political clout, another example of how such influence could negate the priorities of the NPS.

Heightened interest in battlefield preservation associated with the Civil War centennial prompted Congress to test a new policy of land acquisition that demonstrated growing concern for the integrity of areas adjacent to park boundaries. Congress offered monies to purchase land near Gettysburg National Military Park on the condition that contiguous counties agree to enact protective zoning buffers around the respective battlefields. The NPS withdrew its Gettysburg purchase proposal after Adams County, Pennsylvania, refused to implement a protective zoning ordinance. Until the county did so, the NPS confined its activities to the acceptance of private donations. During this time the House Interior Committee once again explored the possibility of developing a more systematic approach to battlefield preservation. It asked NPS officials to conduct a study of all Civil War battlefields and to make policy recommendations for their protection. Gradually, as the centennial drew to a close, Congress and the NPS lost interest in the project. The study was never completed.[32]

In the 1970s, congressional activity relating to Civil War battlefields followed the pattern of benign oversight first established in 1933. Various committees simply asked the NPS to perform park boundary studies as problems arose at individual sites. In general, Congress heeded the NPS's ensuing recommendations for the acquisition of additional parkland. Senator Alan Bible, chairman of the Senate Appropriations Subcommittee on Interior and Related Agencies, slightly altered this case-by-case acquisition system in 1974 when he requested that the NPS conduct boundary studies for five different Civil War parks. Soon thereafter, representatives from the Department of the Interior and the Senate oversight committee signed a letter of agreement stating that Congress would authorize the expansion of the park boundaries as recommended by the study, but that "implicit in this approval is the firm understanding that the depicted boundaries will not be subject to change in the future except for substantial and compelling reasons that are not now apparent. Thus, subsequent alteration or deviation must be subjected to the full legislative process." This gentleman's agreement paved the way for a series of boundary disputes to be discussed in forthcoming chapters.[33]

Today, the NPS protects Civil War battlefields and fort sites in forty-three different areas. Only sixteen Civil War battlefields are protected within national military parks, battlefield parks, battlefields, and battlefield sites. Those NPS battlefields not protected as parks or battlefield sites are typically commemorated with a small parcel of land and a monument. Both Richmond National Battlefield Park and Fredericksburg-Spotsylvania National Military Park function as multiple-site parks. Richmond National Battlefield Park contains battlefield sites at Chickahominy Bluff, Beaver Dam Creek, Gaines's Mill, Cold Harbor, Malvern Hill, Fort Harrison, Drewry's Bluff, and Parker's Battery. The Fredericksburg park includes sections of the battlefield at Fredericksburg, the Wilderness, Chancellorsville, and Spotsylvania Court House. A complete list of all NPS Civil War battlefield and fort sites is provided in appendix A.

Any historian who confronts a gap in the record of bygone days knows moments of despair when he complains bitterly that no one took the trouble to dig out and assemble all of the facts while those facts were still available. To use unlimited resources in order to make record for history, a record as broad and as all-inclusive as it possibly can be, to do it while everything is still fresh, and to do it with no other earthly motive than a desire to establish the full truth—this is the sort of thing that only government[s] can do, and they almost never dream of doing it.

—Bruce Catton

3

The Current Preservation Landscape: An Example of Flawed Public Policy

BATTLEFIELDS protected through the NPS are threatened by in-holding disputes, inappropriate development on adjacent lands, acquisition difficulties, and discord within the NPS arising from a conflict between politics and professionalism. While scholars, preservationists, and tourists might prefer that Civil War sites, battlefields, and resources be owned and controlled by the NPS in a logical and comprehensive way, the reality is that service ownership of its "landscape" is a hodgepodge of mechanisms and arrangements.

NPS Protection

Inholdings

The NPS does not own or directly manage all of the lands within official park boundaries. Lands within official boundaries but not owned by the NPS outright (that is, in fee simple) are classified as inholdings. Interior Secretary Franklin Lane, who presided over the creation of the NPS, established the service's first inholding policy in a 1918 letter drafted by Horace M. Albright and sent to NPS director Stephen T. Mather: "There are many private holdings in the national parks, and many of these seriously hamper the administration of these reservations. All of them should be eliminated as far as it is practicable to accomplish this purpose in the course of time, either through Congressional appropriation or by acceptance of donation of these lands."[1] This NPS policy was modified in 1979 to accommodate acquisition of parks from privately held land, but inholding acquisitions were prohibited four years later by President Ronald Reagan. As a result of the ban, NPS officials have had to use alternative approaches as means of managing inappropriate activities on inholdings.

In parks with inholdings, superintendents must create a delicate balance between inholders' exercise of their private property rights and NPS protection of resources. Their management tools consist of easements, lease-back agreements, and voluntary cooperation. For example, to preserve the historic setting, farmers within the boundaries of Fredericksburg-Spotsylvania National Military Park operate under strict guidelines that forbid the planting of some modern crops such as soybeans. While groups like the National Inholders Association protest what they describe as government meddling in private interests, the NPS would be hampered in its preservation efforts without land-use controls. Richard Rambur, superintendent of Antietam National Battlefield, believes that "within 15 to 20 years, the only people farming in this area will be the National Park Service."[2] He predicts that urban development will gradually encroach on most of the agricultural land outside the park's boundary.

Examples of incompatible inholder activities abound. To cite just one, at Gettysburg National Military Park a 310-foot observation tower rises from a 4.5-acre parcel behind Cemetery Ridge and the Union line. This gigantic gilled mushroom of steel has dominated the scenery since it was constructed in the early 1970s. Fortunately, its days may be numbered. In August 1990 Congress extended the park's boundary to include the tower area and 1,900 additional acres. The legislation also provided for the development of conservation incentives and cooperative planning efforts in the Gettysburg Battlefield historic district, an area of approximately 7,300 acres surrounding the park. Even though Congress has approved this expanded boundary, the NPS now faces the difficult task of how to protect the new areas with a land-acquisition budget of only one million dollars in fiscal year 1993 for Gettysburg. For instance, within the new boundary there are many other areas that may be of greater historic significance than the tower parcel. One developer plans to establish a commercial campground within the park. Another intends to construct a shopping mall on the park's periphery which will be visible from such key vantage points as Benner's Hill and East Cemetery Hill.[3] Should the NPS acquire and subsequently dismantle the obtrusive tower, or should it concentrate on purchasing the most historically significant areas? Alternative-management techniques rather than outright purchase may provide the best answer to this preservation dilemma.

Adjacent Lands and Viewsheds

Development on adjacent lands represents the most common source of resource degradation in the United States. Local governments and individual developers are not the only culprits. Federal agencies such as the Bureau of Land Management, the U.S. Forest Service, and the Department of Housing and Urban Development frequently fund projects leading to resource degradation. Moreover, the separate statutory mandates and constituencies of each government department hinder interagency cooperation. In any case, until

RT 15 SOUTH

STEINWEHR AVE.

BALTIMORE PIKE

NATIONAL CEMETERY

Fourscore and seven years ago...

BALTIMORE PIKE

RT 134 SOUTH

TANEYTOWN ROAD

LINCOLN SPEECH MEMORIAL

NATIONAL TOWER

ALI PACKER '92

GETTYSBURG 1992: TOWER LOOMS OVER TRANQUIL CEMETERY

The intersection of Baltimore Street and Steinwehr Avenue, Gettysburg, looking southward. By the 1880s the area south of town was already being developed. The prominent building at center is the old Wagon Hotel and Tavern (later enlarged and named the Battlefield Hotel), an establishment that dated back to the 1840s. The building at the far left was the residence of Dr. David Study, who helped care for the wounded after the battle. The structures along the righthand side of Emmitsburg Road (now Steinwehr Avenue)—except for the one-story house beyond the brick house at right—are all post-battle construction. (Gettysburg Historical Society)

development began rapidly to encroach on park boundaries, NPS concerns rarely went beyond their boundaries. Superintendents now find it difficult to maintain park values when parkland is surrounded by such nuisances as tall buildings, industrial noise, and wastewater treatment plants. Jerry Rogers, associate director of cultural resources at NPS, remarked, "The units of the National Park System in large measure rely upon an eighty-year-old assumption that has been invalid for forty years—that the parks are protected by their locations in remote areas."[4] Accordingly, NPS officials are beginning to recognize that resource protection must extend beyond core historic areas to include adjacent lands. For instance, the general man-

The Study House and Battlefield Hotel (both destroyed by fire in the twentieth century) have been replaced by a motel and a gas station. What was once open battlefield has been replaced mostly by restaurants, ice-cream parlors, gift shops, utility poles, traffic lights, and road signs. The brick house at the right, seen immediately beyond the "open" flag, is the same building seen in the 1880s view. (Elwood W. Christ)

agement plan for George Washington's Birthplace National Park explicitly calls for the NPS to "promote conservation of the adjacent landscape that is critical and essential for maintaining the integrity of the setting in which George Washington was born and lived, as viewed from the George Washington Birthplace National Monument and the Route 204 approach to the monument."[5]

Recently, the NPS expanded its resource management policy by recognizing that visible lands outside a park but not adjacent to its boundaries can have a detrimental effect on park resources. Incompatible development on land directly visible from within the park, commonly referred to as the viewshed, can impair the conservation of features of the landscape essential for maintaining the interpretive potential of a particular site. Unless an NPS unit has been granted

Chambersburg Pike and Seminary Ridge, Gettysburg, looking west-northwest from the west end of Chambersburg Street. Along the ridge in the distance, Union troops made a last stand on July 1, 1863, before they were forced back toward the camera position. In the foreground is the wooden culvert over Stevens Run, and at the right is the home of Perry J. Tate, built around 1860. (Gettysburg Historical Society)

broad latitude over easement acquisition, there is even less control over viewsheds than over adjacent lands and inholdings. A detailed examination of Harpers Ferry National Historical Park, which appears later in the chapter, demonstrates the need for historic viewshed preservation.

Acquisition Needs

Nearly all NPS boundaries represent political compromises. Few if any boundaries accurately reflect the limits of what should be a protected resource. Indeed, almost all national battlefield parks encompass smaller areas than recommended by historians and master

Similar to the Steinwehr Avenue strip, the open battle area between the historic west end of town (camera position) and Seminary Ridge has been replaced mostly with residential development. Within the last forty years, several commercial outfits have appeared, including a Pizza Hut, two insurance/real estate offices, a hair styling salon, a typewriter-repair shop, and the new Gettysburg Post Office (site of the Tate House). (Elwood W. Christ)

planners at the time of establishment. Brices Cross Roads National Battlefield Site, near Tishomingo Creek in northeastern Mississippi, provides an excellent example of this phenomenon. Early in June 1864 a Union force of 8,400 men, under the command of Brigadier General S. D. Sturgis, left Memphis to seek out and destroy the implacable Bedford Forrest and his mounted infantry. Notified of Sturgis's move, Forrest discarded his plans to raid Sherman's Middle Tennessee supply line, reconnoitered, and struck the federals at Brices Cross Roads. Outnumbered more than two to one, Forrest won a stunning victory, forcing his opponents to break ranks and retreat. His booty was enviable: sixteen of Sturgis's eighteen cannons and most of his train of 250 vehicles, along with hundreds of horses and mules, rations and ammunition. Today the battlefield is merely a roadside stop. Only one acre is protected of a field where eleven thousand men engaged in a bitter struggle that resulted in three thousand casualties.[6]

Another serious problem relates to the precipitous drop in park acquisitions that began with Interior Secretary James Watt's 1981 proposed moratorium on all parkland acquisitions. The Reagan administration was characterized by a curtailment of Interior Department acquisitions from which the NPS has still not rebounded. While Congress disregarded the administration's ban, legislators have consistently failed to institute a comprehensive acquisition program. More importantly, various boundary studies, land acquisitions, and analyses of park transportation problems have been authorized by Congress but never funded. The national battlefield at Monocacy, located just south of Frederick, Maryland, is a classic example of an underfunded project.[7] The park was authorized in 1934, but Congress never funded its development. One-third of the battlefield's 1,647 acres is now privately owned. The site of the Battle of Five Forks is another such example. In 1962 Congress authorized a maximum of 1,200 acres at Five Forks, Virginia—five miles northwest of Dinwiddie Courthouse and seventeen miles southwest of Richmond—for inclusion in the Petersburg National Battlefield.[8] Funds were never appropriated, but in 1990 the Conservation Fund acquired the lands and donated them to the United States.

According to the NPS regional directors' budget directive for fiscal year 1984–85, the backlog of authorized acquisitions amounted to more than 306,000 privately owned and unprotected acres, excluding Alaska. In all, approximately 2,077 have been authorized for six Civil War battlefield acquisitions. Between 1987 and 1989 the White House requested less than $20 million each year from the Land and Water Conservation Fund. Although Congress raised each request to $200 million, a substantial amount of money in the fund was left unappropriated. A similar resource-protection program, the Historic Preservation Fund (HPF), had an unappropriated balance of $1.5 to $1.6 billion in 1990.[9] Adding to the confusion is the absence of final legislated boundaries in many parks.

Politics and the NPS

The NPS is divided into three major resource categories: natural, recreational, and historic. These represent a park concept significantly broader than the one envisioned in 1916. Before the 1933 transfer of battlefields from the War Department to the NPS, parks were principally mandated to include natural wonders such as Yellowstone and a few archaeological sites. Since a separate national monuments program existed at the time, many conservationists initially questioned the advisability of including historic sites in the national park system, fearing their addition would lower its overall quality. Even though 57 percent of NPS units are now classified as historic, the focus on natural areas has continued. The Conservation Foundation describes this approach as follows: "The service's central mission is associated with the great western parks, not military battlefields; with Old Faithful, not the Liberty Bell."[10] Because Civil War battlefield parks fall into the historic category, they have received less funding and research support than natural areas.

In the constant tug of war between multiple-use advocates in the Bush White House and the preservationist faction in Congress, the priorities of the NPS have been frequently overlooked. One NPS official bitterly commented, "When you're a small agency, you're a target."[11] Republican members of Congress, typically from Western states, often vote "against" the NPS in order to keep public lands free from restrictions. Most adamantly refuse to support park acquisition bills for Civil War battlefields to avoid setting precedents that could be applied to Western parks. Recently, the U.S. House of Representatives Post Office and Civil Service Committee's subcommittee on civil service opened an inquiry into alleged political manipulation of NPS activities by members of the Bush administration and Western legislators. The former director of the NPS Rocky Mountain region, Lorraine Mintzmyer, testified before the committee that several influential politicians intervened to prevent the release of an innovative planning document for the greater Yellowstone area. Area lawmakers and commodity (agricultural and mining) groups found the document's ecosystem management approach contrary to their own economic-development goals. Senior NPS officials subsequently altered the draft document and asked Mintzmyer to accept an involuntary transfer to NPS's mid-Atlantic regional office in Philadelphia.[12]

The NPS is further burdened by its association with the Department of the Interior. The Interior Department has an unusual mandate of concurrently serving as a protective and an exploitative agency.[13] Political appointees within the Interior Department have tended to override NPS traditions of service and preservation. George B. Hartzog, Jr., replaced as NPS director by a political appointee in the Nixon years, has described the "incursions during the last 15 years [that] have undermined . . . the Service [and] have created a management house divided against itself—pitting career bureaucrat against political bureaucrat."[14] The NPS director is a political appointee, exempt from Senate confirmation. Consequently, that person and upper-echelon Interior Department officials often favor multiple-use alternatives over the preservationist viewpoints of park professionals.

A multiple-use policy is inconsistent with the goals of a national battlefield park. As testaments to fallen soldiers, battlefields are cemeteries without headstones and should survive for contemplative purposes, not for recreation. Barbecue picnics were disallowed at Antietam and community concert programs were halted at Chickamauga. When NPS personnel recently cleared timberland at Manassas National Battlefield Park, public outrage was immediate and heated. The NPS's objective was to restore the landscape to its Civil War–era appearance. Passing motorists and visitors alike were against a return to the open-field concept of the 1860s, favoring instead isles of sylvan green. The NPS ignored the public's response and continued its restoration project with an eye for continuity and historic preservation rather than aesthetic pleasure.

Other Federal Preservation Programs

The federal regulatory framework offers a number of historic preservation programs and legal mechanisms that go beyond the protection granted through the NPS. At best, these rather innocuous regulations supply a minimal degree of protection. Selective enforcement and perfunctory implementation account for only a portion of regulatory failure. A more solid explanation points to inherent weaknesses in regulatory design. For example, listing a property in the National Register of Historic Places or as a national landmark may generate publicity when a resource is threatened, but it cannot *prevent* alterations or demolition unless federal funds or a license is involved. The national register program simply mandates that certain federal agencies must consider the impact of their actions on national register properties. Some property owners refuse to accept even the limited benefits associated with national register listing. Nellie Longsworth, president of Preservation Action, explains that "there's still the incorrect perception that listing in the National Register takes away an owner's property rights. So we have a lot of educating to do."[15]

Most federal statutes regulating historic properties, such as the amended National Historic Preservation Act of 1966, the National Environmental Policy Act of 1969, and the Department of Transportation Act of 1966, are purely advisory. Although some degree of federal protection can be attained through each of these laws, the scope is restricted to federal agencies and federally funded, subsidized, and licensed undertakings. Threats from private individuals and businesses against national register properties are exempt from all federal regulations. Robert Bush, executive director of the President's Advisory Council on Historic Preservation, remarked, "Until there is a federal action, we [ACHP] can do nothing. Let's face it . . . I really don't have a whole lot to go on. It's like being a bridesmaid, but not quite invited to the wedding."[16] As it stands, a developer may destroy a national register or national landmark property without any type of legal repercussion. After reviewing the suggestions of the ACHP, a federal agency may follow a similar course of action.[17] Appendix B provides a more detailed description of federal historic preservation regulations.

Historic Preservation at the State Level

The type and degree of state protection bestowed on historic resources varies. Despite the enormous diversity of state historic preservation programs, they all share a number of features. In accordance with the amended National Historic Preservation Act, all states operate a federally funded historic preservation office. Within each office a historic preservation officer coordinates almost all activities, which include the certification of rehabilitation projects for receipt of federal tax incentives and the dissemination of information regarding historic preservation programs. Upon request, these officers assist interested parties with the procedures required to nominate a property to the national register. Several states manage a register of historic places listing properties of both national and state significance.

Aside from implementing national preservation policies, many states have devised their own preservation programs and regulatory guidelines. Most state programs have features that parallel the federal preservation program, including outright acquisition of land, easement trusts, and historic preservation laws. Even though outright (in-fee) acquisition of historic properties is allowed in most states, it is rare. A more common and financially attractive policy of land preservation involves the creation of easement programs. Many states have already established land trusts to hold conservation easements, while others have granted such powers to local governments. State preservation regulations are similar to federal regulatory programs in that they govern actions by government agencies rather than private individuals, but in form and process their similarity to federal regulations is far from uniform. Like their federal counterparts, state regulations are largely advisory. H. Bryan Mitchell, deputy director of the Virginia Department of Historic Resources, observed that in spite of numerous limitations state and federal regulations have been "responsible for hundreds if not thousands of decisions more favorable to resource protection than would otherwise have been the case." Still, preservationists do have cause to worry since these government regulations can be summarily dismissed by private parties.[18]

A key component of most state preservation programs is the passage of legislation that allows state or local governments to preserve historic sites. Under the dictates of such legislation, most states have delegated primary preservation authority to local governments. Equipped with technical, educational, financial, and regulatory assistance provided by the state's historic preservation officer, along with the state legislature's approval, municipalities have been allowed to establish local historic districts. Local governments have also been permitted to create architectural review boards, enact zoning overlays (special zoning districts), and implement various techniques to rezone property for lower-density use (downzoning). Several states have even authorized local historic commissions to acquire and maintain historic properties. Unfortunately, in many cases states have neglected their historic preservation responsibilities in favor of local preservation programs. This forfeiture of responsibility is aggravated by the fact that many local entities are ill-equipped to meet the demands of protecting nationally significant historic resources.

The overall level of state-sponsored historic protection does not necessarily correlate with the number of historic resources within a given state. For example, more Civil War battles and skirmishes were fought in Virginia than in any other state. However, only one battlefield site, at Sayler's Creek, has been preserved by that state. Although such a limited level of activity may be justified by the fact that Virginia's major battlefields are preserved within the national park system, officials seem unable to manage the only state-owned battlefield site. The Sayler's Creek park facility is poorly maintained and open less than six months a year. In contrast, while just eleven Civil War battles occurred in North Carolina, three battlefield sites have been preserved there as state parks.

Another impediment to historic park protection at the state level concerns the conflict between the recreational mission of state parks and the sanctity of battlefield sites. Gathland State Park in Maryland, which encompasses a portion of the battlefield of South Mountain, typifies this conflict.[19] Because the state established the park to serve as a buffer for the Appalachian Trail rather than as a historic park, state officials have been reluctant to acquire any portion of the battlefield beyond that which was randomly included in the park's original boundary.[20] Most states have been reluctant to spend funds for the protection of land that cannot be utilized for recreational purposes aside from walking, hiking, and contemplation.

Historic Preservation at the Local Level

In the absence of federal or state ownership, local zoning, comprehensive plans, historic districts, landmark ordinances, and local historic registers determine the extent to which historic areas will be protected. William Penn Mott, Jr., former NPS director, cautions, "For better or for worse, effective control of the surroundings of many national parks is in the hands of local jurisdictions. . . . [They] have enormous power to help or harm nationally significant elements of America."[21] A locality's land-use options are limited only by the state's enabling legislation and the creativity of local planners. Properly construed, local controls provide the ideal remedy for expensive and often controversial government ownership.

Zoning on grounds of historic preservation is a fairly recent phenomenon. The use of local government regulation to control the placement of certain types of buildings, such as slaughterhouses and tanneries, has been accepted as a legal right since medieval times. Yet the question of whether the government could regulate to preserve the aesthetics of an area, without financial compensation, was not conclusively decided until 1978. In the case of *Penn Central Transportation Company v. New York City* the Supreme Court upheld the constitutionality of local preservation ordinances. It ruled that aesthetic concerns alone can serve as the primary basis for government regulatory authority. Penn Central had opposed a New

York City landmark law that prevented it from constructing an addition on top of the Grand Central terminal. The court rejected Penn Central's "taking" claim because the company had not been denied "all reasonable economic use of the property."[22] Before this ruling the main objection raised against preservation ordinances concerned the unconstitutional taking of property. Landowners and developers alleged then and now that zoning regulations impose excessive burdens on the individual landowner and thus violate his or her constitutional rights.

There are now more than 1,700 cities and towns with local historic districts across the United States. Local historic districts provide one of the most comprehensive forms of protection. These districts usually require the establishment of a local historic preservation commission or architectural review board and the promulgation of a preservation ordinance. After that, an owner must seek the commission's approval before altering, demolishing, or removing historic properties within the district. Cities and towns are far more inclined than rural counties to implement historic preservation ordinances. Largely isolated from obvious development threats, rural counties are reluctant to issue zoning regulations until historically significant areas are threatened or destroyed. Harry Stokes, president of the Gettysburg, Pennsylvania, Borough Council, described this problem during a hearing before the House Committee on National Parks and Public Lands: "Gettysburg has excellent planning and zoning within its borough. It is surrounded, however, by townships that have weak zoning or no zoning at all. Moreover, they have no effective local historic district regulations. . . . The local leadership is behind the times and reluctant to put controls in place. Gettysburg is vulnerable to unchecked commercial strip development beyond our borders that directly undermines our downtown business sector."[23]

A state's enabling legislation generally determines the range of zoning options available at the local level. However, zoning laws are fluid, often responsive to the political vagaries of local boards. Harpers Ferry NPS chief historian Dennis Frye noted, "To base preservation decisions on zoning is to guarantee preservation disaster."[24] Surprisingly, agricultural zoning does not always serve as a reliable preservation tool. In many cases the allowable density is too high to ensure the maintenance of a farming landscape. Innovative zoning controls such as transfer of development rights (TDR) and conservation easements offer more reliable options by balancing the competing interests of development and preservation.[25] A TDR program provides economic compensation for owners of historic property by allowing them to sell their development rights. The purchaser of these rights may then use them to increase the development potential of a nonhistoric area beyond what the previous zoning regulations would have allowed. In essence, a TDR program allows property owners to transfer the development rights from one property to another through sale or through a rezoning of personal properties. Conservation easements do not involve a transfer of development rights. Instead, a government or private entity purchases a landowner's development rights and holds them in trust. Conservation easements may be held in perpetuity or for a set period of time depending on the type of agreement. The amount of development allowed by an easement varies substantially, but the property itself remains on the local tax roll. Some states do not permit localities to utilize TDRs, and some do not accept conservation easements.

Civil War battlefield preservation has been impeded at the local level for a variety of reasons beyond the constraints imposed by state legislatures. Many localities lack the financial resources to acquire historically significant tracts of land for county or municipal parks. Others are unaware of the historic resources located within their midst. The most serious impediment concerns the attitudes of some local officials. Many planning commissions and boards of supervisors, especially in rural areas, have been reluctant to enact protective ordinances for historic resources. Residents of rural communities commonly deplore the idea of land-use controls even when such protection would guarantee the maintenance of rural values. The dearth of historic preservation zoning in rural areas poses a particularly serious problem for Civil War battlefields, many of which are located in the countryside.

Case Studies: The Reality of Historic Preservation Policies

While the previous sections of this chapter explore the advantages and disadvantages associated with local, state, and federal historic preservation programs, it must be pointed out that federal, state, local, and nonprofit preservation programs are designed to function as complementary units. Supposedly, they interact to achieve the highest possible degree of protection. Regrettably, the system is incapable of addressing our nation's current preservation dilemmas. A detailed examination of four case studies will vividly illustrate the limited strengths and major weaknesses of America's historic preservation policies. While it is impossible to pinpoint a particular policy failure in any one case, collectively they demonstrate the need for a fundamental change in our nation's program of Civil War battlefield preservation.

Fredericksburg-Spotsylvania National Military Park

Virginia's Fredericksburg-Spotsylvania National Military Park was established in 1927 to commemorate four major battles: Fredericksburg (December 11–13, 1862), Chancellorsville (April 27–May 6, 1863), the Wilderness (May 5–6, 1864) and Spotsylvania Courthouse (May 8–21, 1864). Together these battles resulted in more than 100,000 casualties. Under the Antietam plan, the park's enabling legislation called only for the preservation of actual fighting lines, earthworks, and roads. Large tracts of the battlefield remained unprotected, intended to always remain in agricultural use. Additional lands were intermittently added to the battlefield until 1974, when Senator Allan Bible's committee approved an administrative boundary. The result was a ten-square-mile battlefield park scattered over three counties and one city and linked by a hundred-mile automobile tour route.

Today, many of the battlefield sites have been engulfed by devel-

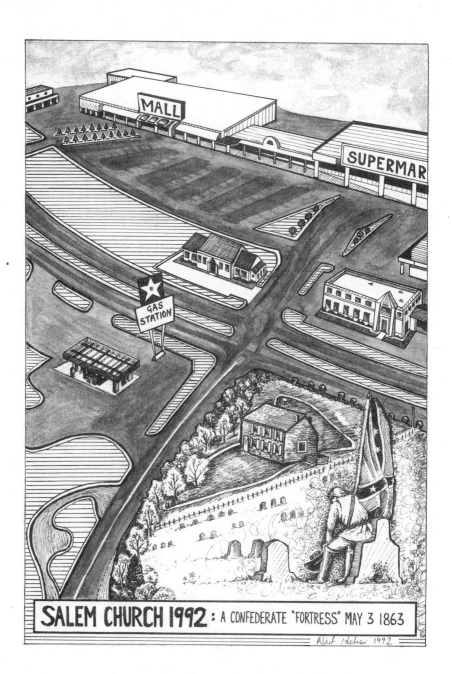

SALEM CHURCH 1992: A CONFEDERATE "FORTRESS" MAY 3 1863

opment. Housing, gas stations, and fast-food restaurants surround the Old Salem Church just west of Fredericksburg where a major part of the Chancellorsville campaign was fought. Spotsylvania County, home to Chancellorsville and Spotsylvania Courthouse Battlefields, is one of the fastest-growing counties in Virginia. The county's population doubled between 1970 and 1980, bringing demands for residential housing, jobs, and recreational facilities. Already, the Commonwealth of Virginia has widened a number of roads running through the scattered units of this battlefield park, and each year an estimated 1.8 million people drive along park roads on their way to work or to nearby subdivisions.[26]

Before historically inappropriate development claimed the site, local park service officials had recommended that the NPS purchase land across the road from the Old Salem Church. After the cost-conscious Washington, D.C., office of the Department of the Interior refused the purchase, the officials attempted to secure buffer zones around the park, but county planning commissioners blocked their effort. By 1989 the federal government had intervened to preserve imminently threatened portions of the Fredericksburg–Spotsylvania County battlefields. President Bush, in December, signed legislation authorizing a 1,900-acre addition to the military park. The administration's carefully crafted bill formally established the park's boundaries and allowed the NPS to acquire new lands through donation, purchase, or exchange. Lands previously acquired by the NPS but technically outside the park's official boundaries were incorporated into the new boundary as part of the expansion. For added protection, the NPS was granted authority to accept donations of conservation easements on lands adjacent to the park.[27] Despite the apparent comprehensiveness of the legislation, significant portions of the Wilderness battlefield were left unprotected. New boundary lines did not take into account the park's historic resources; instead, political expediency reigned. Only the additional 1,900 acres were deemed politically palatable to Congress. On February 13, 1990, Fredericksburg-Spotsylvania National Military Park superintendent Maria Burks editorialized in *The Civil War News*: "Development pressures in central Virginia are affecting every battlefield and historic site in the region, as you and your

THE WILDERNESS

5~6 MAY 1864

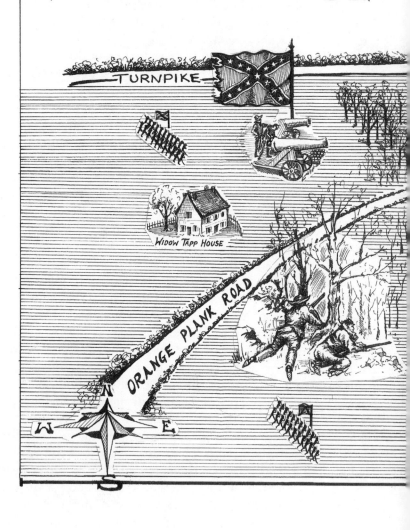

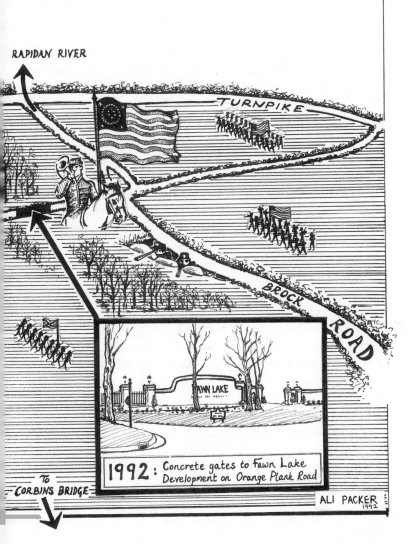

RAPIDAN RIVER

TURNPIKE

BROCK ROAD

TO CORBINS BRIDGE

1992: Concrete gates to Fawn Lake Development on Orange Plank Road

FAWN LAKE

ALI PACKER
1992

readers know. We face an enormous task in protecting the surviving core elements of the battlefields around Fredericksburg and welcome all of the support we can muster."

Recent actions by the NPS may have even accelerated development on the unprotected land. More than 3,000 acres of the Wilderness battlefield, in the vicinity of an "unfinished" railroad grade, is slated to be transformed into a high-density housing development called Fawn Lake. Fearing that this development would encompass the extremely significant but unprotected land on Orange Plank Road, across from Widow Tapp Farm, the NPS proposed a compromise: In return for access off Orange Plank Road into the development, it accepted a ninety-acre elongated buffer parcel running along the south side of Orange Plank Road. This 600-foot-deep zone stretches from Widow Tapp Farm past the entrance to Fawn Lake, thence to the intersection of Brock Road. The developers, the NTS Corporation, subsequently constructed an intrusive powder-pink brick wall along the park's boundary to serve as the entryway for Longstreet Drive, a boulevard trailing deep into the heart of the development. The wall actually lies in part on land owned by the NPS.[28] While the NPS certainly made a critical error by omitting adequate easement protection in the agreement, it is a sad commentary on the current land acquisition process that park officials were forced to sacrifice an extremely significant historic tract in hopes of saving another.[29]

Thus, in this telling landscape of stunted cedar and pine, are buried the memories of Winfield S. Hancock's savage attack on A. P. Hill's Confederate lines. Hill's troops were effectively driven back— almost a mile—to Lee's headquarters along Orange Plank Road. The situation was critical; disaster loomed as firepower from small arms ignited tangled underbrush. A dozen small forest fires consumed stricken soldiers. Longstreet's corps arrived just in time, advancing north past the Tapp house. A vicious counterattack ensued. Hancock's federal advance was blocked, the flank turned. In the confusion Longstreet was accidentally shot by his own men near the present-day entrance to Fawn Lake development.

The NPS did not request acquisition of the NTS Corporation land as part of the boundary bill because it was concerned such a request would jeopardize the bill's chance of passage.[30] As a result of inadequate boundary legislation established by a "whatever-will-fly-in-Congress posture," other historically significant lands have been sacrificed as well. There continues to be no reliable formula for determining the boundary lines of national battlefields.

Harpers Ferry National Historical Park

Although Harpers Ferry National Park in Jefferson County, West Virginia, is most commonly known for its historic association with abolitionist John Brown and the Civil War, the park's location offers one of the most breathtaking views available in the national park system (see Map 1). Thomas Jefferson described it during a visit in 1783: "On your right comes up the Shenandoah, having ranged from the foot of the mountain a hundred miles to seek a vent. On your left approaches the Potomac, in quest of a passage also. In the moment of

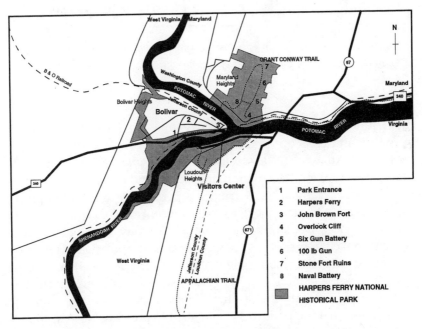

Map 1: *Harpers Ferry National Historical Park, a management challenge for three states. (Brian Huonker, from the U.S. Department of the Interior/NPS)*

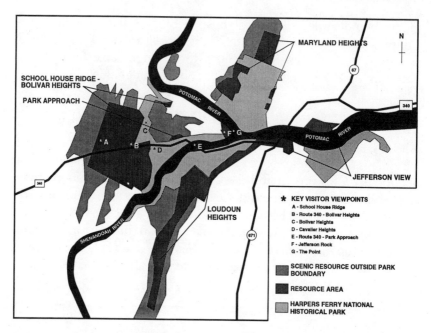

Map 2: Scenic resources at Harpers Ferry National Historical Park. (Brian Huonker, from the U.S. Department of the Interior/NPS)

their junction they rush together against the mountains, rend it asunder, and pass off to the sea . . . this scene is worth a voyage across the Atlantic" (*Notes on the State of Virginia*, 17). Incompatible development along the surrounding ridges and rivers now promises to destroy the famous view from Harpers Ferry. Indeed, unprecedented growth to meet the demands of recent arrivals who commute to Washington, D.C., and Baltimore is presently altering the rural, agricultural character of the area. By 1998 the population of Jefferson County is expected to be triple that of the early 1950s. Park officials openly acknowledged in a 1989 newsletter that development is "threatening not only the resources outside the boundaries, but the very values that the park was established to preserve" (see Map 2).[31]

In the summer of 1988, Jefferson County commissioners passed a new zoning ordinance allowing high-density residential develop-

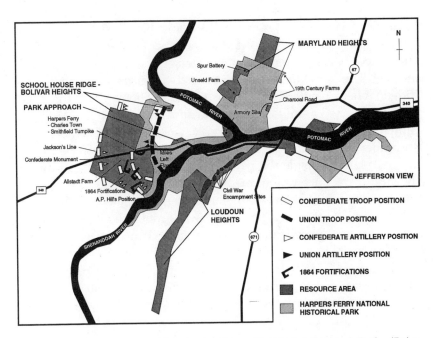

Map 3: Cultural resources at Harpers Ferry National Historical Park. (Brian Huonker, from the U.S. Department of the Interior/NPS)

ment in historically significant areas such as Chambers Farm, Cavalier Heights, and Schoolhouse Ridge. Prior to the official announcement, the NPS had provided the five-member county commission with detailed maps outlining battlefield lines. In an effort to protect the cultural and scenic resources bounding the park on the west and southwest, it asked the county not to alter agricultural zoning for historically significant battle areas (see Map 3). Such a request was within the NPS's professional interests as delineated in the official Harpers Ferry management objectives, which called for the park "to protect existing cultural/historic resources as nearly as possible to [*sic*] their appearance in mid-19th century times . . . [and] to protect the aesthetic values of the park by ensuring that development within and around it is compatible with the historic and natural scene."[32] The county refused the NPS's recommendations on grounds that it could zone land only for its "highest and best" use. A developer subsequently purchased a fifty-two-acre tract of the battlefield and submitted plans to the commissioners for a 150-home development.[33] The developer's tract covers two-thirds of Schoolhouse Ridge, where Confederate Major General Thomas J. "Stonewall" Jackson directed a military operation as a prologue to the Antietam campaign. By seizing Harpers Ferry, Jackson effected the largest surrender of U.S. troops during the Civil War. A 1988 boundary study of lands outside the park's perimeter identified this ridge as the largest tract needing immediate protection. Fortunately for it, a sour economy held plans for the housing development in abeyance.

In a similar dispute a half mile away from Schoolhouse Ridge, developers announced plans to construct a communication tower on a highly visible ridge called Bolivar Heights. On the afternoon of September 14, 1862, Union commander Colonel Dixon S. Miles found his troops trapped on this ridge by Jackson's artillery, situated on Schoolhouse Ridge. Mercilessly the Confederates bombarded Bolivar Heights, cornering a 12,500-man Union garrison. Only the cloak of darkness extinguished the relentless firestorm. An impasse ensued. The Union standard remained visible in the distance, illuminated by an occasional star shell. Undaunted, Jackson sent Major General A. P. Hill to end Yankee resistance and seal the fate of Harpers Ferry, thus assuring Lee's invasion of the north.

The hundred-foot communication tower was to be constructed within ten feet of the park's boundary. Although many area residents welcomed the prospect of cable television, the NPS and other interested parties protested. The dispute delayed construction of the tower for two years until the Federal Communications Commission entered the picture, invoking the National Environmental Policy Act of 1969 as well as section 106 of the National Historic Preservation Act. Resolution came with the construction of a thirty-foot tower barely visible above the tree line. The compromise enabled the area's television audience to satisfy their entertainment needs without damaging the integrity of Bolivar Heights.

Almost all threats to the integrity of Harpers Ferry National Historical Park have originated in nearby counties. The park is situated in West Virginia with the surrounding viewshed located in Maryland and Virginia. While Washington County, Maryland, has enacted a number of preservation ordinances, neither Jefferson County nor the State of West Virginia has responded to guarantee the park's integrity. Community leaders in the town of Harpers Ferry have been much more progressive than county officials. The town has been listed in the National Register of Historic Places and the town council has enacted a historic preservation ordinance.

Congressman Harley Staggers, Jr. and Senator Robert C. Byrd, both representing West Virginia, reacted to the development threats by submitting a boundary study bill for Harpers Ferry. The legislation, passed in 1988, authorized a special study for the identification of significant cultural and scenic resources adjoining but not within the park's boundary. Members of the study group solicited public opinion during two open hearings and devised a series of land-protection options. An independent economic analysis completed in conjunction with the boundary survey revealed that park-generated revenues exceeded those lost by "taking away" the county's tax base. The Harpers Ferry study, completed in the fall of 1989, was available for review on Capitol Hill in January 1990. Undertaken to provide a basis for future in-fee acquisitions and easement purchases, the study was never released by the Department of the Interior. Why? Perhaps because the newly enlarged park boundary includes controversial areas formerly outside the park, such as the fifty-two-acre Schoolhouse Ridge parcel and Chambers Farm. At Harpers Ferry, developers and politicians seem to have joined forces to thwart historic preservation efforts.

No action can be taken by the NPS to expand the Harpers Ferry park boundary since no formal request has been submitted to Congress. Park superintendent Donald Campbell offered a concise summary of the current situation: "Harpers Ferry National Historical Park and the lands adjacent to it are at a crossroads due to dramatic changes in population and settlement. . . . Change is inevitable; there remain only choices."[34] Unless Congress and the public decide to enact protection, the more than one million people who visit Harpers Ferry each year will be unable to enjoy the magnificent view from Jefferson's Rock where the eponymous president beheld it over two centuries ago.

Chickamauga and Chattanooga National Military Park

The historic preservation goals of the national government occasionally conflict with state interests. Recent debate over Chickamauga and Chattanooga National Military Park exemplifies how the burdens of preserving nationally significant resources are shared between the state and federal governments. Located three miles south of Chattanooga, Tennessee, the park covers more than eight thousand acres (see Map 4). Approximately five thousand acres of the total park area encompasses the Chickamauga battlefield in Georgia. The Battle of Chickamauga, which began on September 18, 1863, was one of the bloodiest of the Civil War. A large portion of the fighting revolved around attempts to gain control of the Lafayette Road. Major General William S. Rosecrans's federal line closely paralleled this road. Major General George Thomas's Fourteenth Corps was strategically positioned north of Major Generals Alexander McCook and Thomas Crittenden's troops. To the east, Confederate General Braxton Bragg's Army of Tennessee shadowed the thickets awaiting reinforcements from Lee's army, commanded by General James Longstreet. Additional manpower arrived late in the evening of September 19. By the next day a break had occurred in the Yankee line, between the Brotherton and Viniard houses. Longstreet charged across the Lafayette Road, piercing a gap in Rosecrans's line. The federal right crumbled and fled back to Chattanooga. Only Thomas withstood the Confederate onslaught, earning his sobriquet, the Rock of Chickamauga.

Each day nearly fourteen thousand commuters and commercial vehicles pass through Chickamauga and Chattanooga National Military Park along a 3.7-mile stretch of U.S. Highway 27 (State Route 1), historically known as the Lafayette Road. An environmental-impact statement jointly issued by the U.S. Department of the Interior/NPS and the Georgia Department of Transportation described Highway 27 as a major artery linking Chattanooga, Tennessee, and Lafayette, Georgia. The highway also serves as a major north-south route for western Georgia. Traffic jams and accidents are common, as four lanes of traffic converge on a two-lane road that passes through the battlefield. Tourist vehicles following the self-guided interpretive

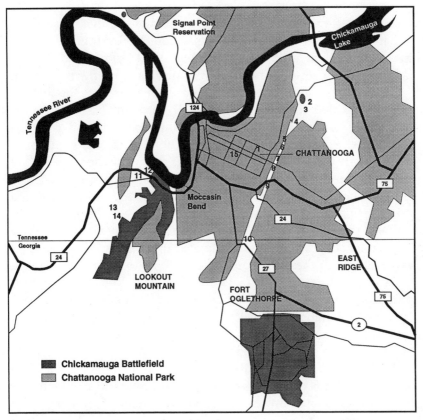

1	National Cemetery	6	Turchin Reservation	11	Wauhatchie Site 1
2	Sherman Reservation	7	Ohio Reservation	12	Wauhatchie Site 3
3	73rd Pennsylvania Reservation	8	Bragg Reservation	13	Wauhatchie Site 2
4	Phelps Monument	9	19th Illinois Monument	14	Wauhatchie Site 4
5	DeLong Reservation	10	Iowa Reservation	15	Orchard Knob Reservation

Map 4: Chickamauga and Chattanooga National Military Park. Route 27 (Lafayette Road) currently bisects the park. (Brian Huonker, from the U.S. Department of the Interior/NPS)

tour route often become ensnared in commuter traffic. Hence, before the passage of congressional legislation, NPS efforts to preserve the battlefield's integrity were simultaneously blocking the transportation needs of several growing communities in northern Georgia.

Following the completion of a comprehensive study, the State of Georgia decided to widen Highway 27 through the battlefield in 1967. In 1972, Civil War markers and cannons positioned along the old Lafayette Road were relocated to the west, along a proposed bypass route that was never built.[35] After reviewing the state-funded proposal, the NPS declined to approve the project and instead suggested a bypass along the western side of the park. Later it modified this decision and maintained that a bypass outside the park boundary was the only acceptable alternative (see Map 5). The Georgia Department of Transportation estimated that the expansion of Highway 27 through the park would cost from $3 to $6 million, while a bypass would cost from $25 to $30 million.[36] Debate over which proposal should prevail culminated in a hearing before the appropriate congressional committees.

Both the state and the NPS agreed that it was necessary to widen Highway 27. In addition to the traffic problems created by the more than 17 million vehicles traveling along the 3.7-mile park section each year, the mix of high-speed commuter traffic and slow sightseeing traffic generated an unusually high number of accidents. The NPS claimed that the congestion diminished the overall experience for most visitors and limited their ability to inspect memorials placed next to the highway. The State of Georgia argued that the economic vitality of the northern Georgia communities of Fort Oglethorpe, Lafayette, Rossville, Noble, and Chickamauga depended on access to a major transportation artery. Hal Rives, commissioner of the Georgia Department of Transportation, stated that the bypass "presents a liability to the State of Georgia and to the local government, and we cannot in good conscience contribute additional state monies to a harmful project when the viable and less harmful alternative of widening the road through the park exists."[37] State officials also contended that a bypass was unacceptable because it would permanently remove land from the local tax base.

In 1987 the preservation interests of the federal government even-

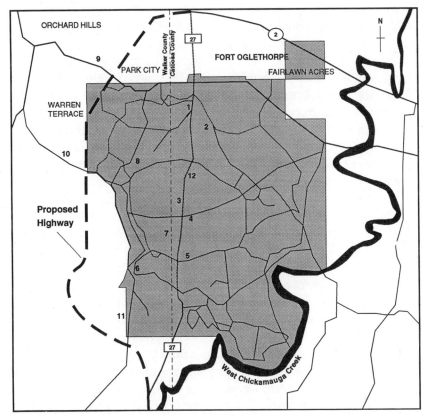

ORCHARD HILLS

N

9

PARK CITY

Walker County
Catoosa County

27

FORT OGLETHORPE

2

FAIRLAWN ACRES

WARREN
TERRACE

10

Proposed
Highway

1

2

8

12

3

4

7

5

6

11

27

West Chickamauga Creek

1	The Battle of Chickamauga	6	Wilder Tower	11 Vittitae - Chickamauga
2	The Battle Line	7	Retreat of the Union Right	Road
3	Mix-up in Command	8	Snodgrass Hill	12 Lafayette Road
4	Confederate Breakthrough	9	McFarland Gap Road	Chickamauga National
5	The Cost of Chickamauga	10	Lytle Road	Military Park

Map 5: Planned relocation of US 27 around Chickamauga and Chattanooga National Military Park. The new US 27 will only enter or touch the park boundary at two locations: McFarland Gap Road (9) and Lytle Road (10). (Brian Huonker, from the U.S. Department of the Interior/NPS, and Lynne Walsh, Chickamauga and Chattanooga National Military Park)

tually prevailed and Congress passed legislation authorizing the
relocation of Highway 27 around Chickamauga and Chattanooga
National Military Park. Senator Wyche Fowler (D-Georgia) effectively argued for federal funding of the bypass on grounds that it was
unfair for local communities to pay for the protection of a nationally
significant resource.[38] The state was authorized to receive federal
support for up to 75 percent of the project. Nearly 50 to 60 percent of
the design work had been completed by January 1993. Since federal
officials are still in the process of acquiring right-of-way tracts, the
construction phase of US 27 is one to two years away. It is assumed
that the Lafayette Road will continue to function as an open thoroughfare, an alternative US 27.

While the prospect of federal funding calmed much of the furor at
the state and local levels, not all parties were satisfied. The bypass is
scheduled to circumvent five blocks of downtown Fort Oglethorpe,
which usually garners the bulk of its business from commuters on
Highway 27. A small but vocal group cried foul. James Ogden, a
historian at Chickamauga and Chattanooga National Military Park,
contended there are no studies available that reflect the difficult
economic aspects of this land-use conflict. According to Ogden,
"Even a casual visit to Fort Oglethorpe will clearly show that the
present and future commercial center of that city is and will be
along Georgia State Route 2, into which bypass U.S. 27 will pass."[39]
Unless the town engages in an aggressive promotional effort to lure
battlefield tourists and area residents, the economic vitality of Fort
Oglethorpe may fall like the Union soldiers at Lafayette Road.

Chantilly

Along a major new thoroughfare in Fairfax County, Virginia, two
stone monuments rest in a 2.4-acre "park" commemorating the
Battle of Chantilly, also known as Ox Hill.[40] Commercial and residential development is planned or has already occurred on 98 percent of the 280-acre battle site. For all practical purposes, the
battlefield is gone. Commuters and passersby need only blink an
eye to miss this unobtrusive slice of Civil War history. Those who
visit the park intent on visualizing the last battle of the Second

Manassas campaign find their view obscured by the Linden condominiums, the Fair Ridge townhouse development, and various high-rise structures. The Fairfax Towne Center, an 870,000-square-foot residential and commercial development dominated by a shopping center, will soon be constructed on land directly opposite the park, its outlets pouring traffic on a battlefield where, on September 1, 1862, 5,500 Union soldiers attacked 15,000 Confederates commanded by Stonewall Jackson. The grim struggle, fought during a blinding rainstorm, ended in stalemate and resulted in 1,500 casualties, including two Union generals. The late Lieutenant Colonel Robert Ross Smith, a military historian and expert on Chantilly, remarked, "The failure of the Confederates at Ox Hill [Chantilly], to push through the meager Union lines simply undid Lee's plans for attacking Pope and Washington."[41] Instead, General Lee initiated the Antietam campaign.

In 1915 a one-legged Confederate veteran named John Ballard, who owned the farm where the battle was fought, donated a 50-× 100-foot plot to honor the soldiers who died at Chantilly. On this plot the First New Jersey Brigade Society erected stone monuments in remembrance of two fallen generals, Isaac Stevens and Philip Kearny. Stevens, a commander of great promise, was mortally wounded while leading an assault on the Confederate positions and fell near a split-rail fence, a short distance from the monuments. Kearny, too, was destined for high command, distinguishing himself with the French in Algiers and at Solferino, Italy, where he was decorated for bravery. With the U.S. Army, he had distinguished himself in the Mexican War and in the Civil War at Williamsburg, Seven Pines, and Second Manassas. Some regarded Kearny as a future leader of the Army of the Potomac. Though Kearny lost his left arm in the capture of Mexico City, he was an accomplished equestrian and fearless leader. On September 1, 1862, in rain and darkness, he rode his horse forward to reconnoiter and accidentally found himself behind Confederate lines. Hell-bent on escape, the general reined his horse to flee when a massive discharge of fire power rent the air. A single bullet struck the general, who fell dead from his horse in a muddy cornfield, about one hundred yards west of the monuments.

Chantilly, May 24, 1937. The Chantilly (Ox Hill) battlefield, unchanged since 1862, is captured in this U.S. Department of Agriculture aerial photograph. Young pine trees are taking over the old cornfield where heavy fighting occurred and where General Kearny rode to his death (A). The Stevens and Kearny monuments (B) are located where General Stevens was killed leading his division in an assault on Jackson's Confederate line. (Photo courtesy Ed Wenzel)

Chantilly, March 1990. The battlefield is virtually destroyed. Townhouses and condominiums blanket the cornfield (A), and Monument Drive cuts a four lane swath along the Confederate line of battle, barely missing two monuments (B). During the townhouse construction, the grave of a Confederate soldier was found at (C). While developers carved up the battlefield, county officials pushed a plan to protect the two monuments by moving them elsewhere. Original plans, in 1983, called for relocating the monuments to a "mini park" at location (D), but this plan was scrapped. Later plans, in 1985, had the monuments being moved 300 yards northeast to location (E). There, the Centennial Development Corporation agreed to build a 2 acre "historic" park within its high-rise project planned for the wooded tract (F). Centennial acquiesced to requests from local preservation activists and donated 2.4 acres surrounding the monuments to Fairfax County, and has also proffered $110,000 toward improvements at the site. The Fairfax County Park authority (FCPA) will design, construct, and interpret the site as a battlefield park. The adjacent 2.5 acre "parcel 5" (G) is the only other piece of the battlefield not owned by developers. The FCPA has attempted to purchase the property for inclusion in the park without success. In early 1992, the high-rise development planned for tract (F) was changed to a shopping center and apartments. (Photo courtesy Ed Wenzel)

Despite the significance of the battle, Fairfax County government never erected a single sign or marker. As of 1986, it did not even appear on Fairfax County historic-tour maps.[42] The state's efforts to preserve Chantilly were virtually nonexistent. Elizabeth David, an official in the Fairfax County heritage resources branch, noted, "Prior to the concerns stirred by protection of the Manassas battlefield, the Commonwealth of Virginia was not active in protection of large open spaces. . . . Since that time, of course, Virginia has become more active in designation of Civil War sites, with the unfortunate backlash resulting in the legislative changes of the last session."[43] At the federal level, U.S. Secretary of the Interior Cecil Andrus expressed no interest in 1979 when John Herrity, chairman of the Fairfax County Board of Supervisors, proposed that the NPS "study the desirability of acquiring park land (200–300 acres). . . . The area in question is the site for the Civil War Battle of Ox Hill. . . . The most important action of the Civil War to take place in Fairfax County. . . ."[44] In the absence of government support at all levels, perhaps an early outpouring of public support could have saved the battlefield. Yet local historians and preservationists failed to guarantee recognition of the site by nominating it for listing in the National Register of Historic Places. Largely unaware of the historic resource, local residents missed an opportunity to save an important battlefield and to preserve precious open space in a densely populated county.

Today a group of concerned citizens, working with the Chantilly Battlefield Association, is lobbying Fairfax County officials to save the only remaining ground—a 2.5-acre tract adjacent to the park. But Chantilly Battlefield really no longer exists. This national treasure, which became a pawn of government officials captivated by the prospects of development, has been lost forever. It should not be allowed to happen again.

Threatened Battlefields

As we have pointed out, virtually all Civil War battlefields, protected or not, are threatened by urban encroachment. A brief account of the history of and development threats associated with Malvern Hill, North Anna, New Market Heights, Cedar Creek, and Spring Hill underlines the gravity of the situation.

Malvern Hill

Malvern Hill, Virginia, located southeast of Richmond, was the site of the last battle of the Seven Days' Battle of the Peninsular Campaign. It was July 1, 1862. The Confederate army of 70,000 had been pursuing McClellan's force of 83,345 as it withdrew southward toward the James River and an entrenched base at Harrison's Landing. Troops maneuvered slowly through heavy woods, over brambles and around thickets. Blood-thirsty mosquitoes and parasitic fleas swarmed in the muggy climate. Southward, the gentle heights of Malvern Hill rolled out before the retreating federals. This elevated natural landscape would serve as an almost impregnable haven for more than a hundred pieces of Union artillery. The battle was on. A confusion of orders to Confederate field commanders resulted in piecemeal attacks. Major Generals John Magruder and D. H. Hill advanced to the base of Malvern Hill, "four hundred yards from the Union line . . . [as] Union artillery switched from solid shot to canister, turning the cannon into giant shotguns." The fiery snouts of enemy cannon decided the day for the Union army. D. H. Hill commented after the conflict, "It was not war, it was murder."[45] The losses were high: 5,355 Confederates and 3,214 Union casualties.

Today Malvern Hill rests quietly in a countrified environment, unaware of its embattled future. Progress intends to pockmark this legendary hill. West Sand and Gravel of Richmond, Virginia, owns mining rights to 700 acres across the road from the Malvern Hill unit of the Richmond National Battlefield Park. In spite of concerns voiced by the county planning staff and Richmond National Battlefield Park employees, in August 1991, the Henrico County Board of Zoning Appeals granted the company a conditional-use permit to excavate a seventy-acre parcel within a ten-year period. The historic composition of the Malvern Hill Battlefield is now at risk. One envisions a constant flow of trucks, grinding gears bouncing over

MALVERN HILL

1 JULY 1862

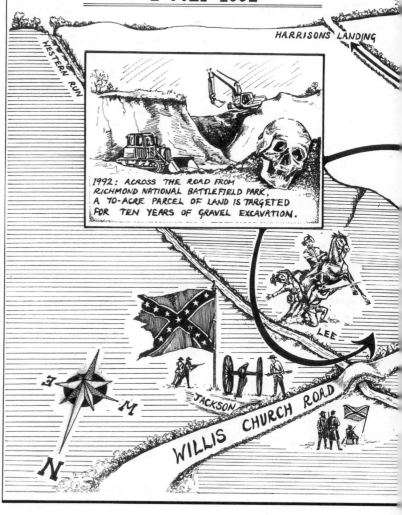

HARRISONS LANDING

WESTERN RUN

1992: ACROSS THE ROAD FROM RICHMOND NATIONAL BATTLEFIELD PARK, A 70-ACRE PARCEL OF LAND IS TARGETED FOR TEN YEARS OF GRAVEL EXCAVATION.

LEE

JACKSON

WILLIS CHURCH ROAD

TO JAMES RIVER

CREWES RUN

MALVERN HOUSE

HUGER

MAGRUDER

D.H. HILL

WESTERN RUN

LEE

LONGSTREET

~Ali F. Packer~ 1992

ever-expanding potholes, and a viewshed blighted by mounds of gravel being continually shifted and scooped; a gravel pit in the middle of the battlefield holding the leached bones of fallen Southern compatriots. Since, after the battle, many bodies were buried where they lay, it is likely that some of their remains are sown about the field.

As expected, the NPS objected to mining on land adjacent to the Malvern unit on two grounds: the defilement of sacred ground, and the disruption of visitors' interpretive experience. At present, Malvern Hill is one of the most important interpretive locations in the Richmond National Battlefield Park. Active mining on land abutting the interpretive site would, in all probability, dilute the experience for visitors. Before excavation begins, the U.S. Army Corps of Engineers must review the application, examining water-quality degradation and wetland disturbances. As of June 1992 the leaseholder had not applied for the corps' permit.[46]

North Anna

A similar dispute has erupted at Virginia's North Anna River Battlefield, also known as Hanover Junction. This privately owned site was once one of the strongest field fortifications of the war. Between May 23 and 26, 1864, Lee maneuvered his army into an inverted-V lineup, with the apex anchored on the North Anna River at Ox Ford. His right arm shielded the North Anna where it merges with the Pamunkey; his left arm fronted the Little River. Lee intended to hold Ox Ford and drive a human wedge between the Army of the Potomac. By splitting it into thirds, he hoped to create an impression that the Confederates had retreated to Richmond, thus enabling the Army of Northern Virginia to assail one of the Union wings. The ruse worked. Major General Winfield Scott Hancock's II Corps crossed the North Anna downstream from Ox Ford and Major General G. K. Warren's forces crossed it upstream. Bloody skirmishes erupted, culminating on May 23 and 24. Casualties were high, approximately 2,600 Union soldiers and 2,500 Confederates. Prudently aware of the inherent danger of enemy fortifications, Grant disengaged on the evening of the 26th and moved southeast toward Hanovertown. Lee lingered at North Anna, incapacitated by intestinal cramps.

The person who owns most of the battlefield has proposed to double the size of his sand and gravel operation. This would lay waste to the heart of the North Anna Battlefield, between Quarle Mill and Ox Ford. To area residents North Anna's vulnerability is apparent. The progressive county affirmed its commitment to preservation by eliciting public "identification of special battlefield districts that could protect the resources and be consistent with their comprehensive plan, economic development and open-space planning endeavors."[47] Initially, conventional wisdom prevailed. The owners halted expansion plans on land earmarked for conservation, agreed to allow limited public access on the land, and offered to provide visual buffering paths as well as interpretive materials. Preliminary discussions between quarry owners and the NPS have addressed management and interpretive strategies for the recently conserved battlefield areas. Nothing substantive has resulted. Moreover, in 1992 expanded mining operations resumed on a portion of the battlefield not set aside for preservation. Conservation of North Anna Battlefield thus hinges on whether or not Henrico County, the NPS, and the local community can launch a successful collective effort.

New Market Heights

Although the land-use debate has failed to reach a crescendo at New Market Heights, all the elements are brewing for the development of a major controversy. Fourteen African-American soldiers and two white officers received the Medal of Honor, the nation's highest military award, for their gallantry during the Battle of New Market Heights, a part of the September 29–30, 1864, attack on Richmond. In fact, this battle prompted Major General Benjamin F. Butler to strike a special medal in honor of the contributions made by African-American soldiers to the Union effort. Fourteen of the sixteen Medals of Honor awarded to African-American soldiers during the Civil War were handed out for heroic action at New Market Heights. Yet most of the battle site is not protected.

The absence of a preserved area could suggest an irreverent disregard for the valiant efforts of those black columns who advanced on

New Market Heights. At this battle, General Butler's Army of the James squared off against the forces of Brigadier General John Gregg. The circumstances seemed to favor the South. Confederate artillery emplaced on the heights bolstered infantry entrenchments hugging the slopes' southern base. Menacing rows of abatis— barricades of felled trees hewed to snare or impale an enemy— defied the Union forces, which included four brigades of United States Colored Troops. The battle commenced before daybreak, as the black brigades waded through Four-Mile Creek toward the heights. Fighting was fierce and the death toll heavy. Colors shifted from hand to hand as the bearer and his ranks fell before a hailstorm of enemy fire. A redeployment of Confederate troops to Fort Gilmore to shore up lines that had been sundered when Union columns stormed Fort Harrison enabled the Union army to crest the heights and subdue the enemy.

Much of New Market Heights consists of privately owned sites without public access. The present owners continue to contravene plans to commemorate a portion of the battlefield. A compromise is desperately needed. No one is suggesting that the battlefield be transformed into a gigantic memorial field, only that a portion be preserved in order to help legitimize the African-American experience in the Civil War. Peter Iris-Williams of the NPS's mid-Atlantic regional office observed, "Of the ten battlefields where black soldiers made a substantial contribution, the New Market Heights Battlefield has the greatest integrity and provides the best opportunity to interpret the story of the battle and the contribution African-Americans made to the Civil War."[48] Like so many other Civil War sites, the fate of New Market Heights rests precariously with the immediate objectives of present landowners.

Cedar Creek

Less than a month after the Battle of New Market Heights, one of the most important battles of the Civil War occurred at Cedar Creek (Belle Grove). It was at this site, on October 19, 1864, that the long struggle for control of the fertile Shenandoah Valley reached a climax. The battle ended major military actions in the valley, capitalized on the momentum from William T. Sherman's September 2 capture of Atlanta, boosted Northern morale, and ensured the re-election of Abraham Lincoln. Long before daybreak on that fateful October morning, four Confederate divisions attached to Lieutenant General Jubal Early's army crossed the north fork of the Shenandoah River and Cedar Creek. Early's force of twenty-one thousand troops, wasting all before them, advanced across the fog-covered grounds of the Belle Grove plantation. With a clash of arms in successive en-counters, the Confederates drove a demoralized and disordered Union army back to a ridge north and west of Middletown. The tide shifted later that day when the diminutive Major General Philip Sheridan rode twelve miles from Winchester, rallied his troops, and effected a successful counteroffensive. Early retreated up the valley.

Much of the Shenandoah Valley is a pristine, rural expanse of undulating hills dotted with checkerboard farms between two paral-lel mountain ranges, but like so many rural landscapes in the United States it is facing development and commercialization. The battle-field at Cedar Creek is no exception. Although 100 acres of this limestone-rich battlefield and Belle Grove plantation are adminis-tered by the National Trust for Historic Preservation, other portions are up against imminent development. Planned construction with heavy grading machinery would obliterate the site's remaining fed-eral earthworks. Another projected development calls for an indus-trial park composed of eight ten-acre lots, which would practically encircle the plantation house that served as Sheridan's headquarters before and after the battle.

To counter development at Cedar Creek, local residents formed the Cedar Creek Battlefield Foundation (CCBF) in 1988. Members based their decision to create the foundation on the assertion that "no ground in America can be more hallowed than this prime develop-ment land, well-watered with the blood of heroes."[49] Each year on the anniversary of the battle the CCBF sponsors a reenactment week-end. Thousands converge on Cedar Creek to watch people from all over the United States reenact battle skirmishes on a portion of the original battlefield. The 1992 event drew seventeen thousand people. Drawing on a growing national awareness of Civil War battlefield preservation, the Marathon Bank of Winchester, Virginia, offers a special credit card called the Save Our Sites (SOS) VISA. The bank has agreed to donate the card's twenty-dollar annual fee to the CCBF.

Most recently, the CCBF joined ranks with the APCWS to preserve the heart of the Cedar Creek Battlefield, a 158-acre tract of unspoiled land. After lengthy negotiations, the CCBF entered into an agreement that required an initial down payment of $125,000, followed by a series of semiannual payments occurring over the next five years. The CCBF is meeting these payment obligations through a combination of noninterest and low-interest loans, contributions from individuals as well as organizations, and proceeds from the Marathon VISA card. The APCWS has already contributed $25,000 to the CCBF as part of a matching grant arrangement. If the CCBF cannot meet each of the $32,500 (plus interest) payments by 1994, the organization could lose the 158-acre parcel. The group also hopes to restore an original antebellum structure known as the Heater House and use it as an interpretive center. Needless to say, the dedicated forces of the CCBF face a difficult task in attempting to preserve the acreage and structure as important pieces of American history.

Spring Hill

Spring Hill, Tennessee, will forever be remembered as the site of General John Bell Hood's greatest blunder. Or will it? The Confederates had hoped Hood's invasion of Tennessee and imminent threat to Nashville would pull General Sherman out of Georgia. It did not. Sherman victoriously marched to the sea while Hood's Army of Tennessee fumbled along, suffering a string of misfires and logistical nightmares. Hood created a stir as he campaigned through middle Tennessee strapped to his saddle, bearing a crippled left arm from Gettysburg and a stump for a right leg following Chickamauga. He loved to fight and was without peer as a combat leader. As an administrator and strategist, however, he did not measure up; his gambit at Spring Hill failed.

On November 29, 1864, Hood bivouacked at Spring Hill, on pastureland owned by Nathaniel Cheairs, and elected to attack unsuspecting federals nearby. It never happened. Union Major General John M. Schofield's columns anticipated entrapment and quietly slipped past the Confederate camp that evening. A disorganized Confederate force hesitated, unwilling to pursue the elusive enemy. The next day Hood's troops assaulted Schofield's Army of the Ohio at Franklin. The upshot was a misguided attack resulting in incalculable losses and a stinging defeat for the Confederates.

As General Hood was deceived by the federals, so too, a century later, most Spring Hill residents believe they were duped by corporate America. The Saturn (General Motors) Corporation's new $1.9 billion manufacturing and assembly facility now encompasses the farmland where Hood bivouacked that luckless night in November. The car company owns about 2,450 acres in Spring Hill, including 900 acres of the Cheairs's property. Saturn spokesperson Jennifer Schettler portrayed her company "as a public-spirited corporation who purchased the Cheairs's mansion to promote preservation in the area."[50] According to Saturn officials, community traffic-flow patterns and environmental concerns were studied before construction began. The corporation went so far as to paint the exterior of the plant in colors suggesting characteristic elements of the Tennessee landscape—limestone, light-blue sky, old red barns. Extraordinary care was taken during the planning of the facility; changes were even made to accommodate a colony of woodpeckers. Saturn officials maintain that they did extensive planning and research to ensure that "the [automobile] facility would not create an eyesore for the community or destroy the rural serenity that exists."[51] Tranquillity is not easily factored into a projected workforce of six thousand. Saturn maintains a "just-in-time" inventory system, meaning few automobile parts are sitting on the plant's grounds. Consequently, the new Saturn Parkway has become a busy thoroughfare for trucks delivering their daily complement of automobile parts. The company produces more than nine hundred cars a day, most of which leave the site by trailer-truck bound for the interstate. Saturn Parkway, also known as State Road 396, boldly bisects Hood's encampment site, linking the auto plant to U.S. Highway 31.

Although the State of Tennessee held several public hearings before building the 4.3-mile-long parkway, Saturn's Schettler noted, "No information presented at the hearings pertained to Civil War battlefields or campsites at Spring Hill. There were no comments or concerns from citizens that lived in this area relative to historic sites."[52] Dennis Kelly, historian at Kennesaw Mountain National Battlefield Park, asserted that not all of Spring Hill's thousand residents were unaware of the historic significance of their locale. Instead, residents became pawns of progress, beguiled by developers and politicians alike. According to him, "Saturn ingratiated itself into the community by promising jobs and prosperity while treating locals like they just fell off the turnip truck."[53]

Saturn donated fifty acres for the construction of Spring Hill High School and built what may be described as the most modern city hall in the country. Such generosity, however, did not produce jobs in the hoped-for numbers. Residents believe a deal was cut with the United Auto Workers whereby laid-off workers from Detroit were given first choice at employment. Saturn conceded that the initial component of its workforce was brought in from other areas of the country. "This fact was presented to the community in the early stages of the project. . . . Without this provision in our partnership with U.A.W., there most likely would not have been a Saturn Corporation," maintained Schettler.[54]

Pastureland along Saturn Parkway has been rezoned for residential, commercial, and industrial development. Realty signs pepper the area, stakes are in the ground, and lots are being offered at Royal Park, a master-planned, mixed-use community under construction to support Saturn. A corporate city may someday supplant Spring Hill, urbanize the provincial environment, and wipe out any of the remaining Civil War heritage. "Only a few made money [from Saturn]; the majority foot the bill—higher taxes, utility rates, crime and loss of culture," observed Kelly.[55] This controversial assessment continues to divide the community. Saturn supporters dispute their critics by pointing out that the proposed corporate city along Saturn Parkway is neither owned nor being developed by Saturn. Indeed, Saturn has contributed over $20 million in-lieu-of-tax payments to the community. Moreover, Saturn's Tennessee payroll in 1991 totaled more than $253 million, most of which is spent in middle Tennessee[144]. As for evidence that the corporate entity can blend with the community, Saturn spokesperson Schettler cited the "continued operation of farm activity on much of the property as part of our site maintenance process."[56]

Saturn believes it is a good neighbor that has infused hope into an economically depressed area. Quite possibly, rancor over the loss of Hood's encampment area is more a case of dissatisfied job seekers or late-blooming grassroots preservation efforts than anything else. Interested parties were just beginning to organize when Saturn's plans were already in place. Many residents have realized that it is impossible to "back into" prosperity and have thus accepted the notion that the price of progress is change. But historian Kelly commented, "What happened at Spring Hill will happen again. . . . Maybe when developers try to hoodwink [people] next time, preservationists can cite the Spring Hill affair to influence local leaders to make the correct long-lasting decision to preserve a historic site and reject the lure of instant progress."[57] The full economic and preservation ramifications of the Saturn project remain to be seen.

Manassas is one of those rare and solemn places where the past is palpable, where ghosts and landscapes silently help us understand who we are as a nation and how we came to be.

—*Robert A. Webb*

 4

Battlefield Preservation in Virginia

THE COMMONWEALTH of Virginia represents virtually all sides in the debate over Civil War battlefield preservation. On one side is a Virginia steeped in tradition. The sentimental obligations inherent in being the site of more Civil War battlefields than any other state bestow a sense of responsibility.[1] On the other side is a state that has allowed land developers to unleash a dynamic spiral of economic growth. Development could bring an unprecedented degree of economic security for those rural communities still on the perimeter of urban corridors. The ongoing conflict between the interests of preservation and development is reaching the most isolated corners of America. Close examination of the battlefield preservation debate in Virginia illustrates how private individuals and governmental bodies interact to determine the effectiveness of historic-preservation policies.

Virginia has one of the oldest legacies of historic preservation in the United States. Strong believers in private property rights, residents of the commonwealth have adhered to a policy of preservation through private initiative. Jamestown, Monticello, Mount Vernon, and Williamsburg were all preserved by private organizations. The success of these endeavors has conveyed the impression that government intrusion is unwarranted. This attitude has been a catastrophe for Civil War battlefield preservation. Unlike preservation of historic buildings or villages, which can be used to generate considerable income, preservation of battlefields involves forgoing the use of otherwise developable land. It does not promise obvious and immediate financial return to a private owner. In addition, the cost of purchasing large tracts in rapidly developing areas greatly exceeds the price of a single building.[2] The staggering number of historic sites within the commonwealth, from the homes of presidents to colonial prisons, simply compounds the problem. Civil War battlefields must compete with a variety of other historic sites for funds and public attention.

Planned-growth advocates and preservationists argue that the right to develop land is a privilege, not a license to destroy.[3] Developers cite Fifth Amendment rights and the tangible benefits of jobs, shelter, and services gained by economic growth. The basic question becomes one of finding a balance between preservation and development. If the private sector cannot achieve such a balance, the responsibility must fall on the government. When government fails to intercede or when it intercedes in an inequitable manner, irreparable harm to historic landscapes typically results.

Local Preservation

Preservation of most historic sites in Virginia will succeed or fail at the local level. Strict adherence to the Dillon rule, however, has limited the number of local land-use options and planning tools normally employed to balance development with preservation.[4] Under the Dillon rule, local jurisdictions can only implement those powers specifically granted by the state.[5] Since the latter part of Charles Robb's term as governor of Virginia, developers have successfully lobbied against a number of bills calling for increases in local land-use controls. In 1992, for example, the Virginia legislature passed a so-called vesting bill favorable to developers as well as a preservation bill requiring owner consent for state designation of historic resources.[6] Furthermore, although a mechanism for acquiring scenic open space was devised, it was passed without requisite funding.

Legislation authorizing local governments to utilize TDRs, impact fees, and tax incentives for historic preservation has all been soundly defeated in the General Assembly. Similarly, measures to increase funding for parks and open-space acquisition have failed because of opposition from the development community. Virginia law requires all local communities to adopt comprehensive plans prior to development. Yet while state law related to comprehensive plans does not explicitly mandate planning for historic resources, the Virginia code on local zoning specifically lists preservation of historic sites as an appropriate object of zoning. Hence preservation efforts devolve upon the residents and depend on the exclusive needs of each locality. H. Bryan Mitchell, deputy director of the Virginia Department of Historic Resources and deputy state historic preservation officer, offered, "Only a minority of Virginia localities has taken the initiative to identify and afford some zoning protection for historic resources."[7]

Cities and towns have been noticeably more successful than rural counties in establishing ordinances to protect historic sites. A brief comparison of county and city historic-preservation zoning ordinances in central Virginia clearly demonstrates the differences. In 1971, a forty-block area of downtown Fredericksburg was placed in the National Register of Historic Places. Over the ensuing years city leaders enacted a historic zoning ordinance for the city of Fredericksburg and granted an architectural review board authority to review all applications for the alteration or construction of properties within the district.

Events in Loudoun County, Virginia, accurately represent the typical obstacles encountered by preservation advocates working in rural areas. In the fall of 1988, a group of concerned citizens submitted an application to the Virginia State Historic Preservation Office to have twenty-five thousand acres of the Catoctin rural historic district in Loudoun County placed in the National Register of Historic Places. Even though national register designation carries no restrictions on private land-use decisions, several landowners feared that the government designation would lower their property values. Aided by the Virginia law firm of Hazel and Thomas, PC, the landowners blocked the designation by presenting the state with the required number of complaints in March 1988.[8] According to the National Trust for Historic Preservation, only fifty-five Virginia localities have adopted historic zoning or architectural review boards.

State Preservation

Virginia's attitude regarding historic sites can be described as a desire to promote but not to protect. Economics, not reverence for historic sites, serves as the driving force behind state preservation policy. The intrinsic contradictions of this policy are puzzling when one considers how the state has engaged in a massive campaign to promote Virginia history for tourism while simultaneously permitting destruction of historic resources. In a 1988 report entitled "A Future for Virginia's Past," members of the Governor's Commission to Study Historic Preservation linked economic and historic interests: "Virginia's historic resources are among the most treasured assets of the Commonwealth and, in the final analysis, are what help to distinguish us from the rest of the nation. They are essential in defining our identity as a people and underlie the present and future economic health of the Commonwealth." The report recommended that the state "invest in and properly manage the capital assets that are the basis for its economic success. Virginia's historic resources are one of those assets. They cannot be duplicated anywhere in the country and they provide a competitive marketing advantage that should not be under-utilized."[9] Thus far the governor and state legislators have been slow to heed the commission's recommendations. In fact, current budgetary difficulties have forced retrenchment from 1989 initiatives to maximize funding for historic preservation and to create an independent department of historic resources. Former Governor Gerald L. Bailes proclaimed, "Preservation is not reverence. Preservation is, rather, a tool to manage change."[10] State officials need to do more than merely rely on the benefits associated with privately preserved historic sites. Instead, they must consider the long-term consequences of limited state activity in the historic preservation sector.

Tourism already generates an enormous amount of revenue for the commonwealth. A 1990 Virginia Division of Tourism study revealed that 83 percent of all tourists interviewed mentioned history as the principal reason for traveling to the state.[11] In the same year, travel-related expenditures in Virginia reached $7.96 billion, while state tax receipts from these expenditures totaled $355.2 million and local tax receipts amounted to $228.1 million. Additionally, in 1989, more than 162,000 Virginians were employed in travel-related jobs.[12] While the economic benefits of tourism have been substantial, only minimal effort has been made to protect the resources luring visitors.

The trend continues. In 1991, findings from the Virginia Tourism Development Group revealed that museums and historic sites drew a higher percentage of tourists than other types of attractions.[13] Interest in the state's historic sites extends far beyond U.S. borders. Following a British broadcast of Ken Burns's television series on the Civil War, more than thirty thousand British citizens contacted Virginia's Division of Tourism seeking information about the state's Civil War battlefields. Thirty-four percent of those making inquiries actually visited the state.[14] Virginia's Division of Tourism and Mobil Oil Corporation responded to this interest by jointly publishing a travel brochure, "Virginia: Civil War Battlefields and Sites." Although in 1991 alone tourist information centers and travel bureaus distributed more than 213,000 copies nationwide, Virginia Division of Tourism spokesperson Sue Bland quizzically responded to the figures by stating that "history is *not* the main motivator in coming to a travel destination, variety is. Our job is to get people into Virginia to see what already exists. We teach people to look at the riches of their own communities. Wrap up what you can market. Develop them with strategic marketing plans and ready communities for new businesses. Once these people are in the business, we support them." Bland also commented that if an unprotected resource is historically significant, it will be preserved by private initiative. Preservation of Civil War battlefields should not be a major concern of the Virginia Division of Tourism because "all of the major sites in Virginia are already preserved."[15]

Preservation of Civil War battlefield sites has never been a priority of the Virginia state government. The Department of Historic Resources does not own or manage any historic properties for public use. State parks created as rustic recreational areas offer one preservation alternative. Yet state officials claim that the ideals of historic preservation conflict with the recreational mission of state parks. Those historic sites now part of the state park system were acquired by unsolicited donation. State officials have even been reluctant to guarantee public access to commemorative site markers erected decades ago. For example, a marker designating the location of Lee's famous conference with Longstreet and Jackson prior to the Malvern Hill battle sits on the roadside a short distance north of Malvern Hill. To read the marker, an attentive driver could toy with suicide by leisurely stopping his car in the middle of the road, or else slow down, rotate his head while maintaining a cockeyed view of the road, and digest the significant information within a tenth of a second. The state does not offer appropriate pulloff areas for visitors to read most wayside markers designating historical sites. More often than not, if a site cannot be transformed into a tourist development, it is neglected.

In 1988, as part of an effort to alter the current image that "protection of its historic resources is not a high priority for the Commonwealth," the Governor's Commission to Study Historic Preservation recommended a number of sweeping changes in state preservation policies.[16] If implemented, the policies could help Virginia's preservation program raise its status in the state's bureaucracy. On the basis of the commission's recommendations, the state has already upgraded the Department of Historic Resources from division to departmental status. Another recommendation implemented was the creation of the Virginia Historic Preservation Foundation, which has authority to acquire and resell threatened historic properties. To guarantee long-term protection, all properties sold by the foundation carry perpetual historic easements. Budgetary retrenchments in the 1990s, however, have reduced the foundation's original appropriation of half a million dollars every two years. Another recommendation was realized with the creation of a grant program designed to provide financial assistance to owners of historic property in Virginia. In the first year, the program's requests for easement purchases exceeded $5 million. Yet the grant program received an initial appropriation of only half a million dollars each year of the biennium. Funding for the program has recently been reduced.[17]

Aside from recommending a structural overhaul of the state preservation program, the commission suggested a number of other policy improvements. It urged Virginia's Department of Historic Resources to engage in an aggressive program of acquiring preservation easements by offering property tax breaks for those persons donating them. The potential impact of the tax break is limited by two regulations. First, Virginia law mandates that local tax assessors consider easement restrictions when assigning property values for tax purposes. Second, the Internal Revenue Service requires owners to grant some degree of public access on such property in order to qualify for a tax break. More specifically, the owner must open the property at least one day every other year. Since 1966, 155 owners have donated perpetual easements to the Virginia Historic Landmarks Board.[18]

The commission has also encouraged the state to simplify the process required to nominate a property to the State Register of Historic Places. Complicated application forms, including 133 pages of directions, and excessive documentation requirements have discouraged citizens from nominating properties. Moreover, the study commission described the state register as "too incomplete to use as an information base for making decisions concerning development, management, and protection."[19] Since state designation requires all the work and forms of its federal counterpart, the commission recommended splitting the process and developing a state register more accessible than the national one. In its overall assessment, the commission called for increased local-government and private-sector participation in state historic preservation programs.

Despite several positive changes, the likelihood of Virginia championing the cause of historic preservation remains highly improbable. Since the release of the commission's report, the General Assembly has implemented only a few of its recommendations.

Most notably, legislators passed a bill requiring that recipients of state grants for restoration work give the state a historic-preservation easement in exchange. H. Bryan Mitchell described the recent overtures as "promising, but not a lot . . . in the great scheme of things."[20] Funding for a statewide survey to identify historic buildings, sites, and districts regarded as essential for effective local planning has been inadequate. The commonwealth also lacks a systematic program for monitoring those preservation easements it currently owns. Admittedly, the review process followed by the Department of Historic Resources has significant weaknesses. For example, state agencies may issue licenses or provide funds to private-sector projects even if they endanger historic resources. Nonetheless, the department's adherence to a formal review process sometimes influences the actions of other agencies. Mitchell maintains, "The process is not regulatory from our point of view. . . . We do not have final authority to permit or bar a project, or to demand that a resource be saved, but we certainly have influenced projects along the way."[21] This influence may be seen in a new regulation advanced by Governor Douglas Wilder that requires the department to review state-funded transportation projects. Nevertheless, additional improvements are urgently required. Unless Virginia fundamentally alters its preservation program the state may preside over a large-scale destruction of historic resources, particularly the remaining unprotected Civil War battlefield sites.

The Influence of Developers

The Commonwealth of Virginia will determine the fate of most Civil War battlefield sites located within the state. Local-government preservation initiatives have been curtailed by financial constraints and the commonwealth's continued reluctance to provide localities with alternative zoning tools. The federal government rarely intervenes in state historic preservation affairs, and when it does the motive can often be traced to politics rather than a site's historic significance.[22] Poised to fill the void left by federal and local programs, Virginia has opted to embrace a minimalist program of historic preservation. Robert Krick, chief historian of Fredericksburg-Spotsylvania National Military Park, remarked that when there "is almost as much bulldozing as there is sunlight" in central Virginia, government must seek an equitable balance between development and preservation.[23] Pressured by enormous financial contributions and the desire to be reelected, political leaders in Virginia have tipped the scales in favor of the development community.

Although it is difficult to show with certainty, there appears to be a direct correlation between prodevelopment voting patterns and political contributions from developers. Virginia state government plays a pivotal role in determining the financial health of the development industry by approving road, water-line-access, and resource-extraction permits along with authorizing local land-use mechanisms. Sociologists John R. Logan and Harvey L. Molotch argue in their book *Urban Fortunes* that "the people who use their time and money to participate in local affairs are the ones who—in vast disproportion to their representation in the population—have the most to gain or lose in land-use decisions."[24] The influence of the development community is restricted only by its monetary resources. Contributions to statewide or General Assembly races in Virginia are not subject to financial ceilings. A look at the official list of General Assembly lobbyists registered with the secretary of the commonwealth reveals that as of March 2, 1990, there were eighty-five directly representing developers, while only thirteen represented causes tangentially related to land-use and environmental concerns.[25]

An examination of political contributions for the 1989 Virginia gubernatorial race demonstrates the potential political leverage of developers. During the Republican primary the eventual winner, Marshall Coleman, received $3.3 million (40 percent of his total) from the development community. His opponents, Congressman Stan Parris and former Senator Paul Trible, received a half and a third of all contributions from developers, respectively.[26] Spokesman J. Bruce Hildebrand defended Coleman's campaign coffers by stating, "Somehow the implication is that these people [developers] want something that benefits them directly, but good roads and effective government benefit everybody." Coleman's Democratic opponent, Lieutenant Governor Douglas Wilder, received $600,000 (12 percent of his total) from developers. Two weeks before the general election, of the $20.6 million raised by all candidates, $7 million had been contributed by developers. Northern Virginia developer John "Til" Hazel and his family contributed $1.25 million alone. Hazel explained, "The only way I know how to accomplish something is to get involved. . . . If it looks like big contributions are evil, I can't worry about that."[27] Hazel's charity toward the Republican party may not have gone unnoticed. President Bush's interior secretary, Donald Hodel, eschewed embroilment in the Manassas controversy until congressional and public pressure became an insuperable embarrassment.

In the 1992 Virginia General Assembly, developers won an impressive victory. Senate Bill 514 (SB 514), drafted by John Foote, a partner in the law firm of Hazel and Thomas, PC (of which John "Til" Hazel is a partner), and introduced by state Senator Charles J. Colgan of Prince William County, radically altered the system of state designation of buildings or sites deemed eligible for historic status. The purpose of official state designation is to inform citizens, potential developers, and local governments of a property's historic significance. Once designation has been granted, local governments can use or ignore such knowledge in making zoning decisions, choosing sites for county services, or devising long-term land-use plans. As far as developers and individual property owners are concerned, state designation places absolutely no restrictions on an owner's use of land or property.

Before passage of SB 514, the Department of Historic Resources decided which properties were placed on the state's list of historic places. From now on the agency must hold public hearings before designating properties or districts as historic. If an individual owner of a historic site or a majority of landowners in a historic area object, the agency cannot place the property on the state list.[28] The new law also requires the state to reconsider the designation of historic districts created since January 1, 1989. Under this retroactive provision, a majority of landowners in two Civil War battlefield areas—Bristoe Station in Prince William County and Brandy Station in Culpeper and Fauquier counties—could vote to have recently approved historic landmark designations revoked.[29] In essence, the bill will allow current landowners (even out-of-state developers) to determine whether or not a property is historic. Til Hazel views SB 514 as a means of restoring democracy to the designation process: "Preservationists had been riding high for five years or so . . . [until] they started telling people they had to paint houses 'colonial buff'. . . . [People were] fed up by bureaucrats who tell landowners 'Your house is in a historic district'. . . . [514] puts the balance back. . . . It will lead to a real discussion on preservation." He also maintains that with respect to drafting and lobbying the bill, he "had zero to do with it."[30]

Proponents of SB 514 claim that historic-site classification was used improperly as a guise for a no-growth agenda; properties classified were of little historic significance.[31] More specifically, bill supporters argue that historic-site designation precipitated a drop in property values and discouraged developers.[32] Evidence concerning the relationship between property values and historic-site designation actually lends support to the contrary. After surveying eighty-seven local assessors and commissioners of revenue, the Virginia Department of Historic Resources recently found that historic designation has no negative impact on individual or historic-district property values. In fact, a study of historic Fredericksburg concluded that between 1971 and 1990 residential and commercial property values had risen 674 percent and 480 percent, respectively, in the downtown historic district, as compared to 410 percent and 281 percent elsewhere in the city.[33] Although Hazel and Thomas lawyer John Foote cites a real-estate-industry view that "once land is designated historic, its marketability is diminished," opponents of SB 514 attribute declining property values to the recession, not to historic preservation.[34]

U.S. Congressman George Allen (R-Virginia) introduced similar legislation that targeted historic designation at the federal level. His bill HR 4849, would amend the Historic Preservation Act in two ways. First, formal responsibility for the determination of national register eligibility would be shifted from the NPS to the secretary of the interior. Historic preservation activists assert that this provision would alter what has traditionally been a technical and professional program housed within the NPS into a highly politicized designation process. Second, the bill would empower local governments to veto the secretary's determination of national register eligibility for any property that is five acres or larger in size, as long as a simple majority of the local governing body objects to such determination.[35] Representative Allen explained the bill's purpose by stating, "Historic preservation is very important for Virginia, nevertheless, the . . . government was instituted for the protection of life, liberty and property, not to come in and diminish people's property without their consent, without local government being involved."[36] In reality, as the *Potomac News* editorialized, "Either Representative Allen has been misled or he simply doesn't understand the law he is trying to bastardize. . . . The Interior Department's review of sites eligible for the National Register of Historic Places is scarcely tantamount to a zoning decision."[37] If passed, historic preservationists allege, Allen's bill will leave protection of nationally significant cultural resources to the whim of individuals whose attraction to short-term monetary gain may overshadow their concern for long-term preservation.

The same type of developer influence found at the state and national levels may be discerned at the local level, as readily demonstrated in Fairfax County. In 1990 the chairperson of the Fairfax County Board of Supervisors, Audrey Moore, who had been elected on a planned-growth platform, proposed a number of measures to restrict the amount of commercial development in the county. Under her leadership the board subsequently downzoned several land areas as a means of controlling traffic-generating commercial development. Fairfax County preservation activist Annie Snyder observed, "We have *many* areas in this County that should be downzoned to be in accordance with the comprehensive plan."[38] Area developers responded, successfully orchestrating a major lobbying campaign in the General Assembly to reverse the county's decision and limit local zoning authority. The state legislature then tried to overturn the Fairfax decision, but to the delight of preservation groups, the courts upheld the downzoning.

Developers also influence local zoning decisions by manipulating the "revolving-door syndrome." Easily attracting former city and county planners with high salaries, major development firms hire employees equipped with invaluable inside information. Developers frequently apply information garnered from this source to exploit local zoning laws. Government officials have been accused of granting especially favorable zoning decisions to major development firms only to resign and become an employee of the same firm a few months later. Roger Snyder, who served as Prince William County planning director for seven years, now works as chief executive of the Northern Virginia Building Industry Association (NVBIA), one of the country's largest development-related lobbyist organizations. As the industry's spokesman, Snyder led the lobbying campaign against Fairfax County's decision to downzone certain industrial areas. His nemesis, Annie Snyder of SBC, has written that the "County's own files are replete with instances where staff abetted the interests of the region's major developers, or so it seems."[39] Former Prince William County executive Robert S. Noe resigned to accept a position with a California-based firm planning a major development project in the county. Fairfax County planning chief Denton Kent departed in 1989 to become executive director of a firm developing a residential and commercial complex on the site of the old Potomac Railyard in Alexandria. Fairfax County approved a code in 1986 that supposedly prevents former county employees who work for private firms from contacting the county about earlier projects. Prince William County has passed a similar revolving-door measure. And in 1991 the Virginia General Assembly passed an ethics law discouraging job-hoppers: a maximum $1,000 fine and/or up to one year in prison for county officials who take jobs with private organizations within a year of leaving county government. The effectiveness of this new law remains to be seen.

The Hazel family is representative of most Virginia developers in that they have been particularly aggressive recruiters of former government officials. Charles B. Perry, chief highway engineer for northern Virginia, accepted the position of vice president of William A. Hazel, Inc., in March, 1989. Likewise, William J. Keefe resigned as Herndon planning director to become director of the land-use division in the law firm of Hazel and Thomas, PC. One northern Virginia planning official explained the power of Til Hazel by commenting, "What Til wants, Til usually gets."[40] As far as Civil War battlefields are concerned, the revolving-door syndrome brings into question whether local government officials can indeed base zoning decisions on the public good. Hazel and Thomas attorney John H. Foote, who ruled that the Manassas shopping mall was a legal use under the William Center rezoning, has been credited with drafting SB 514 on behalf of his current client, Lee Sammis, the California developer of Brandy Station fame.

The Fight over Manassas: A Case Study

By the end of the summer of 1988, an unprecedented number of Americans had heard of the Civil War battles of First and Second Manassas. Television images depicting bulldozers ravaging hallowed ground catapulted Civil War buffs, historians, celebrities, and politicians into action to save the battlefield. The fight over Manassas, however, represented a perversion of public policy. Congress passed a legislative taking measure only after all other means of preservation had been exhausted. Other local, state, and federal policies failed to preserve the historic site. Close inspection of the Manassas debacle dramatically reveals how the interplay of economic need, political influence, and differing values operates to the detriment of Civil War battlefield preservation.

The controversy, as we have seen, centered around a 542-acre parcel of land adjacent to Manassas National Battlefield Park. In 1986 Prince William County officials, with the assistance of the developer's attorney, rezoned the tract as a "planned mixed-use district" to permit construction of an integrated business community and a high-quality, campuslike office park. Manassas National Battlefield Park superintendent Roland Swain and other area residents reluctantly supported the development proposal as the best available alternative.[41] Less than two years after the rezoning, Hazel/Peterson Companies announced that a 1.2-million-square-foot shopping mall would be constructed on the site as part of the William Center development project. The Prince William County Board of Supervisors subsequently interpreted local zoning ordinances to accommodate the change in plans.

Journalists seized on the forthcoming debate, labeling it the Third Battle of Manassas. (In reality, the battle was one of a series that began when the park was first established in 1940.) Every master plan completed by the NPS since the early 1970s had recommended preservation of the William Center tract, but all attempts to acquire the land had been thwarted by county government officials.[42] Furthermore, the NPS's 1959 decision to acquire additional parkland had been contingent on the promulgation of local government regulations to protect the William Center tract and other adjacent lands from development.[43] Despite promises of adequate protection in return for continued private ownership, Prince William County approved plans for a Marriott Corporation amusement park on the tract in 1973. A judge later overturned the rezoning on procedural grounds. Again, during Senate hearings in 1980, the vice president of the board of supervisors opposed NPS acquisition of the William Center tract because "the county . . . has absolutely no intent whatsoever of doing anything to violate the integrity of the park."[44] Just eight years later, the county approved the Manassas Mall.

Few historians disputed the historic significance of the William Center tract, which encompassed Stuart's Hill, Lee's headquarters, and a field hospital (see Map 6). On August 30, 1862, General Lee launched a fateful counterattack from Stuart's Hill that thrust Major General James Longstreet and the First Corps into the left flank of the Union army. Historic and archaeological study mandated by the county's 1986 rezoning and financed by Hazel/Peterson Companies revealed that as many as 43,000 soldiers had camped around and were deployed from Stuart's Hill. In addition, up to 19 Union and 147 Confederate soldiers "may have been killed or buried" on the land. The development firm concluded, however, that the site was "typical unutilized northern Virginia farmland" that was "historically insignificant."[45] Hazel's paid archaeologist, Daniel Koski-Karell, was the only professional academic who denied the existence of un-

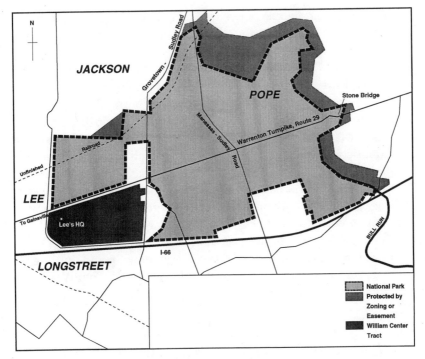

Map 6: Manassas National Batttlefield and William Center Tract, 1988. (Brian Huonker, from U.S. Department of the Interior/NPS)

marked graves on the William Center tract. Incidentally, Koski-Karell's application for admission to the Council of Virginia Archae-ologists had been rejected on three separate occasions.[46]

Prince William County officials welcomed the proposed mall as a source of tax revenue and jobs. County supervisor Ronald Cole commented, "It excites me in the sense that we're no longer going to stand in the shadow of Fairfax County."[47] Over a twenty-year period, it was projected, the mall would generate 2,900 new jobs and $87 million in net revenue.[48] County officials found the prospect of commercial development especially appealing as a means of offset-ting residential demands associated with a population growth rate of fourteen thousand people per year. At the time, tax revenue from the average Prince William County home covered approximately 60 percent of service costs.[49] County officials also deplored the possibility of additional federal ownership in the county. In 1987 the federal government already controlled 20 percent of Prince William County's land base, for which the county received annual payments of $20,139 in lieu of taxes.[50] On the other hand, Prince William County officials never acknowledged publicly that federal expenditures at the Quantico Marine Base and a government lab pumped more than $500 million into the county, and that Manassas National Battlefield Park generated tourism dollars without demanding costly services.

Some opponents of the proposed mall argued against desecration of the battlefield in principle. "What price are we willing to put on our heritage?" asked Congressman Robert Mrazek (D-New York). "You can't hallow the sacrifice of those soldiers who died fighting for freedom with a Burger King and Bloomingdales."[51] Civil War historian James M. McPherson told senators,

> What was at stake in the Civil War and at Second Manassas and in the William Center tract was the very fate of the nation, whether it would be one country or two, would it be a nation with slavery or without slavery. That part of our heritage can best be understood by studying it and Civil War battles, in my opinion, can best be studied by going to the battlefields, walking them as I've gone to this one several times . . . I would have liked to go on the property that is part of the William Center tract. . . . That has not been my opportunity in the past, but I hope as a result of Congressional action it will be my opportunity in the future.[52]

The NPS expressed anger over a breach in a "good-faith agreement" concerning the original development plan.[53] NPS officials worried that the mall, accompanied by the eighty-five thousand extra automobiles it could draw to the area on weekends, would detract from the park's nineteenth-century setting. George Berklacy of the NPS complained that building a mall next to the hallowed ground of a battlefield was "like booking a roller derby in the Sistine Chapel."[54] Public opinion, as determined by a June Mason-Dixon Opinion Research poll, overwhelmingly supported federal acquisition of the tract. A postcard poll taken June 1, 1988, by the *Prince William Journal* found that 80 percent of the 1,711 respondents opposed the mall.[55]

Preservation advocates attempted to foil the mall proposal with three separate strategies. Congressmen Mrazek and Michael Andrews (D-Texas) introduced legislation to deprive the site of access to two major transportation routes, I-66 and Route 29. At the same time, they requested that the secretary of transportation implement section 4(f) of the U.S. Department of Transportation Act to protect the historic site from the harmful impact of federal road projects. On another front, the congressmen requested an investigation of possible violations committed by the developer under section 404 of the Clean Water Act. After finding the developer guilty of damaging wetlands along Youngs Branch without permission, the U.S. Army Corps of Engineers issued a temporary cease and desist order on June 22, 1988. Meanwhile, on May 4, Congressmen Mrazek and Andrews introduced legislation to authorize the Department of the Interior to purchase the 542-acre William Center tract.[56]

Interior Secretary Hodel opposed NPS acquisition of the tract. His solution to the Manassas controversy involved closing the two major roads running through the national park, Routes 234 (Sudley Road) and 29 (Lee Highway), and subsequently directing traffic onto a new bypass. He also proposed that NPS and local officials develop a cooperative arrangement to ensure compatible development on adjacent lands. In return for NPS support of the mall, the developers, Hazel/Peterson Companies, agreed to preserve the Stuart's Hill area and move the mall to another location on the tract. Opponents effectively criticized the Hodel proposal on grounds that construction of the bypass would cost up to $500 million, require large land acquisitions, and take years to complete.[57] When it became apparent that congressional legislation would prevail over the compromise, Til Hazel announced that the mall would be constructed atop Stuart's Hill. During this period of time, the Commonwealth of Virginia and members of the Virginia congressional delegation declined to take a position on what they termed a local zoning issue. The relative inaction of Governor Gerald Bailes and the delegation brings into question the role of political contributions. Representative Stan Parris received several thousand dollars for his reelection campaign from the Hazel family, as did Republican Representatives Frank Wolf and French Slaughter and Senator Paul Trible.[58] Congressman Andrews commented, "One very important elected official that I talked with about Manassas told me he couldn't help me because an interested party was one of his biggest contributors. . . ."[59]

In May 1988 Congressman Frank Wolf reversed his earlier position and introduced legislation authorizing the federal government to acquire the 542-acre tract through a legislative taking. Under the rarely used measure, the government would immediately take title to the property with a "fair price" to be determined at a later date. A highly publicized compromise offered by Senator John Warner (R-Virginia), involving federal acquisition of 136 acres and prohibiting construction of the mall on the remaining land, failed in committee.[60] Following a decisive win in the House, supporters of the Wolf bill anxiously awaited Senate action on the measure. Senator Dale Bumpers's (D-Arkansas) much heralded history lesson on the floor of the U.S. Senate has been credited with swinging the vote in favor of the bill. On November 10, 1988, preservation advocates emerged as victors when President Reagan signed the Wolf bill as part of the veto-proof tax revision bill. In addition to the taking, the law authorized the government to share the cost of building a bypass necessitated by the closing of Routes 234 and 29, and mandated cooperation with the local government to protect the scenic viewshed.

In the midst of congressional hearings, Hazel/Peterson Companies continued to escalate the value of the William Center tract. Working day and night under spotlights, the firm installed sewer lines and graded ground for two hundred houses.[61] Hoping that President Reagan would veto the bill, Til Hazel continued operations on the property until the bill became law. The predicted cost of acquiring the "improved" William Center tract under the legislative taking ranged from $50 to $200 million, even though county tax records assessed the property at just over $13 million. If the government had acquired the tract in 1981, as recommended by NPS professionals, it would have been considerably cheaper, for tax records then listed the property's value at $2 million. By comparison, the entire fiscal year 1989 budget for all acquisitions in the 334-unit NPS amounted to $52.6 million.[62] After Til Hazel had been notified of the president's decision he remarked, "As I ride by the property tonight, I can look at an investment drawing interest—compounding quarterly."[63]

The apparently successful fight over Manassas vividly demonstrates the failure of America's historic preservation policy. Local, state, and federal-executive-branch historic preservation policies failed to prevent a dramatic and extremely expensive legislative taking. Prince William County supported construction of the mall on the William Center tract. Similarly, the Department of the Interior later offered the developer tacit, if not open, support with a compromise plan. The Commonwealth of Virginia refused even to participate in the debate and maintained a position of absolute neutrality. In the absence of preservation action at the local, state, or federal-executive-branch level, credit for preserving the battlefield must be granted to a band of citizen activists and the leadership exercised by several members of Congress. The SBC served as the focal point for grassroots support. Led by feisty Annie Snyder, it embarked upon a nationwide public relations campaign. Snyder, "considered the nation's grande dame of historic preservation," demonstrated that one person can energize and organize legions of citizens for a common cause.[64] Within ten months the SBC group obtained signatures from eighty-two thousand people who supported preservation of the battlefield. After the successful campaign Snyder commented: "They all said we can't win. I don't go into a fight expecting not to win. If your cause is right, and this was clearly a right and wrong thing in the beginning, people will come in behind you. . . . To me, that [the petition drive] was one of the most rewarding parts. That people did have a right to petition against their grievances and that's what we did."[65] Assisted by national preservation groups, sympathetic congressmen, and national media attention, the SBC's unyielding zeal paved the way for successful preservation. Given the unprecedented outlay of federal funds, such a feat is unlikely to be repeated.

The fight over Manassas persists. To date, Congress has paid $118 million to stop development on hundreds of acres earmarked for a regional shopping mall.[66] In 1990 Hazel/Peterson determined that the Manassas property was worth well over $100 million. Since the Justice Department assigned a significantly lower value to the property, federally appointed appraisers were asked to intervene. One placed a $55 million price tag on the property, while another valued the land at $63 million. Given this large differential, Hazel and Peterson filed suit in federal court seeking just compensation for the legislative taking of the William Center tract. They were well positioned to negotiate against a colossus. Congress had promised to pay developers whatever the land was worth in November 1988, which was several months before the land boom of the 1980s came to a screeching halt. Ironically, "If Til Hazel had built the mall, he might well have lost his shirt," wrote Karl Rhodes, associate editor of *Virginia Business.*[67]

In December 1990 federal officials agreed to pay Hazel/Peterson about $81 million—$67.6 million for the 404-acre tract and $13 million in accrued interest. The return on Hazel/Peterson's investment at Manassas exceeded 700 percent.[68] Prince William County sought $5 million in damages when the government confiscated the mall site. The court ruled that the county could not claim losses for incentives that Hazel/Peterson had guaranteed in exchange for approval of the project. Judge Moody Tidwell ruled in this precedent-setting case, "Once the development was canceled, the proffered conditions were no longer required."[69] Less than a year after the settlement Stephen Potter, an NPS archaeologist, announced that the William Center tract "provided more significant insights into antebellum African-American slave life than the studies at any other individual sites in the area, including Mount Vernon and Monticello." The discovery of what has been described as one of the most important pre–Civil War sites in America occurred after the mall project had been stopped.[70]

Remarkably, future residential, commercial, or industrial development on unprotected adjacent lands could once again threaten the integrity of the park and result in yet another battle of Manassas. As it stands, less than half of the park's boundary is protected by conservation easements. Amidst the favorable publicity generated during the Manassas controversy Congress could have enacted a comprehensive park protection plan. Instead, it has continued to address threats to Civil War battlefields and other natural, cultural, and historic resources on a piecemeal basis. This approach is not only uneconomical but unwise. Unless Congress creates a comprehensive solution to ameliorate the clashing forces of development and preservation, haphazard government intervention to protect America's Civil War legacy may be too costly or too late.

Developers are producing an unbelievable amount of short-term, inefficient, uneconomic junk that is going to be like a great slag heap around us.

—Jacquelin T. Robertson,
Dean, University of Virginia
School of Architecture

 **5**

The Costs and Benefits of Battlefield Preservation

O N FIRST inspection, the advocates and adversaries of Civil War battlefield preservation appear to be diametrically opposed. Their arguments are not quite as distinct as one would imagine. Advocates cite historic values, aesthetic merits, economic and social benefits, environmental concerns, and military education as reasons for protecting Civil War battlefields. Opponents rarely confine their argument to economic growth. While formulation of a Civil War battlefield preservation policy is problematical, the economic concerns shared by both factions provide a solid foundation for development of a viable policy.

Arguments in Favor of Preservation

Most Civil War historians, buffs, and activists are persuaded that the Civil War was the United States' definitive moment as a nation. For them, preserved battlefields are more than just dry history lessons.

Not only do these sites commemorate the bloody ordeals of battle but they also translate into capital assets.

The Economics of Preservation

The economic arguments in favor of preservation significantly bolster the preservation case for those citizens ambivalent about historic values. Before examining the ways in which Civil War battlefield preservation can generate revenue, it is helpful to explore the cost of rapid development. Development does not bring jobs and tax dollars without social and economic costs. New residential development creates temporary construction jobs and draws added spending power to a community but at the same time requires additional municipal services. Costs associated with school construction, police and fire protection, sewer lines and other types of infrastructure can simply overwhelm a local government's budget. In the Commonwealth of Virginia, for instance, local communities must provide an average of $1.20 in residential services for every dollar they collect in property taxes.[1] Residential developments, which demand an enormous number of municipal services, must be constructed near industrial and commercial facilities to house employees. A 1984–85 study conducted by the Loudoun County, Virginia, planning staff revealed that on tax revenues of one thousand dollars the net to the county would vary as shown in the following table:[2]

	Required County-Government Expenditures	*Net to County*
Residential Sector	$1,234	−$234
Industrial/Commercial Sector	$ 304	$696
Agricultural Sector	$ 49	$951

Evidently the county accrues the least cost in the agricultural sector. This suggests that counties could protect Civil War battlefields for relatively little cost by placing protective easements on historically significant agricultural lands.

Since the scenario depicted in the table is only applicable when agriculture constitutes the principal form of land use, Loudoun County has adopted a more sophisticated form of computer analysis designed to estimate the direct fiscal consequences of new development at both the regional and project level. The program, called the Fiscal Impact Model, helps planners determine the direct and indirect cost of commercial development. Milton Herd, former director of planning for Loudoun County, summarized the fiscal impact of urban development: Jobs (employers) locate near people (labor force), which attracts more people, which in turn attracts more jobs. As more people and jobs locate in areas, the demand for public services goes up (in quality and quantity), thus increasing the tax burden on all local residents.

There is no conclusive evidence that growth pays for itself: Development can produce either positive or negative results. Personal values and priorities dictate whether better job opportunities, higher income, and enhanced public service outweigh higher taxes, increased congestion, and more expensive housing. In the short term, an invigorated economy has a positive effect on a local government's net tax revenues. Over the long haul, growth attracts new residents with sundry needs that negatively influence net tax revenues. According to Peggy Maio of the Piedmont Environmental Council in central Virginia, ultimately any "development requiring infrastructure and services creates a tax demand. Battlefields open to the public are no exception."[3] A distinction must thus be made between urban battlefields and rural battlefield sites immune from immediate development. Counties can protect arcadian Civil War sites for relatively little cost by placing protective easements on historically significant agricultural lands. The idea of directing development toward places where service and facility needs are most effectively served while steering growth away from sensitive natural and cultural resources is gaining favor in growth areas.

Civil War battlefields preserved as parks or protected agricultural land could minimize the social costs of surrounding development. Preserved battlefields not only save a locality tax money but with proper promotion can generate revenues through tourism. Although location certainly influenced the results, in 1980 the NPS found that the number of people visiting its historical, archaeological, and military areas exceeded those visiting its natural parks by 46 percent.[4] In particular, Civil War battlefields were immensely popular vacation destinations. Updated tourist-survey figures published by the Virginia Tourism Development Group revealed a 5 percent increase in visits to the state's Civil War sites between 1990 and 1991. Another study conducted between September 1990 and December 1991 confirmed the powerful influence of Ken Burns's Civil War television series, which first appeared on PBS in September 1990: Virginia received nearly half a million additional tourist visits.

In 1989, the U.S. Travel Industry Data Center examined the impact of 100 additional visitors a day on the average American community. The study revealed a direct economic impact of $1,294,000 annually in tourist-related sales and services.[5] Some tourism analysts claim that every dollar spent on tourism produces $3.65 elsewhere in the U.S. economy.[6] Tourism already serves as the largest single employer in thirty-nine states, and the trend shows no sign of reversing. More than 11 percent of all American jobs created in 1988 were directly related to the industry.[7] For many communities, the development of a tourist-based industry offers a particularly appealing economic alternative. More than 90 percent of U.S. travel-related firms can be classified as small business, and income generated from these firms is pumped back into the local economy while developers and other major industries often transfer their profits to another location.[8] Furthermore, tourism can be a "clean" industry; it does not necessarily harm the environment, nor does it always require a massive infrastructure of expensive services.

Of course, many tourist attractions spawn support services, namely, gas stations, convenience stores, and restaurants. In the absence of proper planning these services may place a financial burden on local governments. Terry Holzheimer, director of the Department of Economic Development in Loudoun County, Virginia, views tourism and manufactured goods as analogous. He recently wrote, "I suspect that 'successful' battlefield preservations, those that become tourist attractions, are most like commercial/industrial development in terms of cost. Infrastructure needs are primarily transportation related." Yet as Holzheimer points out, unlike manufacturing centers battlefields are typically regarded as public goods with all up-front costs supported by public funds. Holzheimer notes that battlefield sites "must recoup all acquisition and development cost indirectly, through the positive fiscal impact of ancillary development which collects the income. This linkage is always difficult to calculate and usually speciously reported."[9] In most cases, however, the financial burdens associated with tourist-related support services pale in comparison to the costs of industrial development.

Other evidence supporting the income-producing capabilities of historic sites is readily available. A study conducted by the Maryland Historic Trust revealed that tourist spending in Maryland for 1989 surpassed $4.3 billion.[10] Civil War battlefields and colonial-era homes were mentioned as the second most popular attractions after Baltimore's Inner Harbor.[11] In a 1990 study of Harpers Ferry National Historical Park and its effect on the local economy and tax base, the NPS found that the economic benefits far exceeded any additional tax income the county would collect if the parkland were developed to its "highest and best use."[12]

Tourism and Fredericksburg-Spotsylvania National Military Park. The City of Fredericksburg, Virginia, has developed a campaign with surrounding counties to promote the area's Civil War history. Visitors to its historic district bring approximately $42.9 million to Fredericksburg each year.[13] For our purposes, it is important to distinguish the economic benefits generated by the Fredericksburg-Spotsylvania National Military Park from those generated by other historic sites in the Fredericksburg area. The most recent data indicates that the military park produces an annual income of $8 million.[14]

In an economic study entitled "The Cash Value of Civil War Nostalgia: A Statistical Overview of the Fredericksburg Park," researchers calculated the net economic impact of the military park on the City of Fredericksburg and the surrounding counties of Orange, Caroline, Stafford, and Spotsylvania. Placing the average market value of land at $3,000 per acre (the average in Spotsylvania County) and applying a 1981 tax rate of 85¢ per $100 assessed valuation, researchers determined that the 5,400-acre military park costs local jurisdictions $1,377,000 in lost tax revenues. If the parkland were put to its highest and best use, which in this case would be agricultural, the regional economy would gain an additional $437,400 in farm income. Because the military park does not require any local government services, the total cost of the unit can be calculated by adding lost taxes to lost regional economic product for an annual total loss of $1,814,000. On the basis of automobile counts, researchers determined that an estimated 1.1 million people visited the park in 1980. Of the 200,000 individuals who came purely for cultural purposes, approximately 18 percent stayed overnight in the Fredericksburg area. According to data provided by the Virginia Department of Transportation, overnight visitors brought a total of $1,340,000 to the community, day visitors $450,000, for a total tourist income of $1,790,000. Utilizing a U.S. Department of Commerce calculation that twenty-four visitors a day to a park community is commensurate with a $160,000 annual industrial payroll, researchers calculated that the military park compares to a company with a $3,680,000 payroll. Park salaries, local purchases of goods and materials, and funds expended for improvement and maintenance of park structures totaled $1,008,000. By applying a multiplier effect (that is, taking into account further economic activity and spending) of 2.0 to tourist-generated income, the researchers discovered that the military park produces $8,068,000 in total annual income as outlined in the following table:[15]

Losses		Gains	
Lost Taxes	$1,377,000	Salaries/Purchases	$1,008,000
Lost Farm Income	437,400	Tourist Dollars	1,790,000
Multiplier Effect	1,537,000	Multiplier Effect	5,270,000
Total	$3,351,400	Total	$8,068,000

In summary, the City of Fredericksburg and surrounding localities obtain an annual net economic benefit of $4.7 million from the Fredericksburg-Spotsylvania National Military Park.

Although the $4.7 million figure is impressive, it probably grossly underestimates the park's current net economic benefits on two counts. First, in the ten years since the economic study was conducted visitation figures have increased substantially. In 1991, 1.86 million people visited the military park, 240,000 of them solely for cultural purposes. Second, it is erroneous to assess current economic benefits in terms of 1983 dollars. Adjustments for inflation and increased visitation would set the net economic benefit of the park much higher. Robert Krick argues that "to use the 1983 figures unrevised does the disservice of under-reporting the facts by a multiple of something like 150%. . . ."[16] Over the past ten years no one has attempted to complete a major economic analysis of the economic benefits generated by area Civil War sites.

Tourism and Gettysburg National Military Park. The economic impact of tourism is easier to gauge in Gettysburg, Pennsylvania, than in many other Civil War battlefield communities because the battlefield is that city's only major tourist attraction. In a study sponsored by Gettysburg National Military Park, four master's degree candidates at Shippensburg University examined the economic impact of tourism generated by the park. They conducted two different types of studies, hoping to obtain identical results. In one, they surveyed tourists to determine how much money was spent during a typical visit. In another, they interviewed owners of local businesses and reviewed tax receipts to establish the amount of money spent by tourists in Gettysburg. A multiplier of 2.0 was used to determine the gross receipts indirectly associated with tourism.[17]

The tourist survey revealed, with 95 percent accuracy, that park-related tourism provided the community with annual revenues of $43,182,301. Results of the business survey, again with 95 percent accuracy, indicated that annual revenues of $39,310,000 could be attributed to tourism. When the annual operating budget of the park was added to the business figure, a total of $42,269,490 nearly replicated the results of the tourist survey. Moreover, economic data obtained from the Economic Development Office of Adams County, Pennsylvania, confirmed the results of the study. A 1988 study determined that total travel expenditures in the county surpassed $48 million.[18]

Environmental Benefits of Preservation

Historic preservation advocates tend not to promote the environmental aspects of Civil War battlefield preservation on the grounds that environmental arguments unnecessarily detract from the more important issue of preserving hallowed ground. Nonetheless, battlefield preservation offers a number of significant environmental advantages. It serves the dual purpose of protecting both historic and natural resources within a battlefield's boundaries. Consider the example of Manassas National Battlefield Park, which includes environmentally valuable wetlands. During the Manassas affair, environmental attorney Harold Himmelman alerted the Army Corps of Engineers that section 404 of the Clean Water Act was being violated by the Hazel/Peterson developers. According to Himmelman, development activity had caused excessive silting in Youngs Branch, which flows through the park into Bull Run, leading to the destruction of beaver ponds in associated wetlands.[19] In the end, no violation notice was issued because the developer modified the operation in compliance with the corps's regulations.

Preservation of agricultural land and Civil War battlefields can occur in tandem through the use of easements. Under easement protection, a family farm that served as a Civil War site might remain insulated from urban encroachment. Battlefields can function as "green spaces" in the midst of residential and commercial development. A. Wilson Greene, executive director of APCWS, averred that conventional wisdom supports green spaces: "I think the quality of life in a community has a lot to do with open space, and it has a lot to do with historic sites, heartlands and all those sorts of things that contribute to making a community more liveable."[20] Economic studies of residential development have supported Greene's assertion. Those published in the *Review of Economics and Statistics* have consistently demonstrated that proximity to undeveloped public spaces increases property values.[21] As a whole, environmental arguments merely add support rather than impediments to battle-field preservation efforts.

Military Staff Rides

In the late 1890s, Congress frequently justified Civil War battlefield preservation on the basis of military necessity. In 1896, President Grover Cleveland signed a bill declaring all national military parks to be "fields for military maneuvers for the Regular Army of the United States and the National Guard of the States."[22] In 1906, members from what is now known as the Command and General Staff College, as well as West Point cadets and students from the Army War College at Carlisle, Pennsylvania, were among the first to engage in military training exercises on battlefield sites. Inter-rupted by World War II and its aftermath, "staff rides" as the equivalent of military exercises were recommended on a small-scale in the late 1960s. (In its current form, a military staff ride consists of a preliminary study of a particular battle, an extensive visit to the battlefield site, and then a discussion to integrate lessons learned from the experience into modern warfare tactics.) Today both the U.S. Army and the Marine Corps employ staff rides for training. Although staff rides have only recently gained popularity within the U.S. military community, foreign military officers have conducted on-site studies of American Civil War battlefields for years. Some historians argue that the Germans profited by study-ing and implementing several Confederate maneuvers during the blitzkrieg of 1940. Between World Wars I and II officers of the German general staff retraced Stonewall Jackson's brilliant Shenan-doah Valley campaign of maneuver and stealth in the spring of 1862. Staff rides enable participants to visualize the realities of war. Many officers have never experienced combat, and it is virtually impossible to recognize the influence of terrain on military maneu-vers and decision-making with just a map. By retracing the steps of troops and commanders, staff riders can begin to grasp, as army chief historian Brigadier General Howard Nelson put it, "the limita-tion on maneuver and sustained combat action imposed by logisti-cal capabilities."[23] Staff rides also allow participants to examine why and how certain leaders and soldiers reacted to different types of combat situations. Equipped with such information, participants emerge from the experience better soldiers.

Staff rides have become essential components of the American military training program in recent years. As General Carl E. Vuono, former chief of staff of the U.S. Army, noted, "History sharpens the vision of the skilled commander. . . . Equally important, it contributes to leader development by narrowing the gap between peacetime and war. That gap is of special concern in today's Army when few below the rank of lieutenant colonel or master sergeant have ever experienced combat. History infuses with living immediacy the matrix of tactics, logistics, command, terrain, and technology. The student quickly realizes that battles are not merely matters of theory or doctrine—they really happened."[24] Some intelligence experts argue that the staff ride concept should be enlarged to include civilian intelligence officers. Walter P. Lang of the Defense Intelligence Agency began taking agency analysts on guided tours of Civil War battlefields after observing their performance during the Iran-Iraq War. According to Lang, intelligence officers accurately reported the events, "but they had trouble understanding that sometimes the outcome of a battle depends upon intangibles like morale more than it does upon weapons and firepower."[25] Without immediate policy action, further loss of America's unprotected Civil War sites to subdivisions, malls, and industrial parks may impair the military's ability to study tactics related to certain battlefields.

Arguments against Preservation

For pro-growth advocates, development is equated with progress. Implicit within the term development are visions of higher productivity, greater wealth, and happier lives. Those who favor development over historic preservation believe it is right to leave the past behind and confront the future. Historic preservation results in stagnation while development brings new jobs, homes, outside income, and services to a community. Developers question the moral right of preservation activists to deprive individuals of economic opportunity. They commonly oppose Civil War battlefield preservation since it may remove large tracts of land from the market.

Opponents of battlefield preservation include developers, local government officials, and private-property disciples. Most developers view open land, regardless of its historic significance, as a potential economic investment. They dismiss the public "right" to green space and an aesthetically pleasing environment in the name of progress and, as we have seen, often influence political decision-making through financial contributions and intensive lobbying. As for local government officials, they frequently speak about development with an air of inevitability. Others aggressively recruit development in hopes of broadening the local tax base and thereby offsetting rising service costs. They argue that tax revenues collected from commercial and industrial development will prevent increases in local property taxes.

Many individuals, especially in rural areas, oppose preservation of Civil War battlefields on grounds of privacy rights. They abhor intrusion into their private lives, especially attempts by outsiders to influence local decision-making. To them, historic preservation mandated by government or an outside group is just as threatening as change brought about by a major developer. Government recognition of a historic site would simply attract unwanted tourists. Instead, individual property owners should decide if, when, and how a historic site should be protected. Oftentimes developers infiltrate areas before supporters of historic preservation can begin to alert local residents of impending change, and too often rural residents oppose the idea of historic preservation until it is no longer an option.

Private Property Rights

The opposition of developers, local government officials, and rural citizens to Civil War battlefield preservation rests primarily on an affirmation of private property rights. The Fifth Amendment to the U.S. Constitution prohibits government taking of private property "without just compensation." Justice Oliver Wendell Holmes's pronouncement in the 1922 Supreme Court case of *Pennsylvania Coal*

Company v. Mahon has been interpreted to mean that any type of government intervention in private property matters involves an abrogation of an owner's constitutional rights: "The general rule at least is, that while property may be regulated to a certain extent, if regulation goes too far it will be recognized as a taking."[26] In accordance with this view, classifying a tract of land as historic can be regarded as denying the owner his or her right to develop it to its highest and best use. Similarly, if a locality refuses to rezone a historic property, which in many cases means devaluing it, the jurisdiction may be accused of taking a property without just compensation. While historic preservation opponents frequently invoke the Fifth Amendment, until recently Supreme Court and federal court decisions tended to uphold the right of a locality to promote the general public welfare through historic preservation regulations as long as some reasonable use for the property remained.[27] This all seems to be changing in favor of property-rights advocates.

The present state of the law is best expressed in the Supreme Court case of *Penn Central v. the City of New York*.[28] In the 1978 decision Justice William J. Brennan commented that historic preservation laws are constitutionally valid as long as property owners retain an economically viable use of their property. He based his ruling on the "widely shared belief that structures with special historic, cultural, or architectural significance enhance the quality of life for all."[29] Recently, a band of property-rights advocates have joined to attack this law and undermine the basic premise of zoning and land-use planning.[30] They adhere to an absolutist concept of property rights—that all landowners have the right to develop their land to its maximum economic potential or its highest density. Moreover, property owners should be entitled to just compensation every time the slightest restriction is placed on their land. Government restrictions that might diminish the future value of land should be forbidden in most instances.

The origin of the property-rights movement can be traced to Richard A. Epstein's 1985 book, *Takings: Private Property and the Power of Eminent Domain*, which detailed the University of Chicago Law School professor's assertion that the government must provide landowners with monetary compensation whenever environmental regulations limit the value of their property. The power of Epstein's book was fueled by two 1987 Supreme Court decisions that facilitated a property owner's ability to claim a taking. Since then the U.S. Claims Court has become the focal point for most such claims filed against the federal government. Today there are more than two hundred property-rights cases pending before the court, totaling $1 billion.[31] Property-rights activists hope to establish a constitutional right to government compensation when bureaucratic regulations prevent an owner from using his property to its maximum profit potential.[32]

The Reagan administration provided additional momentum to this movement with the promulgation of a 1988 executive order requiring the federal bureaucracy to consider how its regulations affect property owners. Property-rights activists like Troy Mader, a member of the Wyoming-based Abundant Wildlife Society, believe that the executive order provides an excellent means of stemming regulatory abuse by no-growth and antidevelopment interests. He asserts that the law "has become the most effective tool of nature worshippers to lock up vast areas and deprive people of their individual property rights."[33] Other groups, such as the ten-thousand-member Fairness to Land Owners Committee, complain that the Bush administration has not fully implemented the 1988 executive order. These groups have sought congressional means to ensure that their property rights are protected. Last year the U.S. Senate passed a bill introduced by Steven D. Symms (R-Idaho) requiring the attorney general to certify departmental compliance with Reagan's executive order on takings. In the House of Representatives, James A. Hayes (D-Louisiana) has repeatedly introduced legislation to restrict federal designation of wetlands and to require compensation when an individual's property is designated as a protected wetlands area.

Most recently, property-rights advocates hoped that the outcome of three test cases before the U.S. Supreme Court would clearly address fundamental assumptions concerning the government's right to regulate land use through local ordinances, environmental legislation, and other controls. In particular, they expected the largely conservative court to expand substantially the rights of property owners subject to takings by the government. The specific cases involved a South Carolina owner who forfeited his right to build on two shoreline lots when the state's Beachfront Management Act, aimed at controlling erosion, went into effect (*Lucas v. the South Carolina Coastal Council*); a trailer-park owner alleging his property lost value after passage of a rent-control ordinance (*Yee v. the City of Escondido, California*); and a Puerto Rican construction company's proposed hotel and restaurant development in a mangrove forest, held in abeyance because of a forest-preserve site designation (*PFZ Properties v. Rodriguez*). Since indemnifying landowners for losses incurred would undoubtedly be exorbitant, environmental activists feared that an expansive interpretation of the Fifth Amendment's just-compensation clause would prevent government bodies from enforcing historic preservation and environmental protection laws.[34]

The decision in these closely watched cases proved far less than a sweeping vindication of property rights. The court adhered to the longstanding opinion that a property owner must be deprived completely of the economic use of his land before claiming just compensation for a government taking. In a six-to-three decision, the court overturned the South Carolina Supreme Court's decision in *Lucas v. the South Carolina Coastal Council*. Speaking for the majority, Justice Anthony Scalia said that in order to be exempt from compensating the owner the state "must do more than proffer the legislature's declaration that the uses Lucas desires are inconsistent with the public interest."[35] To avoid paying compensation, the state would have to prove that it acted under an "abatement-of-nuisance" standard (that is, the elimination of a nuisance in a particular jurisdiction), a legal tool that has been used in the past to regulate beachfront property. Justice John Paul Stevens suggested that such regulation "is a traditional and important exercise of the state's police power. . . ." The court decided the case of *Yee v. the City of Escondido* on more limited grounds than sought by the plaintiff, and altogether declined to rule on *PFZ Properties v. Rodriguez*.[36]

In the absence of a broad, comprehensive ruling on the takings issue, both property-rights activists and members of the environmental community claimed victory. Chip Mellor of the Institute for Justice maintained that "the *Lucas* decision is another evolutionary step toward greater protection for property owners," whereas Jerold

Kayden, a senior fellow at the Lincoln Institute of Land Policy, stated that "by no stretch of the imagination is this a radical property rights decision. . . . It continues to allow government to go quite far in regulating land use."[37] Despite the court's relatively narrow interpretation, the Lucas ruling implies that states and localities will have to justify land-use regulations under more intense public scrutiny.

The growing property-rights movement is spearheaded by organizations like the Center for the Defense of Free Enterprise (CDFE), the Multiple-Use Land Alliance (dedicated to opening all public lands to private enterprise), the National Inholders Association (created to advance the rights of those who own private property within federal parks), and the American Freedom Coalition (founded by the Unification Church to serve as a third political party). Ron Arnold, one of the founders of CDFE, explained that his organization's goal is to "systematically destroy the environmental movement." In August 1988 these groups and two hundred other organizations, companies, and individuals held a conference under the auspices of the "wise-use" movement. They have concentrated their efforts in three principal areas: the private property movement, pro-jobs economic development, and multiple-use of federal lands.[38]

The National Trust for Historic Preservation has taken an unusually active role countering the "attack on established law launched by this militant property rights group," filing numerous *amicus curiae* ("friend of the court") briefs that helped persuade the Pennsylvania Supreme Court to reconsider a case in which the court ruled that the mere designation of a Philadelphia theater as historic was an unconstitutional taking.[39] The trust has established a toll-free hot line to garner information about other attempts to abrogate local historic preservation regulations, and it has been attempting to defuse the power of the property-rights movement by forming alliances with environmental, land-use control, and growth-management groups.

Members of the property-rights movement have been quite vocal in the Civil War preservation debate. Their arguments are problematical, often disingenuous, and sometimes fallacious. Organizations such as the Fairness to Land Owners Committee allege that the NPS achieves its conservation and preservation goals by confiscating historically significant property from unwilling sellers. The facts speak otherwise. Since 1980, the federal government has initiated condemnation proceedings in only five of the country's twenty-one national parks related to the Civil War. With two exceptions, the 1,293 acres acquired in the process were obtained through "friendly" condemnations.[40] The exceptions involved the rare legislative taking of the William Center tract near Manassas National Battlefield Park and the condemnation of 2.96 acres of a developer's building lots at Harpers Ferry National Historical Park.[41] The 557.95-acre Manassas parcel represented 43 percent of 1,293 acres acquired through condemnation proceedings. Because federal law requires the government to compensate property owners at fair market value, regardless of whether the condemnation is friendly, in a depressed economic market landowners may profit from a taking. This situation was most recently exemplified in the Manassas affair.

Brandy Station: A Case Study

The ongoing controversy over the Brandy Station Battlefield in Culpeper County, Virginia, provides an ideal opportunity to examine arguments against and in favor of preservation. All elements of the typical preservation dispute are present: the outside developer, a pro-growth county government, a dedicated band of preservation advocates, "planned growth" county residents, and environmentally oriented public-interest groups. With the factions engaging in a seemingly irreconcilable war, the case of Brandy Station again suggests why a comprehensive Civil War battlefield preservation policy should be enacted. Meanwhile, in the absence of immediate government intervention we may soon add Brandy Station to the growing list of lost battlefields.

Culpeper County lies sixty-five miles southwest of Washington, D.C. Still largely agricultural, it is just beginning to feel the pressure of urban encroachment. In the past two years alone, Culpeper residents have watched their real-estate taxes escalate 55 to 60 percent. Without an adequate school infrastructure to absorb a growing population, local children must attend elementary school in modular trailers. County officials have taken few steps to protect the rural character of the area from development. "Developers think they can do things much easier in Culpeper than Fauquier . . . because of lax land-use regulations" and higher zoning densities, claims Art Larson, a former Piedmont Environmental Council staff attorney.[42] Although closer to Washington, D.C., than Culpeper County, nearby Fauquier County has enacted zoning regulations that require developers to leave up to 80 percent of a property as open space. In addition, only 862 acres of Culpeper County have been placed under protective easements while over 26,000 acres are protected in Fauquier. Already ill-prepared to manage the needs of a growing population, Culpeper County officials have been reluctant to consider the fate of historic resources.[43]

Culpeper County is the site of the largest cavalry battle ever waged on the North American continent. At Brandy Station on June 9, 1863, more than 11,000 Union soldiers launched a surprise attack on approximately 9,500 Confederate cavalrymen. The battle marked the first time Union horsemen managed to hold their ground against the highly touted Confederate cavalry under the command of Major General J. E. B. Stuart. Some historians maintain that Stuart was so humiliated by the attack that it may have influenced his performance during the Gettysburg campaign. Culpeper County also served as the site of the Union Army of the Potomac's winter encampment of 1863–64. And Fleetwood Hill, near Brandy Station, was the headquarters of Major General George Meade, commander of the Army of the Potomac. Relatively undisturbed by Civil War relic collectors, the encampment holds a wealth of invaluable archaeological resources. James McPherson observed that the Brandy Station battlefield and encampment "are among the most important Civil War sites that still remain virtually unmarked and unprotected from potential destruction by commercial or residential development."[44] The entire battlefield site is commemorated by a lone marker at Fleetwood Hill.

By the spring of 1990 Lee Sammis, a California-based developer, had acquired 5,800 acres of land in Culpeper County. A large portion of the Brandy Station Battlefield was included in the tract. After initially stating that "Sammis has immediate plans only to farm his Culpeper tracts and for the near future no intention of developing the land," his company spokesman later announced plans to construct a massive business and industrial complex on the land to be known as Elkwood Downs.[45] Around the same time, a group of land speculators acquired a significant portion of the Union encampment site with plans to build 290 exclusive homes on the 800-acre parcel. Bill Bryant, trustee for the encampment property owners, declined to allow Virginia historic preservation officials or professional archaeologists to inspect the land.[46]

While the developers were purchasing land in the area, Culpeper County officials were in the process of updating the county's zoning ordinance. As a result of a year-long study they conducted, which incidentally did not include historic-resource analysis, the county rezoned large tracts of land for less intensive use. However, despite protest from local citizens and historic preservation activists, the board of supervisors allowed the Sammis property to retain its more intensive residential zoning.[47] County officials eagerly welcomed the Sammis project and felt the promise of a broader county tax base justified the Sammis exemption.[48] Sammis then requested industrial rezoning for an office/warehouse/industrial park to be constructed directly on the battlefield. In September 1990, the Culpeper County board of supervisors approved the Sammis plans. The Sammis industrial/residential complex will include a total of 6.2 million square feet of industrial development and nine thousand housing units. The completed development will nearly double the county's population.[49] Although Chris Mothersead, director of development for Culpeper County, maintains that the county requested historic-planning assistance from the Commonwealth of Virginia before Sammis filed his new rezoning application, a member of the county planning commission argues that their efforts were "superficial" until Sammis "galvanized us into action."[50] The county now asserts that it has officially identified its historic resources and encourages their protection. But Russell Aylor, chairman of the planning commission, commented, "Even if historical significance were not an issue," Sammis's proposal is "still a big project for Culpeper."[51]

In the wake of impending development, a group of local residents and Civil War buffs formed the Brandy Station Foundation "to foster protection of the historic rural character of the Brandy Station area of

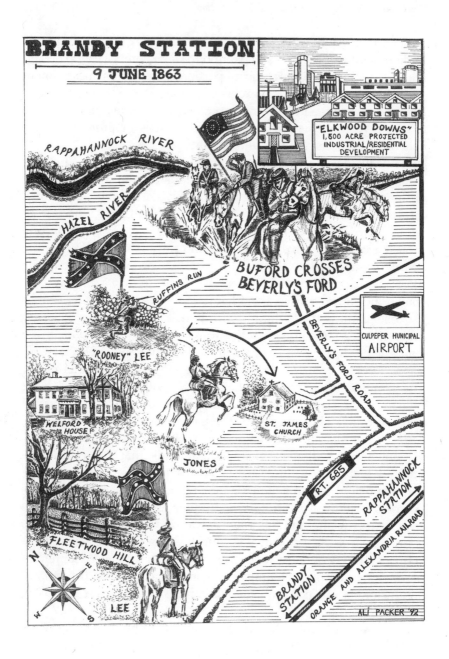

BRANDY STATION

9 JUNE 1863

RAPPAHANNOCK RIVER

HAZEL RIVER

"ELKWOOD DOWNS"
1,500 ACRE PROJECTED
INDUSTRIAL/RESIDENTIAL
DEVELOPMENT

RUFFINS RUN

BUFORD CROSSES
BEVERLY'S FORD

CULPEPER MUNICIPAL
AIRPORT

BEVERLY'S FORD ROAD

"ROONEY" LEE

ST. JAMES
CHURCH

WELFORD
HOUSE

JONES

RT. 685

RAPPAHANNOCK
STATION

FLEETWOOD HILL

N

E

W

S

LEE

BRANDY
STATION

ORANGE AND ALEXANDRIA RAILROAD

ALI PACKER '92

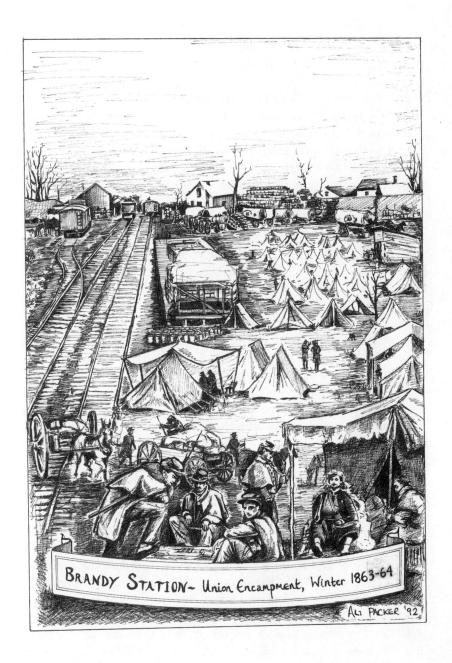

BRANDY STATION~ Union Encampment, Winter 1863-64

ALI PACKER '92

Culpeper County." When it became apparent that the board of supervisors did not share their historic preservation interests, foundation members initiated a public relations campaign to focus national attention on the battlefield's status. With assistance from the APCWS, preservation attorney Tersh Boasberg, and the Piedmont Environment Council, the group nominated Brandy Station Battlefield for placement on the Virginia Historic Landmark Register and the National Register of Historic Places. Provided with state or national recognition, the foundation planned to refute claims advanced by the developer and county officials that the tract was historically insignificant. When criticized for ignoring the historic significance of the Sammis plot, Mothersead responded, "There are very few attributes of the Civil War on this property. What we are going to have to have is a balance between historic preservation and development opportunities. . . . Historical preservation is a serious issue. It should not be used for no growth [agendas]."[52] Michael Armm, a spokesman for Sammis, asserted, "I think the interpretation of what is historically significant is highly subjective."[53] Aside from county government opposition, the foundation encountered resistance from several local residents. These citizens objected to the proposed Elkwood Downs development *and* the potential for official government recognition of the historic site. During the past ten years, all attempts to adopt a historic zoning ordinance for Culpeper County have failed because of opposition from county residents.[54]

The Virginia State Board of Historic Resources not only accepted the foundation's nomination but decided to expand the nomination to include historic sites at Stevensburg and Kelly's Ford. On October 30, 1989, a 14,000-acre rural historic district including Brandy Station Battlefield was designated as a Virginia historic landmark. The commonwealth approved a historic district three times larger than that recommended in the initial nomination. Citing lack of evidence and inadequate research, the Culpeper County Board of Supervisors voted to reject Brandy Station's nomination to the National Register of Historic Places. Mothersead explained that the "impetus" for county leadership in historic preservation "has died since the State has become so heavy handed."[55] H. Bryan Mitchell, director of preservation programs for the Commonwealth of Virginia, retorted that the county's "argument that the state did not consult with localities simply means we didn't agree with the project as envisioned by the Board of Supervisors."[56] In February 1991, the NPS echoed the state's sentiments by adopting the boundaries of the Virginia historic landmark.

The conflict over the Brandy Station Battlefield has now reached a critical stage. Preservation advocates have filed a lawsuit against the county contesting the legality of the Sammis zoning exemption. Hoping to quell the opposition, Sammis offered to donate 248 acres of battlefield land along with some funds for a museum. Historic preservation advocates assert that the 248 acres are completely unacceptable. Located in areas the developer could not develop, such as steep hillsides and floodplains, the proffered land consists of a series of small, noncontiguous tracts. Property-rights groups such as Virginians for Property Rights have also entered the fracas. Patricia Bradburn, a member of that group's board of directors, argued in a *Potomac News* editorial that "in Virginia, when government agencies designate land as historic, no compensation is required, but the property's value is diminished and its use controlled. The poor landowner is helpless. . . . In Culpeper, preservationists are suing the county to protest its rezoning about 1,500 acres of Brandy Station Battlefield. But with proper legislation, there need be no litigation. The law should hold accountable any person, group or government agency that affects the value of one's property without providing just compensation. . . ."[57] Recent developments in the Virginia statehouse related to Senate Bill 514 have further frustrated the efforts of local preservation activists. The new law requires the Virginia Department of Historic Resources to reconsider the historic landmark status it granted to Brandy Station Battlefield. If a majority of landowners at the battlefield site object to the landmark status, the designation will be revoked prior to June 1993. Brandy Station's eligibility for national historic register designation remains unaffected by the Virginia action.

The Brandy Station Foundation wants to preserve 2,000 to 3,000 acres of the most crucial areas of the battlefield and to enhance the value of surrounding historic resources through the creation of local historic districts. They also want to promote tourism as an economic alternative to unplanned and incompatible development. As it stands, even with state or national register designation, the historic resources of Culpeper County are unprotected. Without in-fee (fee-simple) acquisition or the more viable alternative of stringent local zoning ordinances, Lee Sammis and his associates can begin construction on their new industrial/residential complex if the pending lawsuit is decided in their favor. In mid-July 1992 the case was decided in the county's favor. It is now on appeal. With a favorable court decision, the California developer could determine the fate of Culpeper County, the water of the Rappahannock, and possibly the future of central Virginia.[58]

Perhaps in the finest way, while standing on ground
where men once fought and died and surrounded by tributes
to their sacrifices, visitors may have a greater sense
of the communal bonds of generations. Then despite the
intervening years, they might be moved by a personal sense
of loss to say [borrowing from Walt Whitman's elegy for
Abraham Lincoln], "Comrades mine and I in the midst,
and their memory ever to keep."

—Richard W. Sellars, NPS

 6

A Battlefield
Preservation Policy

As CURRENTLY conceived and implemented, America's historic
preservation policies cannot guarantee the protection or in some
cases even the existence of Civil War battlefields. The decentralized,
piecemeal policy program designed to protect historic buildings,
districts, and other components of the built environment falls short
of its objectives where Civil War battlefields are concerned. Given
the prevailing conservative fiscal climate, future NPS acquisition of
Civil War battlefields seems unlikely. Moreover, state and local preservation efforts are not consonant with the significance of historic
resources within their respective jurisdictions. It is naive to assume
that localities and private conservation organizations have the resources necessary to preserve all unprotected Civil War sites. One of
national government's responsibilities is to protect the integrity of
nationally significant resources.

There must be a fundamental reevaluation of national historic preservation policy before any further attempts are made to preserve remaining Civil War battlefields. Local, state, and federal historic preservation programs must be improved, incorporating new opportunities for public- and private-sector partnerships. This would include a systematic identification of significant Civil War battlefield sites, followed by a considered and balanced approach to delegation of protective responsibility. Assignment of protective responsibility to federal, state, local, or private authorities would rest on the notion that historic preservation is a valued public good and all should share its costs. By linking the economic interests of tourism and agriculture with Civil War battlefield preservation goals, the policy would provide an alternative acceptable to both economic-growth and preservation advocates. The value of the policy suggested in the following sections is that it can be used to protect all of America's precious resources, not just Civil War battlefields.

The First Step: Improving the Current Preservation Program

The Federal Level

The NPS is charged with protecting America's natural, cultural, and historic resources for the benefit of all citizens. Yet in recent years its mission has been compromised by factions within the Department of the Interior who support the multiple-use approach. Several conservation groups have recommended separating the NPS from that department and establishing it as an independent agency.[1] As such the NPS would be afforded greater political and fiscal clout. In 1989 Representative Bruce Vento (D-Minnesota) and Senator William Bradley (D-New Jersey) introduced legislation designed to protect the NPS from external political forces. The bill called for creation of a new advisory board to review NPS programs and contained a provision that would have made appointment of the NPS director subject to Senate confirmation.[2] This bill, however, did nothing to resolve internal inconsistencies in the NPS mission.

In the early years of the NPS, management concerns rarely extended to areas beyond park boundaries. Over time its mission was interpreted as requiring park managers to expand their concerns first to adjacent-land issues and later to viewshed problems. Pressures related to urban encroachment, burgeoning population, and pollution now demand additional expansion and refinement of park management policies. NPS personnel can no longer guarantee the protection of resources without becoming involved in local activities outside park boundaries. The National Parks and Conservation Association described this policy as "ecosystem management," which requires "goal setting for an individual park, definition of boundaries, developing and maintaining inventories to monitor success, and establishment of the information base necessary to understand and predict the behavior of the system and its components. One explicit assumption of such management is that ecosystem boundaries often differ from political or ownership boundaries."[3] According to Harpers Ferry National Historical Park chief historian Dennis Frye, from a practical perspective ecosystem management entails "looking at the whole when you are making decisions about your island in the whole. The park has to be involved with county government, town government, state regulations, state government issues, with local tourism, the Chamber of Commerce, and highway plans. All have nothing to do with management of the park, but they have everything to do with the integrity of the park."[4] Since Congress has repeatedly refused to grant the NPS full authority to address zoning problems arising outside park boundaries (for fear of creating a "national zoning board"), NPS officials must work closely with local zoning boards to ensure that park needs are incorporated into land-use plans. Ecosystem management is a means of achieving cooperative management goals.

To begin this process, all parks should complete a study of adjacent lands to provide "information to landowners and local, state and federal land-use permitting agencies on the effects of proposed development, construction, tree-cutting and other land-use and design changes, as well as how to minimize negative effects."[5] At the same time, the NPS should use educational programs and other public-outreach activities to cultivate an appreciation for park resources among the residents of surrounding communities. Unless a community understands the value of park resources, it will not be inclined to enact protective zoning ordinances. Each NPS unit should establish educational goals and attempt to expand the informal NPS motto: *Interpretation* (education) leads to *understanding* which leads to *appreciation* which culminates in a desire to *preserve*. Implementation of ecosystem management will require superintendents to step beyond park boundaries and participate in community affairs. (Richard Rambur, superintendent of Antietam National Battlefield, acknowledges that the notion of NPS park superintendents functioning in a purely custodial manner is already more fiction than fact.)[6] Taken together, these ecosystem-management activities can have a positive impact on local zoning decisions.

An excellent model of NPS outreach activities can be seen at Harpers Ferry National Historical Park. Rangers there have worked with local school systems to develop an educational program about the park for inclusion in the high-school, junior-high-school, and elementary-school social studies curriculum. Each year thousands of area fifth-graders are bused to a five-acre plot on School House Ridge for a one-hour action-packed lecture on T. J. "Stonewall" Jackson's siege and the subsequent capture of the Union garrison.

Obviously, ecosystem management's effectiveness is related to the degree of cooperation exhibited by local officials. Since the inclination to engage in cooperative management varies from one election year to the next, long-term resource protection demands additional enforcement powers. The power of a temporary court order (injunction) offers one extremely effective alternative management tool. If granted, Civil War sites and other nationally significant resources would receive protection through the injunctive powers of the secretary of the interior when threatened by private development on adjacent lands. Implementation of this policy would invite questions of taking property without just compensation, but a temporary work stoppage would enable NPS representatives and other relevant officials to meet with the developer before the resource suffered additional damage. Under current law, the National Advisory Council on

Historic Preservation can only intervene if *federal* agency actions threaten a property listed in the National Register of Historic Places or as a national landmark. Another alternative policy would allow the NPS to acquire easements, without congressional authorization, on sites threatened by immediate development.[7]

Lands and sites outside NPS boundaries can be protected by acquisition or by a range of less-than-fee options, including conservation or agricultural easements, purchase by a third party who then leases or sells the land to the NPS (purchase and lease- or sell-back), donation of land to the NPS by someone who keeps the right to live there during his or her lifetime (life estates), and private-landowner agreements. In a time when local governments are seeking enhanced revenues from taxes on privately held property and federal officials are operating under severe budgetary cutbacks, less-than-fee options seem to offer an attractive alternative. Yet preservation activists such as Bruce Craig of the National Parks and Conservation Association believe that despite the recession, these options cannot replace outright purchase of endangered Civil War battlefields. He argues that the public "could buy *all* the endangered National Park Civil War battlefields for about $50 million and that's chicken feed in the federal budget."[8] Although Craig's proposal represents the most fail-safe form of battlefield protection, at present it is politically unpalatable. Moreover, before accepting any new in-fee acquisitions, the NPS must receive additional staff and financial support. Over the past twenty years the amount of acreage in the national park system has more than doubled, while additional hiring for management and protection has not kept pace.[9]

Another institutional recommendation has to do with how federal land ownership affects local economies. As we have seen, localities garner net tax dollars from agricultural land. When a historic property is protected by federal ownership rather than by easements or other preservation alternatives, the local government does indeed lose a portion of its tax base. Disregarding for the moment the potential economic and aesthetic benefits a locality receives through a preserved park, the amount of compensation offered to communities for federal land ownership is simply unreasonable. Increased federal in-lieu-of-tax payments, perhaps tied to a park's entrance-fee structure, could assist local economies and diminish the likelihood of an adversarial relationship between local government and park officials.[10] Endangered Civil War properties could be further protected by altering the section 106 review under the amended National Historic Preservation Act of 1966 so that federal funds for highways, airports, and other local and state projects would be withheld from jurisdictions encompassing such sites (see appendix B).

The State Level

State historic preservation programs have commonly been regarded as adjuncts to the national historic preservation agenda. Varying in stringency and breadth, state preservation programs cannot ensure the preservation of nationally significant Civil War battlefields. Most states lack adequate financial and administrative resources to engage in a comprehensive program of historic-site acquisition. State officials are also averse to incorporating Civil War battlefields into state park systems. They believe the hallowed nature of battlefield land conflicts with the recreational purpose of state parks. A successful Civil War battlefield preservation program demands a new role for the state historic preservation officer.

There are two ways of substantially improving state historic preservation policies. The first is the use of tax abatements to increase public participation in historic preservation initiatives. The Reagan administration canceled or abridged many federal tax credits, leaving a significant gap in the historic preservation tax-incentive program. By offering charitable deductions to those property owners who place permanent conservation easements on historic properties, states could achieve a high level of preservation without excessive expenditure.[11]

The second and most promising policy for Civil War battlefield preservation requires state creation of rural agricultural or preservation land trusts. Although Virginia residents can donate conservation easements to the Virginia Outdoors Foundation or the Department of Historic Resources, other land-trust programs involve state purchase of conservation easements. The Vermont Land Trust, for example, which is funded as part of Vermont's Housing and Conservation Trust Fund, acquires conservation easements to protect agricultural land from incompatible development. Similarly, Montgomery County, Maryland, has set aside a 100,000-acre "fertile crescent" reserve solely for agriculture, open space, and recreation. More than a quarter of all private land within the reserve has been protected by perpetual conservation easements. Edward Thompson, chairman of the Montgomery County Agricultural Preservation Advisory Board, notes, "By managing growth, Montgomery is saving its taxpayers countless millions of dollars in the cost of providing services to far-flung subdivisions."[12] If the reserve happens to contain Civil War battlefield sites, Montgomery County is also preserving a piece of America's heritage.

The Local Level

Local zoning decisions will determine the fate of most Civil War battlefield sites. The appearance of state or federal influence is misleading: Control over land use lies in the hands of local government. When authorized by a state's enabling legislation, local communities have a number of creative options in managing the competing interests of growth and preservation. A brief description of alternative zoning techniques will illustrate their potential as historic preservation tools.

The most obvious type of protective zoning requires the establishment of a local historic district. In most instances, a local architectural review board must approve the demolition or alteration of any structures contained within the district. Because historic districts offer protection without compensation to the property owner, other zoning techniques frequently provide a more practical alternative acceptable to both developers and preservation advocates. Lower-density zoning or downzoning of specific areas are two such options, but their implementation is limited by the taking clause of the Fifth Amendment. If, however, a locality allows a property owner to transfer the development rights of a property, the issue of taking no longer applies. As we have seen, TDR simply involves severing the development rights from the land and trading them in the open market. Equipped with TDRs, a community can zone certain areas for growth and designate others for historic preservation. A similar option, usually called planned-unit development, permits developers to cluster structures, which is less costly, in return for leaving the rest of their property as open space. In many cases, protection afforded by agricultural or other downzoning alternatives cannot guarantee the integrity of historic resources. Supplementary protective mechanisms such as easements may be required when the maximum allowable density of agricultural zoning is too high to preserve a farming landscape. Value-taxation programs are yet another preservation option. They enable property owners to pay taxes on current-use value as opposed to fair-market value. This special assessment commonly applies to owners who intend to use their property for agriculture or horticulture, or as forest or open space. Civil War battlefield preservation can easily be achieved through implementation of any one of the aforementioned zoning alternatives.

Preservation and Private Conservation Groups

A fourth type of historic preservation, aside from local, state, or federal government programs, emanates from the actions of private individuals and conservation groups. Some property owners protect historic resources on their premises merely by refusing to sell or develop. The reliability of these protective measures is extremely variable; in the case of death or a change of heart on the part of the owner, for example, resources may lose their protected status. Private conservation organizations are a far better alternative. Groups such as the APCWS buy, or acquire through donation, historically significant properties. Other organizations, like the Nature Conservancy, The Trust for Public Land, and The Conservation Fund, purchase threatened properties and later donate the land to the NPS. Destry Jarvis of the Student Conservation Association explains that private organizations "can move faster and cheaper than the Park Service. [They] act in areas that are high priority in resources, but low priority for acquisition."[13] Other groups like the Piedmont Environmental Council rarely hold easements but readily promote them.[14] While the ultimate goals of these groups differ, ranging from a desire to "complete" national parks to the hope of maintaining the rural character of an area, each can incorporate Civil War battlefield protection into their programs. Approximately five hundred private land trusts have preserved nearly 3 million acres across the United States.[15]

Additional Tools

The preservation technique of education, which holds the greatest potential to influence the course of battlefield preservation, has been underemphasized by government and private organizations alike. Ways to unleash the power of public education warrant immediate attention. Most Americans are aware of the national landmark and register programs, but few realize that such designation places absolutely no restrictions on the activities of private property owners unless federal funds or licenses are involved. Likewise, most people do not fully understand the section 106 review process or the difference between local, state, and federal historic preservation programs. Some private-property-rights groups have used this ignorance to fuel their respective causes. National and state register designations have been portrayed as highly restrictive government regulations that precipitate an immediate drop in property values, while the activities of the NPS have been represented as confiscatory. Perpetuation of such misinformation has done much to retard the cause of Civil War battlefield preservation.

An aggressive public information campaign could serve two separate but related purposes. First, by clarifying the stipulations associated with major preservation programs, government organizations could diminish the influence of militant property-rights groups in a single stroke. Second, and perhaps more importantly, a public relations campaign would apprise the general public of the number of alternatives that can be used to preserve historic properties. In a recent newspaper article John Foote, a land-use attorney for Hazel and Thomas, PC, argued that because there are few laws governing historic preservation, historic lands can often be preserved only by condemnation or by a landowner's "willingness to give up the land."[16] This statement suggests that the preservation challenge is an all-or-nothing debate. In contrast, a simple and broad-based public relations campaign would help members of the general public view the preservation challenge in terms of a continuum of options. Rather than adopt a defensive posture, historic preservation officials should seek to explain all major elements of a preservation program by using every available forum, including television talk shows, newspaper interviews, public debates, brochures, telephone hot lines, and signs posted at historic sites. Provided with such information, people could then make informed decisions about the merits of historic preservation.

The Second Step: A New Approach

Even if all these policy recommendations were enacted and all existing historic preservation policies were carried out to the full extent of the law, Civil War battlefield sites would continue to vanish. Successful preservation of the Stuart's Hill tract at Manassas National Battlefield Park conveyed the false impression that government preservation programs are not only adequate but effective. The legislative action over Manassas, however, was a once-in-a-lifetime solution that will probably not be repeated. As preservation activist Brian Pohanka laments, "It often takes a horrendous occurrence, a preservationist's Pearl Harbor, if you will, to galvanize opposition to the destruction of a Civil War site."[17] Crisis management for the protection of Civil War sites is no longer pragmatic. It is time to capitalize on the favorable publicity generated over Manassas to formulate a long-term, systematic protection plan for America's Civil War battlefields. Fortunately, recent federal initiatives have provided a few signs of hope.

Civil War Sites Advisory Commission

Time and time again since resolution of the Manassas debacle, Congress has dealt with imperiled Civil War sites on a piecemeal basis.

Malvern Hill, Harpers Ferry, Cedar Creek, and Brandy Station all demand immediate attention. In response to such policy incoherence, Tersh Boasberg, a historic preservation attorney from Washington, D.C., made a discerning recommendation—the creation of a congressionally chartered Civil War sites commission. Partially as a result of Boasberg's *Washington Post* article on the subject (April 8, 1990), U.S. Interior Secretary Manuel Lujan, Jr., and Senator Dale Bumpers of Arkansas publicly acknowledged the merit of approaching battlefields on a more comprehensive basis. In a highly welcomed move, Senator Bumpers tacked an amendment onto a bill calling for a study of Civil War sites in the Shenandoah Valley. His amendment resulted in the creation of the Civil War Sites Advisory Commission.

Congress mandated the commission to make a two-year comprehensive study of historically significant sites and structures in the United States associated with the Civil War. Comprised of scholars, political leaders, and prominent citizens, the commission first met on July 17, 1991. Public Law 101-628 (1990) charged them with identifying important remaining, unprotected Civil War sites, listing them in order of significance, assessing short- and long-term threats to their integrity, developing innovative alternatives for their preservation and interpretation, and formulating open-space and land-use preservation techniques. NPS personnel who staff the commission are presently compiling data from field studies and historical research to identify and evaluate individual Civil War sites as well as locations of various campaigns. Land-use information supplied by Geographic Information Systems (GIS) databases has enabled staff members to access the integrity and threats at each site with state-of-the-art technology.[18] After analyzing the results of field studies, historic research, and GIS mapping, the commission must report its findings and recommendations to Congress by the spring of 1993. It is hoped the results of the commission's unprecedented survey will serve as a blueprint for further action by the NPS, the American Battlefield Protection Program (ABPP), and the Civil War Trust (CWT).[19]

The Secretary of the Interior's Proposal

In July 1990, on the occasion of the 129th anniversary of the Battle of First Manassas, Interior Secretary Lujan called for the creation of the ABPP. The program, housed within the NPS, was designed to complement rather than compete with the activities of the Civil War Sites Advisory Commission.[20] Marilyn Nickles, staff director of ABPP, explained that "Secretary Lujan knew about and supported the congressional effort, but recognized . . . critical issues were present. An in-depth study was desirable; battlefields are disappearing every day. . . . In order to avoid a two-, three-, four-, five-year delay, [the secretary of the interior] wanted immediate action."[21] Of course, the secretary's action provided an additional benefit to the administration by demonstrating its commitment to Civil War battlefield preservation.

The ABPP has evolved workable partnerships with federal, state, regional, and local officials as well as private organizations to explore preservation options for the secretary's priority list of twenty-five endangered Civil War battlefields. These were selected on the basis of their historical importance, the degree to which they are threatened, and the probability of saving them. Port Hudson, Louisiana; Fort Fisher, North Carolina; Franklin, Tennessee; Perryville, Kentucky; and Prairie Grove, Arkansas, are a few of the sites receiving assistance under this program. Lujan's priority list is, however, subject to modification depending on the exigencies of specific site degradation. Site studies undertaken by the congressionally chartered advisory commission will aid ABPP in compiling a priority list of threatened battlefields. Nickles notes that ABPP staff members "work in the same office as Commission staff [and] coordinate efforts. . . . [We] hope the program will have experience [sic] in dealing with critical issues so that by the time the Advisory Commission report is complete . . . [ABPP] can move ahead quickly."[22] A complete list of the twenty-five priority battlefield sites may be found in appendix D.

Aside from developing preservation partnerships, ABPP has received federal funding to promote conservation interests in imminently threatened Civil War battlefield sites and viewshed areas. In 1991 ABPP contributed several thousand dollars to the State of Kentucky for planning at Perryville Battlefield. Additional planning assistance has come from NPS personnel. For the 1992 fiscal year ABPP was allotted $250,000 to distribute among pending grant applications involving a variety of battlefield preservation projects. Although ABPP has submitted a total budget request of $10 million for 1993, officials also hope to leverage the purchase of land by private conservation organizations and government bodies.[23] Other preservation activities will be funded through ABPP's public/private partnership with the recently formed nonprofit Civil War Trust (CWT).

The Civil War Trust

The CWT was established in 1991 to lead a national fund-raising campaign for the preservation of Civil War sites.[24] As a private, nonprofit, tax-exempt organization, the CWT is designed to operate in conjunction with the ABPP to "protect, once and for all, Civil War and other significant battlefield sites—with a strategic cost-effective approach."[25] It is hoped that the public/private partnership will eliminate the need for emergency land purchases such as occurred with the legislative taking at Manassas in 1988. The federal government eventually paid $250,000 per acre to protect 542 acres adjacent to Manassas National Battlefield Park. Modeled after the Statue of Liberty/Ellis Island Foundation, the CWT plans to raise $100 million by 1996 for the preservation of Secretary Lujan's twenty-five priority sites, to raise another $40 million by the year 2000, and to leverage $60 million from other sources for the preservation of an additional twenty-five sites. The fifty sites will be preserved as part of a network of local, state, and federal battlefield parks, the "Civil War legacy system."

The CWT hopes initially to solicit contributions from individual donors, major corporations, and regional foundations, to obtain revenues from corporate sponsorship and major foundation grants as well as from the sale of commemorative coins produced by the U.S. Mint. The coins will be minted in commemoration of the 100th anniversary of the first Civil War battlefield preservation legislation. Members of the CWT's board of directors project that the sale and issuance of the coins will generate $10 to $30 million in private funding for battlefield preservation.

The CWT is also spearheading the development of a national data base of Civil War soldiers' personal histories. Working with the NPS, National Archives, Church of Jesus Christ of Latter Day Saints, National Federation of Genealogical Societies, and other interested parties, the CWT plans to develop the "Civil War soldiers' system," which would enable battlefield visitors to recount the steps of their embattled ancestors. When completed, the database will link the regimental histories of 3 million Civil War soldiers to particular battles and battlefields. These sites now serve as living memorials to the ancestors of an estimated 100 million Americans.

Although the CWT is still not ready to accept official applications for funding support, grants have already been announced to protect historic properties in three states. Save Historic Antietam Foundation of Sharpsburg, Maryland, became the CWT's first grant recipient with an award of $100,000 toward the purchase of Grove Farm. Tony Zaccagnino, formerly of the CWT, explained, "This is how we intend to do business. We are not going to go into areas looking for battlefields to save, we want to make money available to local groups that have identified properties and have set specific goals."[26] Preservation of Byram's Ford, also known as the Big Blue Battlefield, outside of Kansas City, Missouri, bears witness to this.[27] Through the cooperative efforts of APCWS and the Civil War Round Table of Kansas City, an eighteen-month-option agreement to purchase the tract was signed in 1991. The Monnett Fund, the nonprofit arm of the Civil War Round Table, has met the challenge of raising half of the purchase price of $42,600 to enable APCWS to complete the acquisition and donate the Byram's Ford Battlefield to the Kansas City Parks Board. The CWT donated $6,000 to the Monnett Fund to help meet its fund-raising challenge. The trust also donated $4,000 to the Central Maryland Heritage League for preservation activities at the site of the Battle of South Mountain and $35,000 to the Mill Springs Battlefield Association for the purchase of land in Pulaski County, Kentucky.

The Shenandoah Valley Study

Several recent policy initiatives undertaken in the Shenandoah Valley of Virginia have been touted as a potential model for future activities of the ABPP and the CWT. In accordance with the Civil War Sites Act passed by Congress in 1990, the NPS has conducted a year-long study of Shenandoah Valley battlefields. Barring future political obstacles, preservation proponents hope that information contained within the final study report will enable Congress to initiate protective measures before external developments make land acquisition politically and economically impossible.

The origin of the Civil War Sites Act can be traced to May 6, 1988, when NPS Civil War historian Robert Krick stood with a friend, Vermonter Howard Coffin, at the edge of a field on the outskirts of Fredericksburg. Krick, the consummate historian, recited how soldiers from the Vermont Brigade had crossed the field while shielding the Army of the Potomac's Sixth Corps, then retreated to the Rappahannock River in the Chancellorsville campaign. Coffin, the great-grandson of a member of that very brigade, listened with rapt attention, especially when Krick offered a concluding caveat to his brief lecture: "Take a good look, Vermonter; in a few months there'll be several hundred houses here."[28]

Back in Vermont, Coffin prevailed upon members of the state legislature to support a resolution calling on Congress to protect those battlefields where Vermonters fought. By unanimous resolution, the General Assembly directed "the federal government to save the national treasures that are our Civil War battlefields." After Coffin notified Krick of his resolve to support battlefield protection in the Fredericksburg area, the latter seized the opportunity to suggest that Coffin pursue preservation of Shenandoah Valley battlefields as his top priority. The Vermonter warmed to the idea, aware that no Northern state had been more energetic in support of the Union cause than his home state. Coffin would do what the Vermonters had done at Cedar Creek—lead the federals to victory to save the Shenandoah Valley battlefields. Senator James Jeffords (R-Vermont) was subsequently contacted and apprised of the urgent need for battlefield preservation in the valley. When Coffin asked Jeffords, "What can you do?" he replied, "Save 'em." "Save what, Cedar Creek?" "Save 'em all," said the senator. Jefford's Shenandoah Valley battle-field study legislation "is credited with spurring the Bush Adminis-tration into addressing, at long last, the need to protect America's Civil War battlefields."[29]

The Shenandoah Valley, located in western Virginia, witnessed some of the most intense and sustained combat of the Civil War. This "bread basket of the South" was the site of two Civil War campaigns. General Stonewall Jackson's brilliant valley campaign in 1862 saved Richmond by diverting Union forces. Two years later, General Philip Sheridan and his ten thousand well-equipped cavalrymen raided the valley. During this devastating campaign the Yankee invaders de-stroyed General Jubal Early's army, pillaged towns, burned barns and crops, and dwarfed Southern pride. Although forty-nine armed conflicts occurred in the Shenandoah Valley, not to mention the minor skirmishes that were a daily occurrence, the valley study focused on assessing the integrity of the fifteen most significant battlefields situated on twelve sites: Cedar Creek, Cool Spring, Cross Keys, Fisher's Hill, Front Royal, First and Second Kernstown, McDowell, New Market, First and Second Winchester, Opequon (Third Winchester), Piedmont, Tom's Brook, and Port Republic. Ten of the fifteen battles were fought on or within a few miles of Inter-state 81 and US 11, the valley turnpike.

The field-survey portion of the study involved the use of computer mapping programs. Preliminary results of GIS analysis found that the fifteen battlefields covered 3.4 percent of the Shenandoah Valley while the core battlefield area amounted to 1.4 percent of the land. As a whole, the study's authors concluded that "the primary losses of integrity have occurred in the Lower Valley in the vicinity of the cities of Winchester and Front Royal. The battlefields of McDowell, Pied-mont, Port Republic, Cross Keys, Cool Spring, Cedar Creek, Fisher's Hill, and Tom's Brook were all rated in good condition. Opequon and Front Royal rated poor. The only battlefield considered lost is First Winchester."[30] Nearly 81 percent of the core battlefield areas were assessed as having maintained a high degree of integrity. This may be attributed to an abundance, however temporary, of unde-veloped private property in the area. Still, after determining the valley's growth potential, NPS officials predicted a 26 percent increase in population by the year 2020. Other features of the study included a comprehensive historical review of each battle site, a discussion of growth and development in the region, and an assessment of the potential for increasing heritage tourism. With respect to policy-making, the most essential aspect of the study involved a review of alternative preservation techniques: no action, creating a national battlefield park, granting NPS-affiliated status to various units with a single battlefield as an interpretive core, or building a local/regional effort that would emphasize cooperation and private ownership of the sites.

Once the draft report had been completed, it was circulated for public review and comment. During this period the APCWS worked assiduously with the NPS and conservation groups to gauge the level of local support for various Shenandoah Valley battlefield preservation options. All groups involved in the series of discussions recognized that successful long-term preservation required solid community support. It is hoped that these exploratory sessions will serve the dual purpose of increasing public awareness and indicating which course of action would be most favorable to area residents. Neither of Virginia's senators, John Warner or Chuck Robb, is willing to introduce Shenandoah Valley battlefield preservation legislation without a clear public mandate.

Senator Jeffords has already begun to prepare legislation "aimed at creating what may prove to be the largest of all of America's national battlefield parks—a national battlefield encompassing all the major battlefields in the Shenandoah Valley."[31] His plan faces an uphill battle on many fronts. The NPS study draft report came to the following conclusions: "In the opinion of the study team, the expense and logistical difficulties involved with [sic] acquiring and maintaining the vast acreage needed to maintain all fifteen battlefields makes federal acquisition and management unlikely. Given the complexity of ownership patterns, current land uses and jurisdictional differences among the fifteen battlefield areas, it makes sense to explore preservation options that allow maximum flexibility of private and public interests."[32] Senator Jeffords and other battlefield preservationists must also contend with an active and vociferous group of resident private-property advocates. Unfortunately, the debate over preservation and land-use strategies in the valley has been clouded by misinformation. Writing in a recent publication, members of Virginians for Property Rights portrayed the NPS as a "predatory, conspiratorial agency preying on innocent Americans to deprive them of their property. . . . NPS is formulating a plan threatening to acquire or control as much as an additional 325,000 acres [in the valley]."[33] The 325,000-acre figure is far higher than any NPS estimate.

Critics of the Shenandoah study suggest that the Interior Department balks perennially at accepting NPS responsibilities and that, accordingly, results of the draft report may be explained by the fact that the department does not want to be burdened with another national park. Other critics view the draft conclusions in terms of budget considerations. Yet to dismiss a new Shenandoah battlefield park on the basis of cost is misleading. There is no need to purchase upwards of thirty thousand acres—the core area of fifteen battlefields—to study Civil War battles in the Shenandoah. A fraction of the battlefields' core area would provide an ideal framework for explaining historic events. Battlefield sites outside the core areas could be preserved through a variety of alternative preservation techniques including local zoning, private-sector acquisition, and voluntary easements. Whatever preservation strategy is eventually adopted, however, should apply to the valley campaigns as a whole; haphazard preservation of individual sites is unacceptable. As Edwin Bearss asserts, the Shenandoah Valley is nationally significant as a unit, not as a conglomeration of individual components.[34] In any case, the time to act is now. Although area land prices are still relatively low, the valley's glacial pace of life will not continue forever.

Recent Battlefield Preservation Developments

The creation of the Advisory Commission on Civil War Battlefields, the ABPP, and the CWT conveys the impression that the battlefield preservation dilemma has been solved, but these programs have achieved more on paper than in fact. Local grassroots organizations deserve most of the credit for recent advances in battlefield preservation. Over the past two years the CWT has only dispersed four grants. Regrettably few preservation groups are aware that such grants exist, let alone how to apply for them. The activities of the ABPP have been limited to conducting research and granting advice. As to the advisory commission, it may not complete its battlefield study until spring of 1993. There are three fundamental reasons why these programs have failed to achieve much-needed results.

The most formidable challenge to battlefield preservation has to do with its inclusion in the broader area of environmental concerns. Battlefield preservation issues have been placed in the same category as disputes relating to wetlands, all-terrain-vehicle access to public lands, and offshore drilling. Battlefield preservationists have thus found themselves confronting not only property-rights activists and developers but also corporate interests, Western politicians, and selective recreational organizations. The issue of Civil War battlefields is different, however, and regardless of the merit of other environmental-protection initiatives, battlefield preservation policy must be formulated independently.

The current state of the economy has not helped the cause of battlefield preservation. With land prices plummeting along the East Coast, disgruntled property owners have been quick to target Civil War battlefield activists and environmentalists rather than the recession for their plight. Ironically, the drop in land prices means that the time is ripe for the acquisition of battlefield land or conservation easements.

The inclusion of Civil War battlefield preservation in the broader context of environmentalism and the current recession have combined to create a third challenge, polarization. In recent years, battlefield preservation issues and objectives have been couched in a cloud of hyperbole produced by preservation activists and developers alike. It is not constructive to describe all historic preservation activists as "nongrowthers" or "not-in-my-backyard" advocates, nor is it helpful to characterize all developers as avaricious businesspeople.

Polarization frustrates the creation of a common platform for discussion and resolution of the issues at hand. The benefits associated with cooperative planning have rarely been addressed.

Future Steps

Despite the scope of the challenges imposed by the environmental connection, the recession, and the polarization of involved parties, the future of Civil War battlefield preservation may not be so dismal after all. Formulation of a viable preservation policy will require three separate components, namely, widespread public support, strong institutional backing, and leadership. Public support and the institutional structure are already in place. What is required is leadership at the national level to start a program in motion.

The real impetus for preservation must come from the general public, and as we have seen, since the Manassas debate public interest in Civil War battlefield preservation has grown at an astronomical rate. Nevertheless, many of the 26 million individuals who visited NPS Civil War sites in 1991 (an increase of over 9 million from the previous year) believe that significant battlefield sites have already been protected or are located in rural areas far removed from the danger of development. A. Wilson Greene, executive director of APCWS, notes that a major difficulty in preserving Civil War battlefields pertains to "conveying the seriousness or the gravity of the situation to those who are unaware of the situation."[35] Only when development threatens to mar a Civil War site does preservation become a heated issue. Battlefield preservation activists and organizations must now draw on public interest in Civil War history to create a powerful lobby for battlefield preservation.

It is not necessary to commission new studies, time-consuming analyses, or additional programs; the information required to develop and implement a preservation policy is either available or being actively sought. With additional funding and a clear mandate from Congress, the ABPP and the CWT could serve as the perfect vehicles for change. Moreover, the dedicated and capable members of the

NPS stand ready and waiting to carry out battlefield preservation activity. Yet despite the wealth of public support and the presence of such a fine institutional structure, battlefield preservation suffers from a dearth of leadership. With several notable exceptions, few members of the administration or Congress have been willing to promote an aggressive Civil War battlefield preservation program. Greater public awareness of the precarious state of America's Civil War battlefields could provide the necessary motivation to prompt immediate policy action.

A National Battlefield Preservation Policy

Development of a comprehensive preservation policy requires access to a highly accurate and dependable data base. The Army War College conducted the last official survey of America's Civil War sites in the mid-1920s. A study commissioned in the late 1960s by the House Committee on Interior and Insular Affairs was never completed. To devise a policy utilizing the military's outdated information would be futile. Not only have our conservation values radically changed since the 1920s, but the military assessed the need for battlefield preservation on the basis of what sites were threatened at the time of the survey. Military education rather than historic significance frequently dictated the priority given to a particular site. Congress recognized the problem when it directed the Advisory Commission on Civil War Sites to complete a comprehensive inventory by early 1993. Although some battlefield preservation advocates may disagree with the standards used by the commission to rate battlefields in terms of historic significance and relative integrity, as long as the inventory is conducted in compliance with congressional legislation, it should provide a solid foundation for development of a national Civil War battlefield preservation policy.

The APCWS has conducted a comprehensive inventory independent of the advisory commission's efforts. Phase one of the inventory, completed in the spring of 1992, involved a survey of forty-five key Civil War battlefields at high risk of being developed. The sites were assessed in terms of their integrity, significance, availability, endangerment, and cost. Phase two will cover thirty more sites.

A. Wilson Greene believes the inventory will "serve as a blueprint for Civil War preservation across the county. Once the sites are identified and evaluated, they won't slip through our fingers and we will all be able to go about saving them in a more organized way."[36] Since the advisory commission and the APCWS employed different criteria to select and evaluate Civil War battlefields in their respective studies, an exchange of results should assist both organizations in the formulation of battlefield preservation strategy.

Thorough analysis of all Civil War sites does more than simply serve as the basis for future policy formulation. Invaluable Civil War resources are often destroyed because people are unaware of them. In April 1989, for example, construction crews at Mary Washington College in Fredericksburg, Virginia, bulldozed an artillery emplacement. Lacking a catalogue of historic resources in the area, the college did not realize it had authorized the destruction of a Civil War site until it was too late. A readily available nationwide inventory of Civil War sites might have prevented this incident. It would also offer future benefits. Provided with a reliable data base, developers could plan their projects fully apprised of an area's historic significance.[37] A reliable data base would allow government officials and concerned citizens to preempt attempts by developers to claim "I had no idea it was there" before giving their bulldozers the go-ahead.

Once all Civil War sites have been identified and evaluated, it must be decided how to achieve protection. By law, the advisory commission is supposed to report back to Congress a plan to protect, preserve, mark, and interpret battlefield sites. After Congress has approved the commission's national battlefield preservation program, the ABPP should be charged with its administration. Management of such a program would validate the role of the NPS (under whose auspices the ABPP comes) as a leader in the area of historic preservation.[38] Senator Dale Bumpers expressed support for NPS leadership: "All these battlefield preservation efforts seem to be initiated by legislators. I'd much rather see you coming up here with a comprehensive plan, setting some priorities, rather than simply reacting to threats as they come along."[39] The NPS should exercise a leadership role, "but they won't without a mandate from Congress and the reason they won't is because they operate under the executive wing of government. The orders of the executive wing of government are, Don't do anything that is going to cost any money. So the only way they'll do it is if we mandate that they do it."[40] Assisted by a reliable inventory of Civil War sites and bolstered by congressional support, the NPS could begin the task of delegating protective responsibilities.

Cooperative management, coordinated by the NPS and involving landowners, interested citizens, and elected officials as well as local, state, and federal agencies, should form the heart of a national battlefield protection policy. Specific management plans would depend on a resource's significance, its ownership, the threat to it, and management objectives. Lands adjacent to battlefields presently protected as NPS units should be managed cooperatively to maintain the integrity of the resources the park is designed to protect. In essence, a park unit would serve as the focus of a broader planning district. Those battlefields deemed to be of historic significance but not appropriate for designation as parks could be managed as affiliate units of the NPS in cooperation with a local organization. Alternatively, the NPS could simply serve in an advisory capacity and provide technical or financial assistance to existing landowners or communities to assist with battlefield conservation. Such a cooperative approach would provide some type of protection for all historically significant battlefields while simultaneously lessening the federal government's administrative and financial burdens. Regardless of what specific local, state, or federal actions are taken, the NPS should participate in the protection of each battlefield recognized by the advisory commission. Every site identified as historically significant will need some level of protection. As Jerry Rogers, NPS associate director of cultural resources, warns, "No place is remote enough to be protected by its remoteness."[41]

The Scenic Byway Program, funded by the U.S. Department of Transportation, and the American Heritage Area Program, funded by the Department of the Interior, are two federal initiatives that could assist the NPS and other conservation interests with battlefield protection. Although scenic byways tend to be limited to highway corridors, heritage areas encompass broad regions that have some level of historic, cultural, environmental, and/or visual significance. The heritage program is an "effective means of targeting the use of limited funds to provide assistance, a stimulus and coordination for extensive local preservation and revitalization efforts."[42] Both programs are supported by a number of legislators who believe that federal historic preservation support should vary depending on a resource's level of significance. Senator Jeffords argues that the national government must determine priorities, but that this should not "necessarily usurp the availability of the expertise and funds or whatever else you can determine from these various other sources."[43]

Protection under the aegis of a cooperative plan succeeds best when landowner, community, and NPS goals of preservation, economic growth, and improvement in quality of life can be accomplished together. This involves demonstrating to a landowner and a local community the direct benefits accrued through coupling battlefield protection with tourism. Economic and recreation programs as well as coordination between private and public preservation efforts would be needed to achieve maximum resource protection and economic benefits. This policy would also demand recognition that while the costs and benefits of protecting historic resources should be shared by all, ultimate responsibility for the protection of nationally significant resources rests with the federal government. By approving and appropriating funds for a comprehensive plan, Congress would virtually eliminate the need for piecemeal acquisition of threatened Civil War battlefields and the costly and politically unsavory policy of crisis management. More importantly, Congress could guarantee the long-term protection of America's Civil War battlefields.

The Role of Nonprofit and Public-Interest Organizations

Broad public participation must be the focal point of any cooperative-management scheme, and nonprofit organizations provide one of the best avenues for achieving such participation. Despite their variety of goals, most public-interest organizations can be categorized in terms of national advocacy, local advocacy, and acquisition. While national advocacy groups like the National Trust for Historic Preservation, Preservation Action, and the Civil War Round Table Associates provide invaluable publicity for battlefield preservation, real power rests with local preservation groups. The fight over Manassas initiated by Annie Snyder and SBC confirmed the effectiveness of grassroots organization. Since then, groups such as the Port Hudson Campaign Committee, the Prairie Grove Battlefield Commission, and the Friends of Fort Fisher have carried forward the preservation fight using highly organized lobbying methods and advance planning. These local groups now recognize that successful preservation requires a proactive rather than reactive strategy.

The power of these grassroots organizations may be attributed to two factors. First, until Congress enacts a comprehensive battlefield preservation policy, local government officials will determine the fate of most unprotected sites. When such officials resist outside interference, local preservation groups frequently provide the most constructive avenue for protest. Second, in contrast to the large national groups, notably environmental, that have embraced regulatory legislation as their main instrument of change, most grassroots organizations rely on direct confrontation. They are able to pursue their goals without worrying about long-term political implications or the loss of a particular constituency. In a recent issue of the *World Policy Journal* Mark Dowie aptly summarized the contrast between local- and federal-level efforts: "[No matter how] big and clever environmental groups become, when it comes to lobbying Congress they will always be outmaneuvered and outspent by chemical manufacturers, oil companies. . . . The heart of American environmentalism is the thousands of regional, local and often ad hoc groups that spring up almost spontaneously to confront a particular environmental assault."[44] The same can be said of battlefield preservation efforts. Still, when forced to operate on a volunteer basis with minuscule financial resources, grassroots organizations cannot be expected to bear all the responsibility for preserving America's battlefield resources.

Many nonprofit private organizations engage in land acquisition. The Conservation Fund represents one organization that has made significant contributions to battlefield preservation with its acquisition of parts of seventeen "endangered" sites, including Gettysburg, Antietam, Five Forks, and Petersburg. Nevertheless, private acquisition of Civil War sites is severely limited by financial considerations and should not be regarded as the ultimate solution to the problem of battlefield preservation. Cooperative management should not entail a complete or even a nearly complete abrogation of government responsibility. Some nationally significant historic resources merit government protection regardless of cost.

As the single national organization devoted solely to battlefield preservation, the APCWS has managed to combine the goals of acquisition, advocacy, and education in a three-part strategy. The loss of Chantilly (Ox Hill) Battlefield led to the founding of APCWS in 1987. Since that time, this nonprofit tax-exempt corporation has grown to post some 4,500 members on its nationwide membership roster. The group concentrates its efforts on imminently threatened and unprotected Civil War sites, using a variety of techniques including acquisition (deeded interest), lobbying for the creation of national and state battlefield parks, and encouraging local zoning boards to adopt historic preservation ordinances. Private donations to APCWS's acquisition fund provide the primary source of financial support for site and easement purchases. In January 1989 APCWS acquired its first Civil War site, the "Coaling," on Port Republic Battlefield in Rockingham County, Virginia. Its most recent acquisition encompassed forty acres of West Virginia's Rich Mountain Battlefield, purchased in the summer of 1992. Aside from acquiring properties, APCWS has taken an active role in advocating legislation sensitive to historic preservation at the federal and state level, as well as in providing technical and financial assistance to local preservation groups. Full details of APCWS activities may be found in appendix E.

Preservation Alternatives

Battlefield protection strategies must be site-specific. In some cases, especially in urban areas, preservation achieved through extensive development of tourism may provide the most viable alternative. For battlefield sites in rural areas, conservation of the landscape through land trusts and easements may be the most appropriate alternative. Coordinated groups comprised of local, state, and federal officials along with private citizens and nonprofit organizations must determine which preservation alternative to implement on a case-by-case basis. Whatever the alternative, the key to success lies in comprehensive economic analysis; the quantification of the costs and benefits of preservation in a logical and professional manner. This is not to say that economics should dictate the selection of alternative preservation strategies. Rather, economic analysis should be used as a tool to find a common ground among apparently conflicting interests. The aforementioned studies on the economic benefits communities such as Fredericksburg, Virginia, and Gettysburg, Pennsylvania, derive from their respective historic sites convincingly demonstrate the power of economic analysis.

All individuals and organizations affected by a cooperative-preservation venture, whether they be local government officials, NPS rangers, or area businesspeople, must have an opportunity to engage in constructive debate. Even if some participants disagree with the outcome, their involvement not only validates the process but also limits the chances of neglecting certain viewpoints or alienating particular constituencies. Cooperative management, though fraught with difficulties, is not impossible. Two recent programs demonstrate the reasonable degree of success that can be achieved through cooperative management.

Richmond National Battlefield Park

The NPS mid-Atlantic regional office's division of park and resource planning has explored the feasibility of implementing cooperative management for related-land programs.[45] Boundary- and adjacent-land studies have been completed at Gettysburg National Military Park, George Washington Birthplace National Monument, and Richmond National Battlefield Park. Projects are currently under way at Petersburg National Battlefield, Fredericksburg-Spotsylvania National Military Park, and Shenandoah National Park. Each project required substantial public support throughout the phases of

resource assessment, identification of alternative protection techniques, and development of cooperative strategies. Officials at the
mid-Atlantic office describe this planning process for related-land
studies as "developing and sustaining broad public involvement in
the planning process to ensure the best consensus possible for an
adjacent lands strategy." Public opinion can serve as the guide for
delineating the "compatible and incompatible land uses for these
[historically significant areas] and for developing alternatives and
actions for resource protection."[46] In the related-land project at Richmond National Battlefield Park, a group of private citizens, public-
interest groups, and landowners, along with state, local, and federal
officials, attempted to forge a historic protection plan that would not
curtail opportunities for economic growth.

The Richmond National Battlefield Park boundary includes
roughly all Civil War battlefield resources within five miles of the
City of Richmond. Of this approximately 250-square-mile area, the
NPS owns 732 acres divided into ten separate units. Like many other
Civil War battlefield parks, the Richmond park was established by
Congress under the Antietam plan, which called for the conservation only of core battlefield areas (ground deemed crucial to understanding and interpreting the sites). Many of the park's significant
outlying areas were left unprotected. Originally surrounded by
farmfields and forests, Richmond's battlefield resources are now
under severe development pressure. Rapid urbanization around the
ten NPS units, coupled with their relatively small size, has created
problems in resource preservation and interpretation. Visitors to the
park face a 100-mile interpretive road, poorly marked sites, and
relatively few services. Not surprisingly, these factors have curbed
visitation.

Two factors have complicated battlefield conservation in Richmond: lack of a specific boundary, and the legacy of a haphazard
land acquisition program. Many NPS units, regardless of resources'
significance, follow existing property lines. Though the original 1936
Richmond Battlefield legislation recognized the broad geographic
areas in which battles were fought, financial and public-policy considerations have limited NPS ownership to core areas. Today some
officials in surrounding jurisdictions worry that battlefield resource

protection may impede local economic goals. They insist that cooperative planning remain sensitive to the rights of landowners.

The related-land study was devised by the NPS to identify common interests so that an appropriate combination of private and public resources could be targeted for conservation. More specifically, study organizers hoped to address structural problems associated with the park's land base and legislative mandate, as well as concerns voiced by local governments and area property owners. To begin the process, representatives from the City of Richmond, Chesterfield, Hanover, and Henrico counties, the Commonwealth of Virginia, and the NPS signed a memorandum of agreement. The document outlined a cooperative plan to evaluate Civil War battlefield resources, develop a conservation strategy, and identify a number of steps for implementing the chosen strategy. Like all related-land studies, the agreement called for public participation throughout the process.

Study coordinators initiated the study by hosting a series of public workshops in each county. These focused on the project's goals: to identify battlefield resources; protect those resources designated as historically important; interpret the battles for area residents and visitors; and find ways that conservation efforts could contribute to the local economy. With the assistance of local experts, county historical societies, and NPS historians, the coordinators identified and located thirty-five battle sites related to the two Richmond campaigns. These were mapped, reviewed at public workshops, and revised. The identification stage was followed by meetings, workshops, and interviews in which interested citizens, historical groups, and public agencies suggested alternative protection strategies and ways of meeting goals. The cumulative results were summarized in a draft report whose conclusions organizers presented to the public in a series of three workshops. They also distributed summary reports to all interested persons for review and comment.

The creation of a Richmond Heritage Trail lies at the heart of the report's recommendations. The trail would connect existing NPS units and a number of other battlefield sites with the business areas of downtown Richmond. This combination of private and public areas would provide visitors with access to important historic sites augmented by a system of welcome centers and other interpretive facilities. Welcome centers could be established in each of the surrounding counties to lure prospective visitors off highways. Many of these efforts would be developed as cooperative ventures among local, state, and federal governmental bodies, the aim being to encourage private investment. The variety of promotional activities seems endless, for example, a reenactment center, an annual cavalry ride coordinated with local equestrian interests, and a heritage radio station. Any successful combination of protection and promotion interests could yield unlimited opportunities for tourist-related businesses.

The effort would involve existing public programs, new initiatives, and private-sector activities. According to Peter Iris-Williams, project manager of the Richmond National Battlefield Park related-land study, most of the historically significant land outside the park would remain in private hands. Conservation and compatible development would heavily rely on incorporating the resource information generated by this study into three major areas: county comprehensive and open-space plans, procedures associated with the development review process, and local and state programs related to economic development or recreation. In addition, study organizers envisage an expansion in the capacity of local, state, and federal officials to provide technical assistance to landowners and developers. It is hoped that these combined efforts will integrate conservation into the existing decision-making process and encourage individual property owners to "retain ownership and . . . [through incentives] take conservation actions on their own land."[47] Given the difficulty of managing such a wide range of conservation strategies, the draft report called for the founding of a heritage council responsible for refining regional strategies, disseminating information, and coordinating private/public-sector efforts in battlefield conservation.

Public reaction to the recommendations has run the gamut from concern that they do not include all heritage resources to deepseated suspicion about federal action. Chesterfield and Hanover counties, the City of Richmond, and the Commonwealth of Virginia have been highly supportive of the related-land study, expressing a desire to build on this foundation for conservation efforts.[48] A number of the recommendations have already been implemented, including the following:

1. Private landowners, county governments, and the NPS jointly initiated battlefield conservation strategies at North Anna, Cold Harbor, Gaines's Mill, and Glendale.[49]

2. The NPS established a new planning position at the park. The planner's responsibilities will relate to adjacent-land issues. A superintendent's job description was also rewritten to include adjacent-land responsibilities.

3. NPS officials have begun working on a general management plan for the park that expands on concepts articulated in the draft report.

4. Representatives who participated in the related-land study have initiated another cooperative-planning effort to examine the potential for development of recreation corridors in the metropolitan area. Battlefield resources are included in the study.

Since public interest has generally remained high, organizers hope to implement at least some of the other recommendations listed in the draft report. Nevertheless, refinement and implementation of these ideas have been slowed by a highly vocal minority that solicited significant political support.

The related-land study seemed destined to alter fundamentally how a visitor would experience Richmond National Battlefield Park and how local communities would regard it. The park might have generated a profitable tourism trade. As it turns out, the experience at Richmond must be described as a case of lost opportunity. In fact, if the objectives outlined in the memorandum of agreement are compared to actual results, the project may even be viewed as a failure. Once the Henrico County Board of Supervisors decided to drop out of the cooperative planning initiative, the financial and political strength that can emanate from regional coalitions was immediately curtailed. State and local agencies use the breadth of support as a major criteria for funding allocations; regional projects that have been proposed with partial support typically receive lower priority. In addition, since battlefields and viewsheds cross county lines, the cooperation of all parties is absolutely essential to establish a federal Greenway program, to develop an extensive trail system, to accrue regional economic benefits, and to guarantee long-term resource protection. Although the NPS achieved a number of independent successes with local entities, it was unable to draw upon the power of a group. This missed opportunity can no doubt be attributed to political intransigence and parochialism. Unfortunately, the small, but vocal group that largely prevented Henrico County from participating in the regional effort was not representative of the community at large.

Although the regional effort did not achieve its desired result, the conservation strategies summarized in the draft report, along with the steps taken to achieve them, have made a pathbreaking contribution to the development of other cooperative-management initiatives. For instance, the working coalition managed to identify and agree upon the 32 key areas where battles occurred. Moreover, the fact that every locality except for one managed to participate in the cooperative planning effort constitutes a remarkable achievement in a Commonwealth state—with no tradition of regionalism. Using these lessons, the NPS has launched a similar battlefield conservation project in the Fredericksburg area.

Antietam National Battlefield

On a September day in 1862 at Sharpsburg, Maryland, more than twenty-three thousand soldiers were killed, wounded, or went missing during the Battle of Antietam, the bloodiest single day of the Civil War. Confederates under General Lee struck north, hoping to retain their initiative and draw border states into the Confederacy. Numerically superior federal forces under George McClellan exploded with fury, ravaging Lee's army. Soon thereafter the North's military fortunes improved, granting Lincoln the needed edge to issue his preliminary Emancipation Proclamation. Abolition of slavery was finally an official goal of the Union's war effort. Popular sentiment now favored the North, dashing the South's lingering hope that European nations would intervene on its behalf.

In 1890 Congress established the Antietam National Battlefield Site to commemorate and preserve important features of the battlefield. For many years, the strategy for acquisition involved roadways (to provide access throughout the battlefield) but not purchases of land. In April 1960 Congress increased the authorized boundaries to 1,800 acres "to assure the public of a full and unimpeded view thereof, and to provide for the maintenance of the site . . . in, or its restoration to, substantially the condition of which it was at the time of the Battle of Antietam."[50] Until recently the Antietam plan, which protected strips of battlefields and left large sections as unprotected agricultural land, served the area's rural setting rather well. But now what has been described by the Department of the Interior as "one of the few Civil War battlefields untouched since the war" is threatened by development northwest of the Baltimore-Washington corridor.[51] Suburban development has steadily progressed from Washington, D.C., toward Sharpsburg.

Here lies Antietam, once named by the National Trust for Historic Preservation as one of the country's eleven most endangered historic sites. Before the establishment of a local, cooperative preservation effort in the late 1980s, a developer planned to construct 1,100 townhouses in the field across from Sunken Road (Bloody Lane), where an outnumbered group of Confederates held off numerous charges by two Union divisions. An infamous field (Miller's Cornfield) that saw some of the heaviest fighting in the war was in danger of being sold to a private party, motives unknown. Developers also planned to construct a mall on the historic Grove Farm. Some of the proposed development has been thwarted by a coordinated effort of local, state, and federal officials, assisted by citizen groups and private conservation organizations.

The cooperative preservation techniques applied at Antietam are fundamentally different from those utilized in areas that hope to develop tourism. In fact, many Sharpsburg residents initially resisted land-preservation programs implemented by state and federal authorities, fearing that their pristine agricultural area would become a tourist attraction.[52] Antietam National Battlefield superintendent Richard Rambur notes that many local residents are "not interested in commercialism. They are very afraid Sharpsburg is going to become a Williamsburg [Virginia]."[53] The NPS continues to encounter resistance among local residents who do not fully grasp the impending threat of development.

The specter of another Manassas and the demographics of the area prompted Washington County (Sharpsburg) officials to convene a twenty-three-member commission to reevaluate the need for stricter zoning to protect the battlefield's environs. This commission, composed of farmers, local residents, state and county representatives, historic groups, and the park superintendent, drafted the "Antietam Overlay," a comprehensive plan to protect the integrity of the battlefield and ensure minimal outside interference in the community's way of life. Completed in June 1989, it is unique among protective zoning ordinances because it aims to preserve both the battlefield and the surrounding viewshed as described in article 20A: "The purpose of the Antietam Overlay is to provide mechanisms for the protection of significant historic structures and land areas by requiring development and land subdivision to occur in a manner that 1) preserves the existing quality of the viewshed of the Antietam Battlefield [and] 2) ensures that development of certain lands adjacent to major roads which provide public access to the Antietam Battlefield is compatible with the agricultural and historic character of the area."[54] Park superintendent Rambur reacted to Washington County's visionary approach: "I am convinced that success in keeping Antietam's visual integrity intact will depend entirely on Washington County's approach to a comprehensive plan—not on Uncle Sam's ability to buy everything the eye can see."[55]

In 1988 Congress removed the congressionally mandated cap on parkland acquisition at Antietam.[56] Aided by $1 million in federal funds, park officials have been able to acquire, through donation or purchase, unprotected lands within the park's existing boundaries.[57] Working with the South County [Southern Washington County] Advisory Commission, the NPS analyzed the viewshed to decide which land inside and outside the park should be protected (see Map 7). County officials adopted the results of this study to

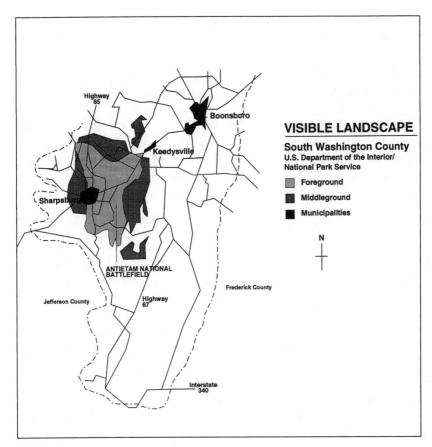

Map 7: Viewshed of Antietam National Battlefield. (Brian Huonker, from the U.S.
Department of the Interior/NPS)

design appropriate regulations for land located within the battlefield
viewshed. Utilizing data obtained from the NPS's viewshed study,
the commissioners approved a zoning-ordinance overlay and inserted a provision requiring an architectural review board to approve all new construction within the overlay. The ordinance did not
change zoning laws, but it did provide basic guidelines for property
owners.

The Antietam Overlay is designed to operate through leverage, regulating architectural appearance rather than controlling density. For instance, the plan cannot prevent construction of a McDonald's near the battlefield, but it can direct where the restaurant's parking lot should be situated. However, according to Save Historic Antietam with Responsible Policies (SHARP), a local property-rights organization, and some area farmers, the threat of a Big Mac franchise suddenly appearing on the battlefield landscape is baseless, propounded by preservationists. Outside the park's boundaries there is no area zoned for development of fast-food businesses, and construction of a McDonald's inside the park's boundary will never happen, since Congress and the NPS have condemnation powers there.[58]

In June 1992 the NPS completed a general management plan for scenic restoration of land inside the congressionally authorized boundaries at Antietam. This twenty-year plan would return the area to the way it looked in 1862 by replicating walkways, removing roads, and creating landscape conditions reminiscent of that era.[59] The plan was recently approved by the regional director of NPS's national capitol region office.

Action at the state level has complemented NPS preservation efforts as well as those taken by the Washington County commissioners to protect the area surrounding Antietam National Battlefield. In January 1990, the State of Maryland announced the allocation of $500,000 through Program Open Space (Department of Natural Resources) to purchase the development rights for land within the battlefield's viewshed.[60] The state pledged another $500,000 for the creation of a private agricultural-land trust in Washington County, Maryland, with initial emphasis to be placed on the Sharpsburg area. The trust is primed to conserve historic scenery around the battlefield but not to compete with other state and county land-preservation programs. By combining charitable contributions and private grants, it will supplement the $800- to $1200-per-acre grants presently paid by the state for the acquisition of conservation easements on agricultural land. As of early 1992, the trust had not received the monies allocated by the Maryland legislature.[61] Unlike the Maryland Environmental Trust, which can respond only to inquiries initiated by the property owner, the Washington County

Quality Foundation Land Trust is authorized to solicit landowners for the purchase of development rights. (The latter trust is largely defunct. The Maryland Civil War Heritage Commission is currently assembling a new easement trust program.) State officials believe local residents are more inclined to participate in a locally administrated land trust than in a program managed by the state.[62]

The Conservation Fund and the locally based Save Historic Antietam Foundation (SHAF) form the final component of this cooperative effort. These groups purchased land outside the protected areas of the battlefield as well as within its boundaries. With support from the Mellon Foundation, the Conservation Fund acquired the historic cornfield and a 118-acre portion of the West Woods. Since both of these properties lie within the park's official boundaries, they were donated to the NPS without the need for congressional approval. The SHAF has also been actively involved in preservation of Grove Farm, site of a famous meeting between President Abraham Lincoln and General McClellan, as immortalized by photographer Alexander Gardner. Two weeks after the battle of Antietam, McClellan's troops rested at Grove Farm while their general ruminated about the lack of supplies and refused to undertake a campaign until heavy reinforcements were forthcoming. Lincoln bristled, traveled to Antietam, and ordered his general to cross the Potomac. McClellan balked and subsequently lost command of the Army of the Potomac. The farm also served as a Union campground, a review field, and a hospital following the Battle of Antietam, and Lee's troops straggled across it once the horrific struggle had drawn to a close. With assistance from the APCWS, CWT, and Maryland Environmental Trust, the SHAF recently purchased forty acres of Grove Farm, which had been previously subdivided and approved for home sites. A sluggish economy provided a unique opportunity for the SHAF to acquire this particular tract for $325,000, about $15,000 below its appraised value.[63] Still, a few years earlier the entire farm of 150 acres plus house could have been purchased for $250,000.

The quasi-success story of preservation at Antietam cannot be attributed to a single group or individual. It was made possible through the efforts of many groups. But like so many cooperative endeavors, this one was not without dissension. A rift developed over who could best ensure Antietam's legacy while protecting fundamental property rights. The result is a polarized community with farmers and landowners pitted against preservation groups. Their goals are similar, their means at issue. The farming community is reluctant to negotiate for easements if the land will eventually be taken by eminent domain. SHARP's Anne Corcoran contends that while the citizens of rural Sharpsburg have labored hard to protect the visual integrity of the battlefield, these efforts have not been recognized by the NPS and other organizations. She believes that the "SHAF and NPS should have acknowledged the great job done by local citizens and their rural neighbors to preserve this quaint hamlet. If NPS had touted our efforts toward protection and preservation, this current adversarial climate might never have surfaced."[64] SHARP representatives have also questioned whether the Antietam Overlay is a legal document. SHAF president Tom Clemens argues that the overlay is "really a weak first step, and protects very little."[65]

While Antietam National Battlefield is among those sites least marred by development, there remain serious threats to its integrity. The government owns or has protective easement rights on far too small a portion of the battlefield to safeguard it adequately. While owners of twelve farms abutting the battlefield expressed willingness to join Maryland's State Agricultural Land Preservation Program to protect the park's viewshed, the SHAF and the NPS maintained that they were asking too much money for easements. Corcoran, who resides on one of the farms, suggests that the "NPS may not be the best steward of our land."[66] Many area farms have been owned by the same families since antebellum times; these families have so far resisted offers to sell their land for development. There is a deep sense of pride in the history of the area, and many property owners have preserved this history as trustees of the land. Preservation of the rural landscape is not necessarily guaranteed by county zoning regulations, either. Although all of the land around Antietam National Battlefield has been zoned for agricultural purposes, county regulations allow for the construction of such ubiquitous businesses as convenience stores and gas stations.

Isolated housing developments and gas stations are not the only threat to the battlefield's integrity. Grove Farm is located two miles southwest of Antietam, near the Norfolk and Southern Railroad Station. For many years this Sharpsburg depot was the stopping-off point for Civil War veterans. Plans are now under way to connect the railroad line there to the MARC commuter rail line into Washington, D.C. Could Sharpsburg become another bedroom community for Washington? Should the preservation of a Civil War battlefield and its viewshed become a growth-control device? Questions such as these, being asked in so many rural communities across the nation, continue to challenge area residents.

Economic self-interest and historic preservation are not always in conflict. Treasured historic landscapes such as Antietam National Battlefield can and should coexist with community concerns transfigured by time. If some type of development is inevitable around Sharpsburg, superintendent Richard Rambur argues, then "counties must recognize the economic value of tourism to the community. Now is the time to get away from talking only of our visceral experiences on battlefields or the value of radiant sunsets. We need to talk about *economics.* . . . Housing per se is not the best medium for raising the tax base, there are too many hidden costs, e.g., schools, sewer hook-ups, roads. . . ."[67] Area residents should reassess which they prefer: preservation of a battlefield and associated tourist-based development, or a conglomeration of shopping malls, planned communities, and light industrial development.

The Ultimate Goal of a Battlefield Preservation Policy

Debate concerning the formulation and implementation of a Civil War battlefield preservation policy should not overshadow the real issue at hand. As J. Jackson Walter pointed out, "It's easy to see why some may characterize the Manassas affair as a growth versus no-growth tussle. But peel back a few layers and you will find the real meaning of Manassas—the safeguarding of our history. Our victory at those 600 acres in northern Virginia was not about development versus no development or federal power versus local option. It was about the protection of a priceless common heritage, the heritage of our country."[68] Cooperative-management ventures, heritage tourism, and agricultural land trusts are simply means of fulfilling what may be described as a moral obligation to Civil War soldiers and future generations alike. A letter published in APCWS's newsletter placed the issue of battlefield preservation in proper perspective: "As I look around at what is left of the countryside and battlefields, I can't help but wonder if the gallant soldiers, both Union and Confederate, could see what we see today, would they have fought as bravely and died so willingly?" Long-term protection of our nation's heritage, in its recorded moments of redolent splendor as well as its periods of wanton brutality, should be the ultimate goal of any Civil War battlefield preservation policy.

Manassas was a harbinger of things to come. An untold number of Civil War battlefields has already been destroyed by waves of development, while others await their fate. These sites, like many of America's other cultural, natural, and historic resources, are finite. Once damaged or destroyed, they cannot be replaced. Only a few years remain for us to decide what value we place as a country on historic preservation. Thomas A. Lewis, author of *The Guns of Cedar Creek*, made an eloquent argument for the cause of conservation: "But these ghosts, you see, are not really immortal. They can be banished forever by asphalt and traffic and factories, or destroyed by indifference. Their immortality depends on our thinking of them now and then, wondering why they did what they did, pondering what they mean to us, giving them space in our lives. And by granting them the repose of the ground they consecrated with their blood and agony. . . . [Civil War battlefields] . . . are densely populated with memories, crowded with lessons and meditations about courage and character and causes for us and our children and all who are or ever will be citizens of this once riven country. These fields are thick with the spirit of America, waiting for us to decide what is worth keeping."[69] Our decision, by default or choice, will permanently determine which Civil War battlefields survive. Will we, as a nation, have the compassionate enlightenment to preserve these sacred lands?

Appendix A: NPS Civil War Battlefield and Fort Sites, 1861 to 1865[1]

National Military Parks

Chickamauga and Chattanooga National Military Park, GA-TN
Fredericksburg-Spotsylvania National Military Park, VA
Gettysburg National Military Park, PA
Pea Ridge National Military Park, AR
Shiloh National Military Park, TN
Vicksburg National Military Park, MS

National Battlefield Parks

Kennesaw Mountain National Battlefield Park, GA
Manassas National Battlefield Park, VA
Richmond National Battlefield Park, VA

National Battlefields

Antietam National Battlefield, MD
Fort Donelson National Battlefield, TN
Petersburg National Battlefield, VA
Stones River National Battlefield, TN
Tupelo National Battlefield, MS
Wilson's Creek National Battlefield, MO

National Battlefield Sites

Brices Cross Roads National Battlefield Site, MS

National Historical Parks

Appomattox Court House National Historical Park, VA
Chesapeake and Ohio Canal National Historical Park,
    WV-MD
Cumberland Gap National Historical Park, KY-VA-TN
Harpers Ferry National Historical Park, WV-MD-VA
Pecos National Historical Park, NM[2]
Yorktown Battlefield (Colonial National Historical Park), VA

National Monuments

Castillo de San Marcos National Monument, FL
Fort Jefferson National Monument, FL
Fort Pulaski National Monument, GA
Fort Sumter National Monument, SC (includes Fort Moultrie)
Fort Union National Monument, NM

National Historic Sites

Eisenhower National Historic Site, PA
Fort Bowie National Historic Site, AZ
Fort Davis National Historic Site, TX
Fort Raleigh National Historic Site, NC
Fort Scott National Historic Site, KS
Fort Smith National Historic Site, AR
Jamestown National Historic Site, VA

National Memorials

Arkansas Post National Memorial, AR

National Capital Parks

Fort De Russey in Rock Creek Park, Washington, D.C.
Fort Slocum, Washington, D.C.
Fort Stevens Park, Washington, D.C.
Fort Washington Park, MD

Miscellaneous Historic Sites

Cape Hatteras National Seashore, NC
Cape Lookout National Seashore, NC
Fort Marcy, VA
Gulf Islands National Seashore, MS-FL

National Cemeteries

Andersonville, GA
Andrew Johnson (Greeneville), TN
Antietam (Sharpsburg), MD
Battleground, Washington, D.C.
Chalmette, LA
Cold Harbor, VA
Custer, MT[3]
Fort Donelson (Dover), TN
Fredericksburg, VA
Gettysburg, PA
Glendale, VA
Poplar Grove (Petersburg), VA
Richmond, VA
Shiloh (Pittsburg Landing), TN
Stones River (Murfreesboro), TN
Vicksburg, MS
Yorktown, VA

Appendix B: Federal Historic Preservation Regulations and Alternative Federal Preservation Programs

Land and Water Conservation Fund of 1964

This innovative approach to natural, historic, and cultural resource protection was created in 1964. Under the dictates of the program, Congress expends a portion of federal taxes collected on motorboat fuel, funds obtained from the sale of federal real estate, and monies accrued from offshore oil and gas leases to support miscellaneous preservation activities.[4] Even though Congress must allocate some funds to state and local projects, at least 40 percent of the Land and Water Conservation Fund (LWCF) annual grants must be used to purchase land in national parks, wildlife refuges, forests, and other federal lands. In accordance with the program's purpose, Congress has followed a policy of purchasing additions to national military parks and other battlefield sites. The acquisition of Manassas National Battlefield Park, for example, was partially funded by the LWCF. Since its inception in 1965, the LWCF has financed the protection of more than 5 million acres in parks, historic sites, and recreational areas all over the United States. The LWCF has an unappropriated balance of several hundred million.[5]

Historic Preservation Fund of 1976

In 1976 Congress created the Historic Preservation Fund (HPF), specifically designed to finance preservation projects. Like the LWCF, monies garnered from federal taxes, leases, and real-estate sales support the HPF. The NPS channels the money to state programs in the form of grants. The National Trust for Historic Preservation receives an annual HPF grant for distribution among various local and state historic preservation projects. As of 1990 the fund contained an unappropriated balance of $1.5 to $1.6 billion.[6]

National Historic Preservation Act of 1966, as Amended

Before Congress passed the NHPA in 1966, the rather innocuous and ineffective Antiquities Act of 1906 and Historic Sites Act of 1935 were the only major federal preservation laws. Preservation under these programs was limited to the national-historic-landmarks designation and the certification of national monument status for certain federal properties. Passage of the NHPA greatly expanded the federal role in historic preservation. According to the authors of *Historic Preservation Law and Taxation*, the amended NHPA "remains that basic federal statute regarding preservation."[7] In the enabling legislation, Congress justified the creation of national historic preservation law as follows:

> (b)(1) the spirit and direction of the Nation are founded upon and reflected in its historic heritage; (2) the historical and cultural foundations of the Nation should be preserved as a living part of our community life and development in order to give a sense of orientation to the American people; (4) the preservation of this irreplaceable heritage is in the public interest . . . ; (5) in the face of ever-increasing extensions of urban centers, highways, and residential, commercial and industrial developments, the present governmental and non-governmental historic preservation programs and activities are inadequate. . . .[8]

The comprehensive program outlined by the legislation called for the creation of the ACHP to advise the president and Congress on all matters related to historic preservation.[9] Congress also directed the ACHP to review all undertakings falling under section 106 of the NHPA. The enabling legislation mandated that the coordination of federal, state, and local agency preservation activities would be a priority under the new law. As a result, most state governments created the position of state historic preservation officer to implement the requirements of the NHPA at the state level.[10] Additional provisions of the NHPA included a national program for identifying historic structures, a historic preservation grants-in-aid program for states, and a stipulation allowing federal agencies to charge federal licensees for all preservation costs associated with a particular project.

Section 106 forms the cornerstone of the NHPA's regulatory scheme. Under the provision, the ACHP must review all federal agency activities affecting properties listed, or eligible for listing, in the National Register of Historic Places. Until the ACHP has completed its report and the federal agency has subsequently reviewed the ACHP's recommendation, a potentially destructive action may not proceed. The ACHP has no authority to regulate private-sector projects unless federal funding or licensing is involved. While section 106 review can be used to increase public awareness regarding federal activities, its effectiveness as a preservation tool is limited in a number of ways. The act applies exclusively to national register properties and can only be implemented when federal agency activities threaten a historic property. Furthermore, the recommendations of the ACHP are merely advisory in nature. After allowing the ACHP to comment on a specific project, a federal agency may technically follow any course it desires without violating the procedural dictates of section 106.[11]

National Register of Historic Places and National Historic Landmarks

Designed primarily as a planning tool, the National Register of Historic Places currently has more than fifty-five thousand entries and serves as the principal source of information regarding America's most significant historic and archaeological resources. The national register expanded the concept first developed with the 1935 Registry of National Historic Landmarks by including properties of state and local historic significance. Their inclusion in the register has fostered an unprecedented degree of grassroots support for historic preservation. Today, less than 10 percent of all national register listings can be characterized as nationally significant.[12] In addition to historic properties of national, state, and local significance, the national register now includes all properties recognized as national historic landmarks, all areas added to the NPS because of the national significance of their cultural resources, and other historically significant federal properties. Before a national register nomination can be forwarded to the Interior Department, it must be reviewed by a state historic preservation officer or a local government official certified to submit such nominations. After the interested parties have filed an application with the preservation officer, the state decides if the application should be forwarded to the Department of the Interior. The secretary of the interior makes the final determination on all national register applications.

As distinguished from national register status, national historic landmark status is granted to those districts, sites, structures, and objects possessing "exceptional quality" as national historic resources. Because the resource must be of historic significance to the nation as a whole, only about two thousand properties have been designated as national historic landmarks. Unlike properties listed in the national register, national historic landmark properties are usually incorporated into the program as part of a specific theme. Before a property is listed as a landmark, the NPS conducts an intensive historic study. If it determines a property is eligible for listing, it must present a report and recommendation to the NPS advisory board. After reviewing recommendations submitted by the advisory board and the NPS director, the secretary of the interior makes a final judgment. Although a state or locality can suggest properties for national historic landmark designation, the NPS ultimately determines all nominations. Designation as a national historic landmark brings more federal protection than national register designation. Section 110(f) for national landmarks supplements the section 106 review by requiring an agency, "to the maximum extent possible, [to] undertake special planning or other action to minimize harm to property" that is threatened by "direct" and "adverse" federal activity.[13]

Localities and property owners obtain three major benefits from listing a property on the national register or determining that a property is eligible for listing. Most importantly, inclusion provides an informational planning tool for governments, private organizations, and businesses alike. Listing also serves as the legal basis for implementation of the NHPA section 106 review.[14] Finally, owners of properties placed in the national register can apply for preservation assistance from a variety of grant and loan programs.[15] However, participation in both the national register and the national historic landmarks programs is voluntary. If a property owner objects to a national register nomination, the property will be declared as eligible for listing but will not be listed until the objection is withdrawn. For purposes of preservation, however, the distinction between listing and being eligible for listing carries no regulatory distinctions. Both designations trigger the application of federal regulations when a property is threatened.

U.S. Department of Transportation Act of 1966

Among federal preservation laws, section 4(f) of the U.S. Department of Transportation Act of 1966 (DOTA) offers perhaps the most stringent form of protection. The act explicitly declares that the preservation and enhancement of lands surrounding roads is a matter of national policy.

A special provision in the act requires the secretary of transportation to avoid destroying or damaging any items listed in the National Register of Historic Places unless "there is no feasible and prudent alternative" and the project "includes all possible planning to minimize harm to such . . . historic sites resulting from such use."[16] Like other federal historic preservation regulations, the overall effectiveness of the DOTA is limited because it only applies to federal agency actions or projects supported by federal funds. Nevertheless, the protection provided under the act significantly exceeds that available under that of the NHPA and the NEPA. For instance, the act prohibits the secretary of transportation from rejecting any feasible alternative that would minimize or prevent damage to historic resources.

National Environmental Policy Act of 1969

The provisions of the NEPA are another legal mechanism for the protection of historic resources. Much broader in scope than other preservation laws, the NEPA protects all aspects of the environment; historic properties are just one of several categories. Section 101 states that NEPA's purpose is to "assure for all Americans safe, healthful, productive and culturally pleasing surroundings; . . . preserve important historic, cultural and natural aspects of our national heritage, and maintain, wherever possible, an environment which supports diversity and variety of individual choice. . . ."[17]

Under the NEPA, if a federal agency or federally supported program threatens a historic property, the agency must consider alternatives to lessen the "harmful impacts of their actions." The involved party must also prepare an environmental-impact statement and disclose the results for public inspection. Protection accorded to historic resources by the NEPA extends beyond the NHPA for two reasons. First, the act applies to significant historic resources even if they have not been placed, or been recognized as eligible for placement, in the national register. Second, the NEPA broadly defines impacts as those "significantly affecting the quality of the human environment."[18] However, like the NHPA and DOTA, it only applies to federal actions. It does not cover private initiatives or the actions of state and local governments. Moreover, the NEPA operates in an advisory capacity without powers to prohibit destruction of historic resources.

Appendix C: Civil War Battlefields Requiring Protection[19]

Protected Battlefields Lacking Adequate Protection

Antietam, MD
Bentonville, NC
Brandy Station, VA
Brices Cross Roads, MS
Byram's Ford District, MO
Cedar Creek, VA
Champion Hill, MS
Chancellorsville, VA
Chattanooga, TN
Chickamauga, GA
Cold Harbor, VA
Corinth, MS
Cross Keys, VA
Dallas, GA
Fisher's Hill, VA
Five Forks, VA
Fort Donelson, TN
Fort Fisher, NC
Fort Morgan, AL
Fort Pulaski, GA
Fredericksburg, VA
Gaines's Mill, VA
Gettysburg, PA
Glendale, VA
Glorieta Pass, NM
Harpers Ferry, WV-MD-VA
Honey Springs, OK
Iuka, MS
Kennesaw Mountain, GA

Malvern Hill, VA
Mansfield (Sabine Cross Roads), LA
McDowell, VA
Monocacy, MD
New Hope Church, GA
New Market, VA
North Anna River, VA[20]
Olustee, FL
Perryville Battlefield, KY
Petersburg, VA
Picketts Mill, GA
Pleasant Hill, LA
Prairie Grove, AR
Port Gibson, MS
Port Hudson, LA
Port Republic, VA
Raymond, MS
Ream's Station, VA
Richmond, VA
Rocky Face Ridge, GA
Shenandoah Valley, VA
Shiloh, TN
South Mountain, MD
Spotsylvania Court House, VA
Stones River, TN
Vicksburg, MS
The Wilderness, VA
Wilson's Creek, MO

Unprotected Battlefields

Atlanta, GA[21]
Averysborough, NC
Big Black River, MS
Blakeley, AL
Cedar Mountain, VA
Cloyd's Mountain, VA
Kernstown, VA
Kinston, NC

Mill Springs, KY
New Market Heights, VA
Piedmont, VA
Resaca, GA
Second Winchester, VA
Third Winchester, VA
Yellow Tavern, VA

Lost Battlefields

Bethesda Church, VA
Chantilly, VA
Fayetteville, AR
First Winchester, VA
Franklin, TN
Knoxville, TN

Lexington, MO
Memphis, TN
Nashville, TN
Roanoke Island, NC
Savage Station, VA
Weldon Railroad, VA

Number by State of Battlefields Lacking Adequate Protection, and of Unprotected and Lost Battlefield Sites

Alabama	2	New Mexico	1
Arkansas	2	North Carolina	5
Georgia	9	Oklahoma	1
Kentucky	2	Pennsylvania	1
Louisiana	3	Tennessee	8
Maryland	4	Virginia	34
Mississippi	8	West Virginia	1
Missouri	3		

Appendix D: The Secretary of the Interior's Twenty-Five Priority Civil War Battlefields, July 1990

Alabama
Blakeley
Fort Morgan

Arkansas
Prairie Grove Battlefield Park

Georgia
Kennesaw Mountain National
  Battlefield Park Resaca

Kentucky
Mill Springs
Perryville Battlefield

Louisiana
Port Hudson

Maryland
Antietam National Battlefield
Monocacy National Battlefield

Mississippi
Corinth
Corinth Siege

Missouri
Byram's Ford Historic District

New Mexico
Glorieta Pass Battlefield

North Carolina
Fort Fisher

Pennsylvania
Gettysburg National Military
  Park

Tennessee
Franklin Battlefield
Stones River National Battlefield

Virginia
Brandy Station
Glendale
New Market Heights
Richmond National Battlefield
  Park
Shenandoah Valley
The Wilderness

West Virginia
Harpers Ferry National
  Historical Park

Appendix E: APCWS Activities

Real Estate Acquired

Name	Number of Acres and Date of Acquisition	Status
The Coaling, Port Republic Battlefield	8.55 acres December 1988	Rockingham County, Virginia. Key Union artillery position during culminating battle of Jackson's Shenandoah Valley campaign.
First Massachusetts Heavy Artillery Monument at Harris Farm	1.5 acres June 1989	Spotsylvania County, Virginia. Monument erected to honor the First Massachusetts Light Cavalry Artillery's bravery on the Spotsylvania Battlefield on May 19, 1864.
White Oak Road	30.3 acres 1989–91	Dinwiddie County, Virginia. Contains excellent fortifications and was the site of action leading to the Battle of Five Forks.
Hazel Run	1 acre March 1990	Fredericksburg, Virginia. Pending donation for inclusion into Fredericksburg-Spotsylvania National Military Park.

Bentonville	7.24 acres August 1990	Johnson County, North Carolina (Newton Grove). Land was donated by the APCWS to the State of North Carolina for inclusion in Bentonville Battleground State Historic Site.
Hatcher's Run (Dabney's Sawmill)	50 acres September 1990	Dinwiddie County, Virginia. Site where Brigadier General John Pegram, CSA, fell in battle on February 6, 1865.
McDowell	126.488 acres December 1990	Highland County, Virginia. Contains almost all important areas of Sitlington Hill, the key position during the May 1862 battle.
McDowell	9 acres December 1990	Highland County, Virginia. Donated by private landowners, these easements follow Stonewell Jackson's route to Sitlington Hill.
Fisher's Hill	194.39 acres March 1991	Shenandoah County, Virginia. Crucial Confederate defenses and Union attack routes during September 22, 1864, battle.
Byram's Ford	38.75 acres October 1991	Kansas City, Missouri. Fifty-fifty partnership with the Monnett Battle of Westport Fund. Battlefield to be donated to Kansas City Parks.
Rich Mountain Battlefield	40 acres July 1992	Randolph County, West Virginia. Site of an early Union victory that placed McClellan into the national limelight.

Grants Awarded

Name of Recipient	Preservation Project
Brandy Station Foundation	Brandy Station Battlefield
Shenandoah Valley Civil War Foundation	All significant Civil War sites in the lower Shenandoah Valley
CCBF	Cedar Creek Battlefield
New Market Battlefield Park/ Virginia Military Institute	Shirley's Hill
J. E. B. Stuart Birthplace Trust	J. E. B. Stuart Birthplace
Society for Port Republic Preservationists	Kemper House
SHAF	Grove Farm

Appendix F: Organizations and Individuals Associated with Battlefield Preservation

National Organizations

American Battlefield Protection
  Program
NPS
U.S. Department of the Interior
P.O. Box 37127
Washington, D.C. 20013-7127
ATTN: 413, Maureen Foster

The Association for the Preservation
  of Civil War Sites
613 Caroline Street, Suite B
Fredericksburg, VA 22401
(703) 371-1860
A. Wilson Greene, Executive Director

The Civil War Foundation
24 N. Buckmarsh Street
Berryville, VA 22611
(800) 247-6253
Thomas A. Lewis, Trustee

Civil War Round Table Associates
P.O. Box 7388
Little Rock, AR 72217
Jerry L. Russell, National Chairman

The Civil War Society
24 N. Buckmarsh Street
Berryville, VA 22611
(800) 247-6253
Tom Lewis, President

The Civil War Trust
1225 Eye Street, N.W.
Washington, D.C. 20005
(202) 326-8420
Grae Baxter, Executive Vice President

The Conservation Fund
The Civil War Battlefields Campaign
1800 N. Kent Street, Suite 1120
Arlington, VA 22209
(703) 525-6300
Frances H. Kennedy, Director

Council on America's Military Past
P.O. Box 1151
Fort Myers, VA 22211
(703) 644-6692
Colonel Herbert M. Hart, USMC
  (Ret.), Executive Director

Fairness to Land Owners Committee
1730 Garden of Eden Road
Cambridge, MD 21613
(410) 228-2316
Margaret Ann Reigle, Chairperson

HERITAGEPAC
P.O. Box 7281
Little Rock, AR 72217
Jerry L. Russell, National Chairman

Name of Your Congressman
U.S. House of Representatives
Washington, D.C. 20515

Name of Your Senator
U.S. Senate
Washington, D.C. 20510

National Inholders Association
233 Pennsylvania Avenue, S.E.
Washington, D.C. 20003
(202) 544-6156
Contact: M. Eball

National Parks and Conservation
    Association
1776 Massachusetts Avenue, N.W.
Suite 200
Washington, D.C. 20036
(202) 223-6722
Paul Pritchard, President
Bruce Craig, Cultural Resources
    Program Manager

The National Trust for Historic
    Preservation
1785 Massachusetts Avenue, N.W.
Washington, D.C. 20036
(202) 673-4000
Richard Moe, President

Regional Organizations

Battle of Carthage Historic
    Preservation
Route 2, Box 226
Carthage, MO 64836

Brandy Station Foundation
Box 165
Brandy Station, VA 22714
B. B. Mitchell III, President

Cedar Creek Battlefield Foundation
P.O. Box 229
Middleton, VA 22645
Kristen Sanders, Executive Director

Chantilly Battlefield Association
P.O. Box 3828
Fairfax, VA 22038
Contact: Ed Wenzel

Friends of National Parks at
    Gettysburg
P.O. Box 4622
Gettysburg, PA 17325-4622
(717) 337-1807
Larry Schweiger, Executive Director

Gettysburg Battlefield Preservation
Association
P.O. Box 1863
Gettysburg, PA 17325
(717) 334-7036
Dr. Walter L. Powell, Executive
Director

J. E. B. Stuart Birthplace Preservation
Trust
P.O. Box 901
Stuart, VA 24171
(919) 789-7557
Tom Perry, Executive Director

The Lee-Jackson Foundation
P.O. Box 8121
Charlottesville, VA 22906
Contact: Colonel Richard B. Smith
(Ret.)

Mill Springs Battlefield Association
P.O. Box 814
Somerset, KY 42502
(606) 679-4589
Contact: William Neikirk

New Market Battlefield Historical
Park
P.O. Box 1864
New Market, VA 22844
Ed Merrell, Director

The North Carolina Committee to
Save Fort Fisher
P.O. Box 330
Wilmington, NC 28402
(919) 762-2611
FAX (919) 762-9765
Paul M. Laird, Project Director

Perryville Battlefield Preservation
Association
1114 First National Bank Building
167 West Main Street
Lexington, KY 40507

Rich Mountain Battlefield Foundation
Route 2, Box 114
Bowden, WV 26254

Save Historic Antietam Foundation
P.O. Box 550
Sharpsburg, MD 21782
(301) 432-2522
Tom Clemens, President

Save Historic Antietam with
Responsible Policies
5564 Porterstown Road
Keedysville, MD 21756
Contact: Anne Corcoran

Save the Battlefield Coalition
P.O. Box 110
Catharpin, VA 22018
Annie Snyder, Chairperson

Shenandoah Valley Civil War
Foundation
114 Russellcroft Road
Winchester, VA 22601

Stonewall Brigade Foundation
338 Walnut Street
Woodstock, VA 22664

Virginians for Property Rights
P.O. Box 986
Madison, VA 22727
Contact: Alice Menks

Notes

Chapter 1

1. Rhodes and Andrews, "Rebels with Cause," *The Free Lance-Star, Town and Country,* 23 July 1988, 13.

2. Senator Bumpers credits Professor James M. McPherson, Edwards Professor of American History at Princeton University, for convincing him to lead the Manassas preservation fight. In the summer of 1988, Senator Bumpers read Dr. McPherson's book *Battle Cry of Freedom.* He later chaired the September 8, 1988, hearing on the Manassas bill and invited Dr. McPherson to testify (Senator Bumpers, interview by Georgie Boge, 22 March 1990, Washington, D.C.).

3. Senate, *Congressional Record,* 100th Cong., 1st sess., 1988, vol. 134, October 7, daily ed.

4. Cited in "U.S. Fights a New Battle of Antietam," *The New York Times,* 10 November 1987.

5. James M. McPherson, "The War That Never Goes Away," *Civil War Chronicles,* 5.

6. Edwin Bearss, interview with author, 1 February 1990.

7. Robert Penn Warren, *The Legacy of the Civil War,* 4.

8. Quoted in Robert Cruden, *The War that Never Ended,* 192.

9. James M. McPherson, *Ordeal By Fire,* viii.

10. In Warren, *Legacy,* 10–12.

11. Quoted in Henry Steele Commager, *Documents of American History,* 428–29.

12. Robert A. Webb, "Storm Over Manassas," *Historic Preservation,* 45.

13. Daryl Lease, "Group Girds to Protect Battlefields," *The Fredericksburg (Virginia) Free Lance-Star,* 9 January 1989, 1, 18.

14. Robert P. Hey, "Shopping Malls Peril Civil War Sites," *Christian Science Monitor,* 6.

15. Frances H. Kennedy, interview with Georgie Boge, 12 January 1990. Full descriptions of the battlefields may be found in *The Civil War Battlefield Guide.*

16. Roger M. Williams, "Save or Pave," *Americana,* 25.

17. Leo Marx, *The Machine in the Garden,* and Joel Garreau, "Earthmover: How Til Hazel Revolutionized the Way We Live," *The Washington Post Magazine,* 21 July 1991.

18. The Civil War Sites Advisory Commission of the NPS places the number of *major* Civil War armed conflicts at 373 (information originally compiled by the editors of *The Official Records;* unpublished material from the NPS, 8 January 1992).

19. Jody Powell, "Battling over Manassas," *National Parks,* 13.

20. Roger Mudd, "The Third Battle of Manassas," news report on the McNeil/Lehrer NewsHour, in Mike Hicklein, *The Third Battle of Manassas: A Video Archive,* Video Vision and Virginia Polytechnic Institute, 1988.

21. Wallace Stegner, "Our Common Domain," *Sierra,* 44.

Chapter 2

1. Charles B. Hosmer, Jr., *Presence of the Past: A History of the Preservation Movement before Williamsburg,* 21.

2. Christopher Duerksen, ed., *A Handbook on Historic Preservation Law,* 1.

3. Hosmer, *Presence of the Past,* 41.

4. "The Origin and Evolution of the National Military Park Idea" (Washington, D.C.: NPS, 1973), 7, photocopied report. Ronald Lee's definitive paper represents the only analysis of the history of the national military park system. The work was not completed before his untimely death in 1972, but it has received high acclaim from Edwin Bearss and Robert M. Utley, former assistant director of park historic preservation, NPS. Because much of Lee's material was gleaned from now inaccessible NPS information, we have heavily cited him.

5. Robert E. Stipe and Antoinette J. Lee, eds., *The American Mosaic,* 36.

6. Lee, "The National Military Park Idea," 19, and Edwin Bearss, letter to Georgie Boge, 25 May 1990.

7. The name Fredericksburg and Spotsylvania County Battlefields Memorial National Military Park was later officially changed to Fredericksburg-Spotsylvania National Military Park.

8. Lee, "The National Military Park Idea," 6, 22, 24. John B. Bachelder may be thought of as the first park historian.

9. Frederick Tilberg, *Gettysburg National Military Park, Pennsylvania,* NPS Historical Handbook Series No. 9 (Washington, D.C.: Government Printing Office, 1954, rev. 1962), 47.

10. Edwin Bearss, letter to Georgie Boge, 25 May 1990.

11. H.R. 8096, 53d Cong., 3d sess., 6 December 1894.

12. H.J. Res. 185, 53d Cong., 2d sess., 1 June 1894.

13. Lee, "The National Military Park Idea," 15.

14. House Committee on Military Affairs, *Chickamauga Battlefield,* 51st Cong., 2d sess., 1891, H. Rept. 51-643.

15. Lee, "The National Military Park Idea," 29.

16. 16 *U.S.C. (United States Code)* §430f.

17. 16 *U.S.C.* §430h.

18. Richard W. Sellars, "Vigil of Silence: The Civil War Memorials," *History News*, 21.

19. Edwin Bearss, interview by Georgie Boge, 1 February 1990.

20. "The National Military Park Idea," 32, 37.

21. House Committee on Military Affairs, *To Establish National Military Park Commission*, appendix C, 58th Cong., 2d sess., 1904, H. Rept. 58-2325, and 57th Cong., 2d sess., 1902, H. Rept. 57-2043.

22. 16 *U.S.C.* §425.

23. House Committee on Military Affairs, *To Establish National Military Park Commission*, appendix C, 58th Cong., 2d sess., 1904, H. Rept. 58-2325.

24. Ibid.

25. Lee, "The National Military Park Idea," 44, and Edwin Bearss, notes to Margie Boge, 16 July 1992. During these years the department was authorized to accept a small tract of land at Cheatham Hill, near Kennesaw Mountain, Georgia, where in 1914 members of Brigadier General Dan McCook's brigade dedicated a monument funded by the State of Illinois.

26. 39 *Stat.* (*United States Statutes at Large*) 535, chap. 408, 25 August 1916.

27. Stipe, *American Mosaic*, 37.

28. Lee, "The National Military Park Idea," 50.

29. 16 *U.S.C.* §461.

30. Horace M. Albright, *The Birth of the National Park Service*, 297.

31. 49 *Stat.* 666, chap. 408, 26 October 1949.

32. Edwin Bearss, interview by Georgie Boge, 1 February 1990.

33. U.S. Department of the Interior, NPS, Gettysburg National Military Park, *Boundary Study, Draft Report to Congress, Environmental Assessment*, 1988, 14.

Chapter 3

1. The Conservation Foundation, *National Parks for a New Generation: Vision, Realities, Prospects*, 124.

2. Richard Rambur, interview by Georgie Boge, 25 January 1990.

3. National Trust for Historic Places, "America's Eleven Most Endangered Historic Places 1992," no date.

4. Jerry Rogers, "Parks and Neighbors," speech before the George Wright Society meeting, Tucson, Arizona, 16 November 1988.

5. U.S. Department of the Interior, NPS mid-Atlantic region, *Conserving the Setting of George Washington Birthplace: An Adjacent Lands Survey*, 1987, 3.

6. Frances H. Kennedy, director, Civil War Battlefield Campaign, the Conservation Fund, letter to Georgie Boge, 28 March 1990.

7. On July 9, 1864, Major General Jubal Early, as part of his Washington campaign, engaged Union troops under Major General Lewis Wallace on the east bank of the Monocacy River. Although Early's Army of the Valley outmaneuvered the enemy, Wallace checked the Confederates' march toward Washington, D.C.

Civil War historian Gary Gallagher contends, "Wallace's troops spared the Lincoln government a potential disaster, and for that reason, the Battle of Monocacy must be considered one of the most significant actions of the Civil War" (Frances H. Kennedy, ed., *The Civil War Battlefield Guide*, 238).

8. Five Forks was a crucial battle on the road to Appomattox. On April 1, 1865, Robert E. Lee ordered Major Generals George E. Pickett and William H. Fitzhugh "Rooney" Lee, son of the Confederate commander, to hold the South Side Railroad running through Five Forks. Confederate loss of this railroad would not only sever the South's last supply line into Petersburg but also eliminate rail access to J. E. Johnson's troops in North Carolina. Perhaps unaware of the immediacy of combat at Five Forks, Rooney Lee, Pickett, and fellow officers enjoyed a shad bake several miles away near Hatcher's Run. Long after the battle erupted, the commanders sallied forth to the Confederate breastworks bordering White Oak Road. This two-mile stretch of log and dirt fortification was being pressed by Major General Philip Sheridan's dismounted troops. Union support also came from one of Major General Gouverneur K. Warren's infantry divisions, which swung north to engulf the enemy's left flank. At the same time, the insolent upstart Brigadier General George A. Custer battled with Rooney Lee on the right flank. Night fell, fighting ceased, and the vanquished Confederates melted into the pine forest. The South Side Railroad subsequently slipped into Union hands, causing the Confederate supply line to Petersburg to cease operations (Kennedy, *The Civil War Battlefield Guide*, 273).

9. Eric Hertfelder, telephone interview by Georgie Boge, 30 March 1990.

10. Conservation Foundation, *National Parks for a New Generation*, 113.

11. High-ranking NPS official who asked not to be identified, Washington, D.C., 1990.

12. "Political Manipulation of NPS Investigated," *National Parks*, 11.

13. The Bureau of Mines and Reclamation and the U.S. Forest Service can be described as exploitative agencies, while the U.S. Fish and Wildlife Service and the NPS function as protective agencies.

14. George Hartzog, *Battling for the National Parks*, 266–67.

15. Thomas J. Colin, "Meet the All-Stars: Key Players in the National Preservation Movement Call Washington Home," *Historic Preservation*, 59.

16. Robert D. Bush, interview by Georgie Boge, 23 March 1990.

17. Out of the 2,903 cases reviewed by the ACHP in 1989, only nine resulted in termination due to federal agency noncompliance (ACHP, *Report to the President and the Congress of the United States 1989* [Washington, D.C.: Government Printing Office, 1989], 96).

18. H. Bryan Mitchell, deputy director of the Virginia Department of Historic Resources and deputy state historic preservation officer, letter to Margie Boge, 15 May 1992. With respect to these regulations, private parties may engage in actions which threaten historic resources with no repercussions.

19. The Battle of South Mountain, fought on September 14, 1862, was part of the Antietam campaign. Brigadier General Alfred Pleasanton's federal cavalry corps encountered D. H. Hill's division at Turner's Gap on the morning of the fourteenth. By midnight, both Turner's and Fox's Gaps were secured by the Union, leaving Major General Jessel Reno of the IX Corps dead on the field. The Confederates proceeded to withdraw from the site.

20. Ross Kimmel, telephone interview by Georgie Boge, 30 March 1990.

21. Robert A. Webb, "Manassas Tragedy: Paving Over the Past," *The Washington Post*, 13 March 1988.

22. Penn Central Transportation v. New York City, 438 U.S. (United States Reports) 104 (1978).

23. Testimony before the House Committee on Interior and Insular Affairs, Subcommittee on National Parks and Public Lands, on H.R. 3248, 26 October 1988.

24. Dennis Frye, interview with Margie Boge, 9 March 1992.

25. Tersh Boasberg, interview by Georgie Boge, 1 November 1989.

26. Robert Krick, notes to Margie Boge, 8 May 1992.

27. H.R. 875, 101st Cong., 1st sess., 1989.

28. Maria Burks, letter to *The Civil War News*, 13 February 1990.

29. One of the developers of the Wilderness land is Joe Gibbs, owner of the Washington Redskins. According to a planner in the Fredericksburg Office of Planning and Community Development, "His request for rezoning in Spotsylvania County was more of a rally for the Washington Redskins than a sober evaluation of land use. . . . One can only speculate if the NPS was concerned that Congress would have been reluctant to limit Gibbs in any way because they were Redskins fans" (name withheld by request, letter to Margie Boge, 14 May 1992).

30. Maria Burks, letter to *The Civil War News*, 13 February 1990.

31. U.S. Department of the Interior, NPS, Harpers Ferry National Historical Park, *Special Boundary Study Newsletter*, July 1989, 2.

32. Ibid., *Special Boundary Study Newsletter No. 2*, October 1989, 1.

33. Dennis Frye, interview by Georgie Boge, 26 January 1990.

34. U.S. Department of the Interior, NPS, Harpers Ferry National Historical Park, *Special Boundary Study Newsletter*, July 1989, 1.

35. The markers now sit in the middle of the battlefield, largely undisturbed. Much farther west, the recently adopted bypass is under construction with a targeted completion date of 1997. This time, houses were moved to make way for the route (James Ogden III, NPS historian, Chickamauga and Chattanooga National Military Park, letter to Margie Boge, 13 May 1992).

36. Mike Snow, testimony before the Senate Committee on Natural Resources, Subcommittee on Public Lands, National Parks and Forests, on H.R. 2121, 29 September 1987.

37. Testimony before the Senate Committee on Natural Resources,

Subcommittee on Public Lands, National Parks and Forests, on H.R. 2121, 29 September 1987.

38. Wyche Fowler, testimony before the Senate Committee on Natural Resources, Subcommittee on Public Lands, National Parks and Forests, on H.R. 2121, 29 September 1987.

39. James Ogden III, letter to Margie Boge, 13 May 1992.

40. The park is essentially a proposed park, since the $110,000 proffered by the Centennial Corporation for design and construction of a commemorative site has failed to materialize. The Fairfax County Park authority is currently awaiting receipt of the donation.

41. Steve Vogel, "How History Is Losing the Battle in Fairfax," *The Fairfax (Virginia) Journal,* 27 October 1986.

42. Barbara Carton, "Confederate Soldier's Remains Sent to South Carolina for Viewing, Burial," *The Washington Post,* 17 November 1986. Elizabeth David, an official in the heritage resources program, Fairfax County Office of Comprehensive Planning, maintains that "due to fiscal constraints, the tour map has not been re-published. The site will appear in the next edition of the map" (notes to Margie Boge, 12 May 1992).

43. Elizabeth David, heritage resources program, Fairfax County Office of Comprehensive Planning, notes to Margie Boge, 12 May 1992.

44. John Herrity, chairman, Fairfax County Board of Supervisors, letter to Secretary of the Interior Cecil D. Andrus, 15 November 1979.

45. Robert U. Johnson and Clarence C. Buel, *Battles and Leaders of the Civil War,* vol. 2, 68, 394.

46. Peter Iris-Williams, mid-Atlantic region, NPS, letter to Margie Boge, 9 June 1992.

47. Ibid.

48. Ibid.

49. Tom Lewis, publisher, *Civil War: The Magazine of the Civil War Society,* telephone conversation with Margie Boge, 2 November 1992.

50. Jennifer Schettler, spokesperson, Saturn Corporation, 22 May 1992. Schettler noted that the Cheairs' property is readily available for use by community organizations such as the Heritage Foundation's symposium on decorative arts and the Association for the Preservation of Tennessee Antiquities Fall Homes Tour.

51. Ibid.

52. Ibid.

53. Dennis Kelly, telephone interview by Margie Boge, 10 February 1992.

54. Jennifer Schettler, fax to Margie Boge, 27 May 1992.

55. "Spring Hill Update," *Blue and Gray Magazine,* 34.

56. Jennifer Schettler, fax to Margie Boge, 27 May 1992.

57. "Spring Hill Update," 34.

Chapter 4

1. The number of Civil War battlefield sites throughout the United States is as follows:

Virginia	2,154	Alabama	336
Tennessee	1,462	North Carolina	313
Missouri	1,162	South Carolina	239
Mississippi	772	Maryland	203
Arkansas	771	Florida	168
West Virginia	632	Texas	90
Louisiana	566	Indian Territory	89
Georgia	549	New Mexico Territory	75
Kentucky	453	California	88

It is important to note that most of the ten thousand military actions were relatively small affairs—big battles like Gettysburg and Vicksburg were the exception ("The Civil War at a Glance," Resource Topics for Parklands [U.S. Department of the Interior, NPS: Washington, D.C.], no date).

2. H. Bryan Mitchell, interview by Georgie Boge, 2 February 1990.

3. Allan Tischler, "Lower Shenandoah Sites Need Preservation," *The Civil War News,* 24.

4. Harry Waters, "End the Dillon Rule," *The Manassas (Virginia) Journal Messenger,* 1 December 1988.

5. Laws similar to the Dillon rule are already used to a limited degree in seven other states, including North Carolina and Kentucky.

6. The so-called vesting measure establishes a point in the planning process beyond which developers cannot have their development rights limited or taken away through downzoning activity (John Harris, "Downzoning Compromise Developing," *The Washington Post,* 7 February 1990).

7. Chris Gay, "Who Was Dillon and Why Does He Have Such a Frustrating Impact on Prince William?" *Prince William County (Virginia) Weekly Messenger,* 6 April 1989.

8. Steve Bates, "Historic-Status Plan Divides Loudoun Area," *The Washington Post,* 10 April 1989.

9. Governor's Commission to Study Historic Preservation, *A Future for Virginia's Past: The Final Report of the Governor's Commission to Study Historic Preservation* (Richmond: Commonwealth of Virginia, 1988), 3, 15.

10. H. Bryan Mitchell, letter to Margie Boge, 15 May 1992.

11. Commonwealth of Virginia, Department of Economic Development, division of tourism, *The Summer Visitor in Virginia* (Richmond, Virginia: Commonwealth of Virginia, 1990), 1.

12. Mark Brown, telephone interview by Georgie Boge, 25 March 1992.

13. Virginia Tourism Development Group, *The 1990–91 Four-Season Virginia Visitor Study* (Richmond, Virginia: Commonwealth of Virginia, 1991), 2.

14. The state spent $223,000 on a brief message about tourism in Virginia that was aired at the end of the television show (Brooke A. Masters, "British Flocking to Va. Battlefields," *The Washington Post, Prince William Weekly,* 8 August 1991).

15. Sue Bland, interview by Georgie Boge, 29 January 1990, and by Margie Boge, 10 March 1992.

16. Governor's Commission to Study Historic Preservation, *A Future for Virginia's Past,* 20.

17. H. Bryan Mitchell, letter to Margie Boge, 9 June 1992.

18. The donation of a preservation easement restricts the development of a property, often reducing its dollar value. The reduction can be claimed as a charitable contribution and deducted from taxable income (H. Bryan Mitchell, letter to Margie Boge, 9 May 1992).

19. Governor's Commission to Study Historic Preservation, *A Future for Virginia's Past,* 23.

20. H. Bryan Mitchell, interview by Georgie Boge, 2 February 1990.

21. H. Bryan Mitchell, letter to Margie Boge, 9 June 1992.

22. Manassas seems to contradict this; the government would not have condemned the land were it not for the site's historical importance. Still, Manassas must be regarded as an aberration.

23. Robert Krick, telephone interview by Georgie Boge, 7 March 1990.

24. John Logan and Harvey Molotch, *Urban Fortunes,* 62.

25. Commonwealth of Virginia List of Lobbyists Registered with the Office of the Secretary of the Commonwealth as of 2 March 1990 for the 1990 General Assembly Session.

26. Donald P. Baker and Thomas Heath, "Developers Power Funds into Virginia Governor Race," *The Washington Post,* 20 January 1989.

27. Kent Jenkins, Jr., "Developer's Money Fuels Race in Virginia," *The Washington Post,* 8 October 1989.

28. Opponents of SB 514 had hoped to achieve a compromise on the issue by persuading legislators to follow the system used for national register designation. In particular, if a majority of owners object to a property's nomination to the register, the property is simply listed as "eligible." (Tersh Boasberg, "History Bulldozed: A New Bill Would Allow Developers to Flatten Virginia's Past," *The Washington Post,* 22 March 1992).

29. In 1989 the Virginia Board of Historic Resources designated 14,000 acres of Brandy Station as a Virginia landmark in recognition of the site's importance as the location of the Civil War's greatest cavalry battle. Two years later, the board designated 1,162 acres of Bristoe Station as a landmark because it served as the location of Confederate General A. P. Hill's failed attack on Union forces.

30. Til Hazel, telephone interview with Georgie Boge, 22 April 1992.

31. If the rationale advanced by developers is examined in context, it is possible to discern a major contradiction. SB 514 was hailed as a means of permitting local landowners to decide how a property should be designated—with minimal state intervention. Yet just two years ago developers heavily lobbied state legislators to overturn a downzoning measure passed by the Fairfax County Board of Supervisors. State intervention in so-called local zoning matters tends to be requested when it is expedient to developers.

32. In an editorial to the *Potomac News* Richard H. Hefter, a former Prince William County planning commissioner, argued, "When Prince William County wanted to locate a debris landfill at Bristoe, landowners cried about the property's historic significance—apparently afraid that a landfill would lessen its value. Mysteriously, when that threat went away, they no longer considered the land to be historic" ("Private-Property Advocates' Arguments Don't Stand Scrutiny," 21 January 1992).

33. More specifically, in 1971 the average residential property value in the historic district was $17,920, and $17,060 in the rest of the city. By 1990 average values had risen to $138,697 in the historic district and $87,011 outside of it. The average value of commercial property inside the district increased from $39,000 in 1971 to $231,675 in 1990. Outside, the average value of historic properties jumped from $77,353 in 1971 to $294,896 in 1990. The difference in value between commercial properties was attributed to the much smaller sizes of commercial properties within the historic district (Government Finance Officers Association, *Economic Benefits of Preserving Community Character: A Methodology* [Chicago: Government Finance Research Center, 1991], 78–80). For information on the economic analysis of historic Fredericksburg, see National Trust for Historic Preservation, *Economic Benefits of Preserving Community Character: A Methodology*, 1991.

34. John F. Harris, "Pulling Up Stakes on Historical Claims: Va. Bill Would Let Landowners—Not Preservationists—Decide," *The Washington Post*, 9 February 1992.

35. Allen established five acres as a base line simply because the section 106 review process only applies to properties five acres or larger ("George Allen Would Weaken Historic Preservation," Piedmont Environmental Council *Newsreporter*, 1, 4).

36. George Allen, "H.R. 4849: Balancing the Concerns of Local Landowners While Protecting Historic Preservation," *Virginia Viewpoint: A Weekly Commentary*, 27 April 1992.

37. "Ganging Up on Our Legacy," *Potomac News*, 27 April 1992.

38. Annie Snyder, SBC, letter to Margie Boge, 9 May 1992.

39. *The Journal Messenger* of northern Virginia, 27 April 1984.

40. Peter Baker, "Fairfax's Hazel: What He Wants, He Usually Gets," *The Washington Times*, 15 June 1987.

41. In retrospect, many observers have argued that Superintendent Swain made a tactical error by attempting to obtain concessions such as buffer zones rather than aggressively opposing the development (Jim Burgess, interview by Georgie Boge, 29 January 1990).

42. Tersh Boasberg, testimony before the Senate Committee on Energy and Natural Resources, Subcommittee on Public Lands, National Parks and Forests, on H.R. 4526, 8 September 1988.

43. House Committee on Interior and Insular Affairs, Subcommittee on National Parks and Recreation, *General Oversight Briefing Relating to Developments near Manassas National Battlefield*, 93d Cong., 1st sess., 3 April 1973, H. Rept. 93-9.

44. Annie Snyder, testimony before the Senate Committee on Energy and Natural Resources, Subcommittee on Public Lands, National Parks and Forests, on H.R. 4526, 8 September 1988.

45. Robert Webb, "Storm over Manassas," *Historic Preservation*, 44.

46. Daniel Koski-Karell, "There Are No Soldiers' Graves on the William Center Tract," *The Washington Post*, 8 May 1988.

47. Cornelius Foote, Jr., and John Harris, "Huge Mall Planned at Manassas," *The Washington Post*, 29 January 1988.

48. "Civil War Battlefield Loses Ground to New Mall," *National Parks*, 10–11.

49. Kathleen Seefeldt, chairperson, Prince William County Board of Supervisors, testimony before the Senate Committee on Energy and Natural Resources, Subcommittee on Public Lands, National Parks and Forests, on H.R. 4526, 8 September 1988.

50. Kenneth Smith, "Blood Runs High at Battle of Manassas Mall," *The Wall Street Journal*, 21 June 1988.

51. Jerome Cramer, "Not on This Hallowed Ground," *Time*, 13 June 1988.

52. James McPherson, testimony before the Senate Committee on Energy and Natural Resources, Subcommittee on Public Lands, National Parks and Forests, on H.R. 4526, 8 September 1988.

53. John F. Harris, "Manassas Mall Plan Pits Future Versus Past," *The Washington Post*, 19 February 1988.

54. John F. Harris, "Officials Battle over Proposed Manassas Mall," *The Washington Post*, 4 March 1988.

55. Tom Wicker, "Mauling the Mallers at Manassas," *The New York Times*, 1 July 1988.

56. H.R. 4526, 100th Cong., 2d sess., 4 May 1988.

57. Senate Committee on Energy and Natural Resources, Subcommittee on Public Lands, National Parks and Forests, *Manassas National Battlefield Park Amendments of 1988*, 100th Cong., 2d sess., 1988, S. Rept. 100-520.

58. Chele Caughron and Peter Baker, "Old Pals Parris, Hazel, Real-Estate Partners," *The Washington Times*, 27 May 1988.

59. Congressman Michael Andrews, interview by Georgie Boge, 22 March 1990.

60. John F. Harris, "Senate Stalks Elusive Cost of Expanding Manassas Battlefield," *The Washington Post,* 9 September 1988.

61. John F. Harris, "War Isn't over Yet for Opponents of Mall," *The Washington Post,* 14 August 1988.

62. Senator John Warner, testimony before the Senate Committee on Energy and Natural Resources, Subcommittee on Public Lands, National Parks and Forests, on H.R. 4526, 8 September 1988.

63. John F. Harris, "Battlefield Fate Settled by President," *The Washington Post,* 12 November 1988.

64. *The Copper Cable* (Copper Mountain, Colorado), November 1990, 6.

65. Annie Snyder, interview by Georgie Boge, 30 January 1990.

66. Not all claims for compensation arising out of the taking have been resolved. In particular, the NPS must pay to relocate two major power lines that stretch across the park and service a large part of northern Virginia. Relocation costs could bring the total cost of the taking to $130 million or higher (Robert Walker, Department of the Interior, telephone interview by Georgie Boge, 28 October 1992).

67. "How to Make a Killing in Land Speculation," *Potomac News,* 27 July 1991.

68. Hazel and Peterson acquired 550 acres adjacent to Manassas Battlefield Park for $10 million in 1986. Later that year, they sold a 150-acre parcel to a second partnership, NV Homes and Equity Resources (a William Center limited partnership), for $7 million; their land settlement was $34.6 million in May 1990. The U.S. Claims Court allocated $2.8 million to Marriot Corporation, since it held a contract to buy 16 acres of Hazel's proposed center (*Historic Preservation News,* February 1991, and Melissa Burns, U.S. Department of Justice, telephone interview by Margie Boge, 29 October 1992).

69. *The Prince William Journal,* 12–13 June 1991.

70. "Almost Asphalt," *Potomac News,* 25 November 1991.

Chapter 5

1. Eric Sundquist, "Land-Use Paradox Hampers Localities in Conservation," *The Richmond (Virginia) Times-Dispatch,* 15 November 1987.

2. R. D. Calderon, "Loudoun County 1984–1985 Revenues and Expenditures by Three Major Land-Use Sectors," photocopied, app., no pages.

3. Peggy Maio, Piedmont Environmental Council, letter to Margie Boge, 28 May 1992.

4. Richard J. Roddewig, "Reaping the Benefits: Historic Sites and Tourism," speech before the Conference on Preserving Historic New Jersey, Princeton, New Jersey, 12 May 1988.

5. State of Louisiana, Office of Tourism, *Louisiana Travel Journal,* October 1989.

6. Richard J. Roddewig, "Reaping the Benefits."

7. *Louisiana Travel Journal,* October 1989.

8. Thomas J. Martin, "The Impact of Tourism," *American City and County,* 49.

9. Terry Holzheimer, director, Loudoun County Department of Economic Development, letter to Peggy Maio, Piedmont Environmental Council, 27 May 1992.

10. U.S. Travel Data Center, *Economic Impact of U.S. Travel on Maryland Counties* (Annapolis: Maryland Department of Tourism and Development, State of Maryland, 1989).

11. Richard J. Roddewig, "Reaping the Benefits."

12. *Special Boundary Study Newsletter No. 2* (Washington, D.C.: U.S. Department of the Interior, NPS, October 1989). The economic study was completed by Dr. Gary Machlis in conjunction with the 1988 boundary study mandated by Congress (Dennis Frye, interview by Georgie Boge, 25 January 1990, and Margie Boge, 9 March 1992).

13. In 1991 Fredericksburg was one of two communities selected by the National Trust to site-test a methodology for analyzing the economic benefits of historic and other community preservation activities. The study organizers analyzed the economic benefits that have accrued to property owners, shopkeepers, and employees in the historic district in three principal areas: construction activity, property values, and revenues from tourism. The researchers also calculated the revenues collected by local governments. Over an eight-year period, the study organizers found, construction activity in the historic district injected $12.7 million into the local economy through job creation (in the construction, sales, and manufacturing industries) and another $11.3 million when the indirect benefits associated with the purchase of construction supplies and materials as well as the spending of workers' wage income are taken into account. Building-permit fees related to new construction brought the City of Fredericksburg an additional $33,442 in revenues while the fiscal benefits obtained by surrounding counties totaled $243,729.

Study organizers found that historic preservation activities provided a similar boon to the local economy in terms of increased property values and tourism. As detailed in chapter 4, researchers determined that "properties within Fredericksburg's historic district gained appreciably more in value over the last twenty years than properties located elsewhere in the City." Tourism sales amounted to $11.7 million in the historic district, and another $17.4 million outside. When secondary impacts of $13.8 million are included, historic-site tourism generated a total of $42.9 million in sales for the local economy. The City of Fredericksburg received fiscal benefits of approximately $1,751,800 in taxes. Although the higher property values had the potential to generate an additional

$478,845 in additional property tax revenues, the city may not have realized all of these revenues because of a special tax-exemption program designed for rehabilitated real estate, which in fiscal year 1989–90 exempted an estimated $241,080 in taxes. Funding for the study was provided by the National Trust for Historic Preservation and the U.S. Department of the Interior (Government Finance Officers Association, *Economic Benefits of Preserving Community Character: A Methodology* [Chicago: Government Finance Research Center, 1991], 2–4, 85–96). Photocopied.

14. Robert Lane, "The Cash Value of Civil War Nostalgia: A Statistical Overview of the Fredericksburg Park," *Virginia Country,* August 1983.

15. Ibid., 44. The study was based on the assumption that agricultural use would be the highest and best use for the parkland. Today, developers would probably receive residential or commercial zoning for the land.

16. Robert Krick, letter to Georgie Boge, 30 April 1992.

17. George Youngblood et al., "The Economic Impact of Tourism, Generated by the Gettysburg National Military Park, on the Economy of Gettysburg." A report of a special study sponsored by the Gettysburg National Military Park and supported by Shippensburg University's masters degree program, August 1987, 11–12, photocopied.

18. Adams County Economic Development Office, "Economic Development Study for Adams County, Pennsylvania," 1988, III–16, photocopied.

19. Philamea Hefer, telephone interview by Margie Boge, 27 June 1992.

20. A. Wilson Greene, interview by Georgie Boge, 29 January 1990.

21. Gardner Mallard Brown, Jr., and Henry O. Pallakowsky, "Economic Valuation of a Shoreline," *Review of Economics and Statistics,* vol. 59, 1977, 272–78.

22. Ronald F. Lee, "The Origin and Evolution of the National Military Park Idea" (Washington D.C.: NPS, 1973), 35, photocopied report.

23. Harold Nelson, "What the Staff Ride Can Depict: Face of Battle, Clash of Wills and Arms, Generalship, and Cause and Effect," *The Army Historian,* 15–16.

24. Carl E. Vuono, "The Staff Ride: Training for War Fighting," *The Army Historian,* 1.

25. Bernard E. Trainor, "Civil War's Fields Are Intelligence Classrooms," *The New York Times,* 19 November 1989.

26. 260 U.S. (United States Reports) 393 (1922).

27. Christopher Duerksen, ed., *A Handbook on Historic Preservation Law,* 353.

28. 438 U.S. 104 (1978).

29. J. Jackson Walter, "President's Page," *National Trust for Historic Preservation News,* February 1992.

30. Tersh Boasberg, "History Bulldozed: A New Bill Would Allow Developers to Flatten Virginia's Past," *The Washington Post,* 22 March 1992.

31. W. John Moore, "Just Compensation," *National Journal,* June 13, 1992.

32. "Property Rights Movement Strikes at Virginia Battlefields: Bitter Fights Seen Ahead," *Society News and Views: The Newsletter of the Civil War Society,* Spring 1992.

33. H. Jane Lehman, "Whose Land Is It?" *Chicago Tribune,* 16 February 1992.

34. Tom Kenworthy and Kirstin Downey, "South Carolina May Have to Pay Compensation in Property Case," *The Washington Post,* 30 June 1992.

35. Linda Greenhouse, "Justices Ease Way to Challenge Land-Use Rules That Prevent Development," *The New York Times,* 30 June 1992.

36. Kenworthy and Downey, "South Carolina May Have to Pay Compensation."

37. Ibid.

38. Thomas Lewis, "The Struggle for America," *Piedmont Environmental Council Newsreporter* (March–April 1992): 1.

39. Lehman, "Whose Land Is It?"

40. Friendly condemnations occur when an owner requests or permits the government to exercise its rights of eminent domain (Mark Stephens and A. Wilson Greene, "Parkland Ruckus Ignores Facts," *Potomac News,* 21 January 1992).

41. According to Stephens and Greene, "The Park Service also condemned a tiny parcel of less than half an acre to obtain a clear title from an unknown owner" ("Parkland Ruckus Ignores Facts").

42. John Harris, "Civil War Buffs, Developers Battle in Culpeper," *The Washington Post,* 20 June 1989.

43. A survey conducted by the Culpeper County government in 1988 found that among those county residents polled, 80 percent did not want development to change the agricultural character of the area. No other official survey of public opinion has been taken in recent years (Audrey Austin, "Readers Respond to Brookes' Column on Civil War Battlefields," *Richmond Times-Dispatch,* 18 August 1991).

44. James M. McPherson, letter to Secretary of the Interior Manuel Lujan and Governor Gerald L. Baliles of Virginia, no date.

45. Christine Neuberger, "Brandy Station, Swords Crossed Again on Battlefield," *Richmond Times-Democrat,* 13 November 1988.

46. H. Bryan Mitchell, letter to John F. Cahill of Hazel, Thomas, Fiske, Beckhorne, and Hanes, 21 September 1989.

47. Thomas L. Cummings, "Changes Not Being Carefully Planned," *Culpeper Star-Exponent,* 15 May 1989.

48. Tersh Boasberg, interview by Georgie Boge, 2 February 1990.

49. "Planners Not Ready to Vote on Sammis Development," *Culpeper News,* 28 December 1989, 1.

50. Chris Mothersead, interview by Georgie Boge, 31 January 1990, and Russell Aylor, interview by Georgie Boge, 31 January 1990. H. Bryan Mitchell

denies that Mr. Mothersead or any other Culpeper County official ever contacted the state to obtain historic-planning assistance (H. Bryan Mitchell, interview by Georgie Boge, 2 February 1990).

51. Aylor, interview by Georgie Boge, 31 January 1990.

52. Mothersead, interview by Georgie Boge, 31 January 1990.

53. Michael Armm, interview by Georgie Boge, 22 March 1990.

54. Neuberger, "Brandy Station, Swords Crossed Again on Battlefield," 5.

55. Mothersead interview.

56. Mitchell, interview by Georgie Boge, 2 February 1990.

57. Patricia A. Bradburn, "Condemnation Cloaked in Past," *Potomac News,* 17 December 1991, A7.

58. Page B. Mitchell, "Readers Respond to Brookes' Column on Civil War Battlefields," *Richmond Times-Dispatch,* 18 August 1991, F7.

Chapter 6

1. John F. Harris, "Manassas: Bittersweet Victory," *The Washington Post,* 29 January 1990.

2. S. 844, 101st Congress., 1st sess., 19 April 1989.

3. *National Parks, from Vignettes to a Global View: A Report for the Commission on Research and Resource Management Policy in the National Park System* (Washington, D.C.: National Parks and Conservation Association, 1989), 4.

4. Dennis Frye, interview by Georgie Boge, 26 January 1989.

5. *Conserving the Setting of George Washington Birthplace* (Washington, D.C.: Department of Interior, NPS, October 1987), 52.

6. Rambur, interview by Margie Boge, 9 March 1992.

7. Bruce Craig, interview by Georgie Boge, 1 February 1990.

8. Notes to Margie Boge, May 1992.

9. Edwin C. Bearss, interview by Georgie Boge, 1 February 1990.

10. Tersh Boasberg, interview by Georgie Boge, 2 February 1990.

11. Easements can also be used to reduce the value of a property for estate-tax purposes. Ironically, family farms are frequently sold in order to pay estate taxes following the death of the principle property owner. Easements not only preserve the rural character of the land but also allow farms to remain in family hands.

12. "Montgomery County's Farmland," *The Washington Post,* 12 January 1989.

13. Destry Jarvis, interview by Georgie Boge, 2 February 1990.

14. Examples of major easement programs include the Montana Land Reliance, American Farmland Trust, and Land Trust Alliance of Washington, D.C. (Peggy Maio, Piedmont Environmental Council, letter to Margie Boge, 28 May 1992).

15. The Conservation Foundation, *National Parks for a New Generation: Visions, Realities, Prospects,* 267.

16. Gary Craig, "Veteran of Mall Battle Answers Call to Arms," *Potomac News*, 2 December 1989.

17. The Shenandoah Valley was excluded from the study simply because the NPS had already completed a congressionally mandated study of the area.

18. GIS allows the user to create a mosaic of modern and historic maps to access current land uses within defined areas, to calculate statistics for land parcels, to identify important viewshed areas, and to change focus easily from a narrow battlefield to a wide region (*Draft, Civil War Sites in the Shenandoah Valley of Virginia, A Regional Assessment of Fifteen Battlefields* [Washington, D.C.: U.S. Department of the Interior, NPS, October 1991], 23).

19. If conducted as envisioned by Congress, the study will be more comprehensive and thorough than any previously performed.

20. The commission was established for the sole purpose of completing a comprehensive two-year study. Members are permitted to hold hearings or host workshops, but no funding was made available for operational activities.

21. Marilyn Nickles, telephone interview with Georgie Boge, 15 July 1992.

22. Ibid.

23. Out of the $10 million request, $8 million is targeted for aiding non-federal organizations in acquisition or protection of vital historic lands. The remaining $2 million would be used to continue technical assistance activities (ABPP, NPS, information sheet entitled the "American Battlefield Protection Program," 25 March 1992).

24. It was originally called the American Battlefield Preservation Foundation. This was later changed to the Civil War Battlefield Foundation, then on June 26, 1992, the CWT.

25. *Strategic Plan* (Washington, D.C.: Civil War Battlefield Foundation, 24 March 1992), 1.

26. "New Foundation Enters Breach at Antietam," *Civil War,* 28.

27. The engagement at Byram's Ford was part of Sterling Price's Raid in the fall of 1864 to recoup Missouri for the Confederacy. Specifically, Byram's Ford and its key Blue River crossing were destined to play an important role in the October 1864 Battle of Westport, possibly the largest Civil War battle west of the Missouri River. The Union victory aided Lincoln's reelection in 1864 and signaled an end to the presence of large Confederate forces in Missouri.

28. Howard Coffin, author and press secretary to Senator James Jeffords, letter to Margie Boge, 1 July 1992.

29. Ibid.

30. *Draft, Civil War Sites in the Shenandoah Valley of Virginia, A Regional Assessment of Fifteen Battlefields* (Washington, D.C.: U.S. Department of the Interior, NPS, October 1991), 1.

31. Coffin, letter to Margie Boge, 1 July 1992. Such legislation, however, will not be introduced until NPS releases the final study report, which was still under review in June 1992.

32. *Draft, Civil War Sites in the Shenandoah Valley,* 2.

33. Thomas A. Lewis, "The Struggle for America," *Newsreporter of the Piedmont Environmental Council,* March–April 1992.

34. *Battlefield Update No. 29* (Washington, D.C.: U.S. Department of the Interior, NPS, January–February 1992). Bearss cites the Cedar Creek Battlefield as an exception to this rule of thumb.

35. A. Wilson Greene, interview by Georgie Boge, 29 January 1990.

36. "Group at Work on Preservation Blueprint," *Civil War* 10, no. 33 (January–February 1992): 29.

37. This idea was suggested by Annie Snyder, interview by Georgie Boge, 30 January 1990.

38. The National Trust for Historic Preservation has traditionally been regarded as the focal point for federal leadership in the area of historic preservation. Unfortunately, most of its activities have involved preservation of the built environment rather than historically significant land. Although the trust has demonstrated an interest in Civil War battlefields, the absence of a substantive acquisition budget and a lack of regulatory power have rendered its actions rather innocuous.

39. Lee Bowman, "Land Developers 'Attacking' Gettysburg Countryside," *The Pittsburgh Press,* 29 October 1989.

40. Senator Dale Bumpers, interview by Georgie Boge, 22 March 1990.

41. "Parks and Neighbors," speech before the George Wright Society Meeting, Tucson, Arizona, 16 November 1988.

42. U.S. Department of the Interior, NPS, "Delaware and Lehigh Navigation Canal National Heritage Corridor," no date, 3.

43. Senator James Jeffords, interview by Georgie Boge, 22 March 1990.

44. "The New Face of Environmentalism," *Utne Reader,* 110.

45. The NPS is divided into ten regions. NPS units in the mid-Atlantic region include battlefields in Richmond, Petersburg, Fredericksburg, Gettysburg, Valley Forge, and Jamestown as well as the site of Appomattox Court House.

46. *Related Lands Projects* (Philadelphia: U.S. Department of the Interior, NPS, mid-Atlantic region, division of park and resource planning, October 1989), 4.

47. Peter Iris-Williams, interview by Georgie Boge, 24 January 1990.

48. In an editorial to the *Richmond Times-Dispatch,* 18 August 1991, Richmond National Battlefield Park superintendent Cynthia MacLeod responded to a letter supporting Henrico County's rejection of the document *Conserving Richmond's Battlefields:*

> He [the author of the letter] mistakenly refers to it as a National Park document when it was in reality a working *draft* publication of a collection of ideas by three counties, the City of Richmond, the

Commonwealth of Virginia and the National Park Service. The ideas concerned matters that Henrico County citizens have in common with thousands of other citizens of this country. The eyes of the nation are looking to Richmond with interest in the preservation and interpretation of Civil War sites. What purpose is served in 1991 to "withdraw from and disavow" the Memorandum of Understanding that was signed in 1988 by the Henrico County Board of Supervisors? The memorandum was an instrument of cooperation and communication and set as objectives the identification of (1) Civil War resources, (2) area growth and development patterns, and (3) conservation options. Implementation of these recommendations was even qualified as . . . "to the extent possible."

There is no intent by the National Park Service to use legislation to give the NPS or the Commonwealth the "power to veto *any* plan of development in a core battlefield area" . . . "Land grab"? Hardly. This cooperative effort in the Richmond area was an attempt to identify ways other than a "land grab," to enlist the brain power and sympathies of people outside the NPS to find alternative ways to NPS acquisition to conserve battlefields. Chesterfield County and Hanover County, in ways different from each other, have both worked to incorporate various methods and instances of conservation. . . .

49. Ibid. Hanover County recognized 50 additional acres of the Cold Harbor site for commemoration. NPS currently owns 149 acres in an area a half mile wide.

50. 16 *U.S.C.* §430oo.

51. Senate Committee on Energy and Natural Resources, Subcommittee on Public Lands, National Parks and Forests, *Antietam National Battlefield*, 100th Cong., 2d sess., S. Rept. 100-529.

52. Eugene L. Meyer, "Antietam's Suspicious Summer," *The Washington Post*, 4 September 1989.

53. Richard Rambur, interview by Georgie Boge, 25 January 1990.

54. "Washington County Zoning Ordinance," article 20A, Antietam Overlay District, revision 13 June 1989, 85.

55. "Compromise at Antietam," *National Parks*, 17.

56. 102 *Stat.* 2649, 25 October 1988.

57. The legislated boundary includes several large parcels that are not owned by the NPS.

58. Anne Corcoran, telephone interview by Margie Boge, June 1992.

59. The SHAF cleared ten acres of locust, cherry, cedar, and underbrush from the approach to Bloody Lane in February 1991.

60. Bill Callen, "Schaefer: Preserve Antietam," *The Hagerstown (Maryland) Morning Herald*, 23 January 1990.

61. Steve Goodrich, interview by Georgie Boge, 25 January 1990.

62. Richard Rambur, "Compromise at Antietam," *National Parks*, 16–17.

63. Tom Clemens, letter to Margie Boge, 19 May, 1992. The Department of the Interior's American Battlefield Protection Foundation contributed $100,000, Maryland's Environmental Trust, $100,000, and the APCWS awarded the SHAF a matching grant of $15,000.

64. Telephone interview with Margie Boge, 23 June 1992.

65. Members of SHARP have challenged the Antietam Overlay in court (letter to Georgie Boge, 19 May 1992).

66. Telephone interview with Georgie Boge, 23 June 1992.

67. Interview by Margie Boge, 25 January 1992.

68. "Forward from Manassas," president's column, *Preservation News Index*, February 1989.

69. "These Empty Fields," *Historic Preservation*, 42–43.

Appendices

1. List compiled from information provided by Edwin Bearss, 5 May 1992, and by the Public Information Center, NPS, U.S. Department of the Interior, Washington, D.C., Fall 1989.

2. Pecos National Historical Park includes the site of the Battle of Glorieta Pass.

3. Contains soldiers' remains from other wars.

4. Pub. L. 88-578, September 3, 1964, 78 *Stat.* 897.

5. William Lienesch, "Parkland Hope Chest," *National Parks*, 14, 15.

6. Eric Hertfelder, telephone interview by Georgie Boge, 30 March 1990.

7. Tersh Boasberg, Thomas A. Coughlin, and Julia Miller, *Historic Preservation Law and Taxation*, vol. 1, pp. 7, 10.

8. 16 *U.S.C.* §470.

9. Pub. L. 89-665, October 15, 1966, 80 *Stat.* 915.

10. 16 *U.S.C.* §470a.

11. Boasberg, *Historic Preservation Law*, vol. 1, pp. 7–8.

12. Robert E. Stipe, *The American Mosaic*, 51.

13. Christopher Duerksen, ed., *A Handbook on Historic Preservation Law*, 207.

14. 16 *U.S.C.* §470f.

15. In the last ten years most of these grant programs have not been funded (Tersh Boasberg, interview by Georgie Boge, 2 February 1990).

16. Boasberg, *Historic Preservation Law*, vol. 1, p. 9.

17. Pub. L. 91-190, January 1, 1970, 83 *Stat.* 852.

18. Ibid.

19. These lists represent the culmination of numerous personal interviews,

responses to questionnaires, and literature reviews. A majority of the information was provided by leaders in the field of battlefield preservation, including Edwin C. Bearss, Robert Krick, Tom Lewis, Frances H. Kennedy, Robert H. Meinhard, and Mark Stephens. We recognize that many readers will disagree with our assessment. Nevertheless, it is essential to note that most experts disagree about how individual sites should be classified. They also continuously debate the criteria that should be used to assess each site. In general, the definition of *threatened* is both arbitrary and relative. Still, we believe that the identification of threatened sites is extremely important in that it is the first step in the historic preservation planning process.

20. Much of this battlefield site has already been lost.

21. A number of individual sites have been lost in the Atlanta vicinity, including Peachtree Creek, Ezra Church, and Jonesboro, as well as the Atlanta city battlefields themselves.

Bibliography

Books

Albright, Horace. *The Birth of the National Park Service: The Founding Years, 1913–1933.* Salt Lake City: Howe Brothers, 1985.

Boasberg, Tersh, Thomas A. Coughlin, and Julia H. Miller. *Historic Preservation Law and Taxation.* Vol. 1. New York: Matthew Bender, 1986.

Boatner, Mark. *The Civil War Dictionary.* New York: Vintage Books, 1991.

Catton, Bruce. *The Civil War.* New York: American Heritage, 1985.

————. *Reflections on the Civil War.* Edited by John Leekley. Garden City, New York: Doubleday, 1981.

Commager, Henry Steele. *Documents of American History.* New York: Appleton-Century-Crofts, 1963.

The Conservation Foundation. *National Parks for a New Generation: Visions, Realities, Prospects.* Harrisonburg, Virginia: R. R. Donnelley, 1985.

Cruden, Robert. *The War That Never Ended.* Englewood Cliffs, New Jersey: Prentice-Hall, 1973.

Duerksen, Christopher, ed. *A Handbook on Historic Preservation Law.* Washington, D.C.: The Conservation Foundation and the National Center for Preservation Law, 1983.

Durant, Will and Ariel. *The Lessons of History.* New York: Simon and Schuster, 1968.

Everhart, William C. *The National Park Service.* New York: Praeger, 1972.

Garrison, Lemuel A. *The Making of a Ranger: Forty Years with the National Parks.* Salt Lake City: Howe Brothers, 1983.

Harzog, George B. *Battling for the National Parks.* Mount Kisco, New York: Moyer Bell, 1988.

Hosmer, Charles. *Presence of the Past: A History of the Preservation Movement in the United States before Williamsburg.* New York: G. P. Putnam's, 1965.

Jefferson, Thomas. *Notes on the State of Virginia.* Magnolia, Massachusetts: Peter Smith, 1976.

Johnson, Robert U., and Clarence C. Buel. *Battles and Leaders of the Civil War*. Vol. 2. New York: Century, 1887.

Kennedy, Frances H., ed. *The Civil War Battlefield Guide*. Boston: Houghton Mifflin, 1990.

Logan, John R., and Harvey L. Molotch. *Urban Fortunes: The Political Economy of Place*. Berkeley, California: University of California Press, 1987.

McCurdy, Dwight. *Park Management*. Carbondale, Illinois: Southern Illinois University Press, 1985.

McPherson, James M. *Battle Cry of Freedom*. New York: Oxford University Press, 1988.

————. *Ordeal By Fire*. New York: Alfred A. Knopf, 1982.

Mulloy, Elizabeth D. *The History of the National Trust for Historic Preservation, 1963–1973*. Washington, D.C.: Preservation Press, 1976.

Stipe, Robert E., and Antoinette J. Lee, eds. *The American Mosaic: Preserving a Nation's Heritage*. Washington, D.C.: J. D. Lucas, 1987.

Stokes, Samuel, and Elizabeth A. Watson. *Saving America's Countryside*. Baltimore: Johns Hopkins University Press, 1989.

Ward, Geoffrey C. *The Civil War*. New York: Alfred A. Knopf, 1990.

Warren, Robert Penn. *The Legacy of the Civil War*. Cambridge: Harvard University Press, 1983.

Journal Articles

"Antietam Supporters Win Shopping Center Battle." *National Parks* 61, nos. 1–2 (January–February 1987): 37.

"Believe It or Not, We Love History." *Historic Preservation* 40, no. 6 (November–December 1988): 8.

"Civil War Battlefield Loses Ground to New Mall." *National Parks* 62, nos. 5–6 (May–June 1988): 10–11.

Colin, Thomas J. "Meet the All-Stars: Key Players in the National Preservation Movement Call Washington Home." *Historic Preservation* 39, no. 5 (September–October 1987): 58–59.

Cramer, Jerome. "Not on This Hallowed Ground." *Time* 131, no. 24 (13 June 1988): 29.

Dowie, Mark. "The New Face of Environmentalism." *Utne Reader* (July–August 1992): 104–9.

Fitts, Deborah. "Historic District Expansion Proposed." *The Civil War News* 16, no. 1 (January–February 1990): 25.

_____. "President Bush Signs Legislation to Expand Virginia Battle-fields." *The Civil War News* 16, no. 1 (January–February 1990): 1.

"Group at Work on Preservation Blueprint." *Civil War* (January–February 1992): 29.

Hall, Clark B. "Season of Change: The Winter Encampment of the Army of the Potomac, Dec. 1, 1863–May 4, 1864." *Blue and Gray* 8, no. 4 (April 1991): 8–22, 48–62.

_____. "The Battle of Brandy Station." *The Civil War Times Illustrated* (June 1990): 32–42.

"House Bill Helps Free Park Service from Politics." *National Parks* 62, nos. 7–8 (July–August 1988): 8–9.

Jacobovitz, Donald D. "Engineers Analyze Antietam." *The Army Historian* (October 1988).

Lane, Bob. "The Cash Value of Civil War Nostalgia: A Statistical Overview of the Fredericksburg Park." *Virginia Country* 1 (August 1983): 44–46.

Lewis, Thomas. "These Empty Fields." *Historic Preservation* 41, no. 5 (September–October 1989): 42–43.

Lienesch, William. "Parkland Hope Chest." *National Parks* 64, nos. 1–2 (January–February 1990): 14–15.

Lord, Lew. "The Search for What Defines Us." *U.S. News and World Report* 105, no. 12 (15 August 1988): 52–54.

Martin, Thomas J. "The Impact of Tourism." *American City and Country* (December 1987).

Meinhard, Robert. "Richmond Battlefield: Dollars or History?" *The Civil War News* 17, no. 7 (September 1991): 34.

Nelson, Howard. "What the Staff Ride Can Depict: Face of Battle, Clash of Wills and Arms, Generalship, and Cause and Effect." *The Army Historian* (October 1988): 15, 17.

"News Update." *National Parks* 62, nos. 11–12 (November–December 1988): 11.

"NPCA Commission Examines Park Science." *National Parks* 62, nos. 7–8 (July–August 1988): 10.

O'Donnell, Mike. "Heritage Lost." *North-South Trader* 2, no. 6 (September 1975): 31–32.

Piccoli, Sean. "Civil War Site Still a Battleground." *Insight* 4, no. 21 (23 May 1988): 22–23.

Piedmont Environmental Council. "The Battle of Brandy Station." *Newsreporter* (June–July 1989): 1.

Piedmont Environmental Council. "Fifty-Six Thousand Acres Protected by Easement." *Newsreporter* (December 1989): 11–14.

"Political Manipulation of the National Parks Investigated." *National Parks* 64, nos. 11–12 (November–December 1991): 11–14.

Powell, Jody. "Battling over Manassas: The Outcome Will Decide the Fate of Historic Parks." *National Parks* 62, nos. 7–8 (July–August 1988): 12–13.

"Public Lands from A–Z." *Sierra* 74, no. 5 (September–October 1989): 16–17.

Rambur, Richard. "Compromise at Antietam." *National Parks* 64, nos. 1–2 (January–February 1990): 1617.

Rankin, Betty, and Annie Snyder. "The Third Battle of Manassas." *Preservation Forum* 3, no. 1 (Spring 1989): 2–7.

Robertson, James. "Our South in Words and Pictures." *Southern Living* 25, no. 1 (January 1990): 54–55.

Satchell, Michael. "The Battle for the Wilderness." *U.S. News and World Report* 107, no. 1 (3 July 1989): 16–25.

Sellars, Richard West. "The Granite Orchards of Gettysburg." *History News* 41, no. 4 (July–August 1986): 22–23.

———. "Vigil of Silence: The Civil War Memorials." *History News* 41, no. 4 (July–August 1986): 19–21.

" 'Sewering' the Countryside around Assateague and Gettysburg." *The Environmental Journal* (June 1979): 21.

"Spring Hill Update." *Blue and Gray Magazine* 8, no. 2 (December 1990): 34.

Stegner, Wallace. "Our Common Domain." *Sierra* 74, no. 5 (September–October 1989): 42–47.

Storch, Marc J. "Wilderness Battlefield Is Threatened." *The Civil War News* 16, no. 1 (January–February 1990): 28C.

Tischler, Allan. "Lower Shenandoah Sites Need Preservation." *The Civil War News* 16, no. 1 (January–February 1990): 24.

Trust for Public Land. "The Local Connection: Serving the Land Where We Live." *Land People* 1, no. 4 (Winter 1990): 1–5.

Vuono, Carl E. "The Staff Ride: Training for War Fighting." *The Army Historian* (October 1988): 1–2.

Watson, Jim. "Civil War Buffs v. the Developers." *Insight* 2, no. 50 (15 December 1986): 53–55.

Webb, Robert. "Storm over Manassas." *Historic Preservation* 40, no. 4 (July–August 1988): 40–45.

Williams, Roger M. "Save or Pave?" *Americana* 17, no. 2 (June 1989): 23–29.

Government Documents

President's Advisory Council on Historic Preservation. *A Plan to Preserve the Historic Resources of the Gettysburg Area of the Commonwealth of Pennsylvania.* Washington, D.C.: Government Printing Office, 1977.

_____. *Report to the President and the Congress of the United States: Twenty Years of the National Historic Preservation Act.* Washington, D.C.: Government Printing Office, 1986.

_____. *Report to the President and the Congress of the United States, 1989.* Washington, D.C.: Government Printing Office, 1989.

Tilberg, Frederick. *Gettysburg National Military Park, Pennsylvania.* NPS Historical Handbook Series No. 9. Washington, D.C.: Government Printing Office, 1954, rev. 1962.

U.S. Congress. House. Committee on Interior and Insular Affairs. *Expanding the Boundaries of the Fredericksburg-Spotsylvania National Military Park near Fredericksburg, VA.* 101st Cong., 1st sess., 1989. H. Rept. 100-144.

_____. Subcommittee on National Parks and Recreation. *General and Oversight Briefing Relating to Developments near Manassas National Battlefield.* 93d Cong., 1st sess., 3 April 1973. H. Rept. 93-9.

U.S. Congress. House. Committee on Military Affairs. *Chickamauga Battlefield.* 51st Cong., 2d sess., 1891. H. Rept. 51-643.

_____. *Establishment of National Military Parks-Battlefields: Hearings before the Committee and Subcommittee No. 8 of the Committee on Military Affairs.* 71st Cong., 2d sess., 21 March and 8 February 1930.

_____. *Study of Battlefields in U.S. for Commemorative Purposes.* 69th Cong., 1st sess., 1926. H. Rept. 69-1071.

_____. *To Establish National Military Park Commission.* 57th Cong., 2d sess., 1902. H. Rept. 57-2043, and appendix C, 58th cong., 2d sess., 1904. H. Rept. 58-2325.

U.S. Congress. House. *Congressional Record.* 101st Cong., 1st sess., 1989. Vol. 135, no. 94, daily ed.

U.S. Congress. Senate. Committee on Energy and Natural Resources. *Antietam National Battlefield.* 100th Cong., 2d sess., 1988. S. Rept. 100-529.

————. *Report to Accompany H.R. 2121*. 100th Cong., 1st sess., 1987. S. Rept. 100-248.

————. *Report to Accompany H.R. 797*. 100th Cong., 1st sess., 1988. S. Rept. 100-179.

————. Subcommittee on Public Lands, National Parks and Forests. *Hearings on S. 858, H.R. 1983 and H.R. 2121*. 100th Cong., 1st sess., 1987.

————. Subcommittee on Public Lands, National Parks and Forests. *Manassas National Battlefield Park Amendments of 1988*. 100th Cong., 2d sess., 1988. S. Rept. 100-520.

U.S. Congress. Senate. Committee on Military Affairs. *Dedication of Chickamauga and Chattanooga National Military Park*. Report prepared by J. M. Palmer. 54th Cong., 1st sess. S. Rept. 637.

————. *Study of Battlefields in the United States for Commemorative Purposes*. 70th Cong., 1st sess., 1928. S. Rept. 70-187.

U.S. Congress. Senate. *Congressional Record*. 101st Cong., 1st sess., 1989. Vol. 135, October 19, daily ed.

U.S. Department of the Interior. NPS. *Antietam National Battlefield: Analysis of the Visible Landscape*. Washington, D.C., 1988.

————. Richmond National Battlefield Park. *Battlefield Conservation Effort Newsletter No. 2* Washington, D.C., 1989.

————. Gettysburg National Military Park. *Boundary Study: Draft Report to Congress, Environmental Assessment*. Washington, D.C., 1989.

————. Gettysburg National Military Park. *Boundary Study Update No. 4*. Washington, D.C., 1989.

————. Mid-Atlantic region. *Conserving the Boundary of George Washington Birthplace*. Washington, D.C., 1987.

————. Civil War Advisory Commission. *Civil War Major Armed Conflicts*. Washington, D.C., 8 January 1992. Originally compiled by the editors of *The Official Records*.

————. Richmond National Battlefield Park. *Conservation Effort Newsletter No. 1*. Washington, D.C., 1988.

————. *Delaware and Lehigh Navigation Canal National Heritage Corridor*. Washington, D.C., no date.

————. Mid-Atlantic region, division of park and resource planning. *Related Lands Projects*. Washington, D.C., 1989.

————. *Draft: Civil War Sites in the Shenandoah Valley of Virginia: A Regional Assessment of Fifteen Battlefields*. Washington, D.C., October 1991, 2.

————. Harpers Ferry National Historical Park. *Special Boundary Study*

Newsletter. Washington, D.C., July 1989, and *Special Boundary Study Newsletter No. 2,* October 1989.

————. Manassas National Battlefield Park. *Statement for Management.* Washington, D.C., 1989.

————. Antietam National Battlefield. *Summary General Management Plan and Final Environmental Impact Statement.* Washington, D.C., April 1992.

————, and the Georgia Department of Transportation. *Final Environmental Impact Statement, MLP-813 (1): Walker-Catoosa Counties, P.I. No. 621190.* 10 August 1990.

U.S. Department of Transportation. Federal Highway Administration. *Scenic Byways.* Washington, D.C., 1988. Publication No. FHWA-DF-88-004.

Interviews*

Andrews, Congressman Michael. Interview, 22 March 1990, Washington, D.C.

Andrews, John L. NPS visitor center supervisor, Gettysburg National Military Park. Interview, 28 May 1989, Gettysburg, Pennsylvania.

Apschnikat, Ken. NPS superintendent, Manassas National Battlefield Park. Interview, 29 January 1990, Manassas, Virginia.

Armm, Michael. Office of Lee C. Sammis. Interview, 22 March 1990, Washington, D.C.

Aylor, Russel. Culpeper County Planning Commission. Interview, 31 January 1990, Culpeper, Virginia.

Bearss, Edwin C. Chief historian, NPS. Interview, 1 February 1990, Washington, D.C.

Bland, Sue. Media relations manager, Virginia Division of Tourism. Interview, 29 January 1990, and by Margie Boge, 10 March 1992, Richmond, Virginia.

Boasberg, Tersh. Boasberg and Norton. Interviews, November 1989 and 2 February 1990, and by Margie Boge, 11 March 1992, Washington, D.C.

Brown, Donald. NPS superintendent, Chickamauga and Chattanooga National Military Park. Telephone interview, 9 March 1990.

Bumpers, Senator Dale. Interview, 22 March 1990, Washington, D.C.

Burgess, Jim. NPS ranger, Manassas National Battlefield Park. Interview, 29 January 1990, Manassas, Virginia.

* All interviews conducted by Georgie Boge unless otherwise indicated.

Burns, Melissa. U.S. Department of Justice. Telephone interview by Margie Boge, 29 October 1992.

Bush, Robert D. Executive director, ACHP. Interview, 23 March 1990, Washington, D.C.

Caldwell, Peter. Office of Senator James Jeffords. Interview, 24 October 1989, Washington, D.C.

Clemens, Thomas. SHAF. Interview, 25 January 1990, Keedysville, Maryland.

Coffin, Howard. Press Secretary, Senator James Jeffords. Telephone interview by Margie Boge, 26 May 1992.

Colgan, State Senator Charles. Telephone interview, 12 March 1990.

Corcoran, Anne. SHARP. Interview, 25 January 1990, and telephone interview by Margie Boge, 23 June 1992, Sharpsburg, Maryland.

Craig, Bruce. Cultural resources coordinator, National Parks and Conservation Association. Interview, 1 February 1990, Washington, D.C.

David, Elizabeth. Heritage resource branch, Office of Comprehensive Planning, Fairfax County, Virginia. Telephone interview, 8 March 1990.

Davidson, Robert. NPS assistant superintendent, Gettysburg National Military Park. Interview, 25 January 1990, Gettysburg, Pennsylvania.

Frye, Dennis. NPS historian, Harpers Ferry National Historical Park. Interview, 25 January 1990, and by Margie Boge, 9 March 1992, Harpers Ferry, West Virginia.

Gibson, Keith. Executive director of museum programs, Virginia Military Institute Museum. Telephone interview, 22 April 1992.

Gilbert, Frank. Senior field representative, National Trust for Historic Preservation. Telephone interview, 1 March 1990.

Goodrich, Steve. Office of Planning, Washington County, Maryland. Interview, 25 January 1990, Hagerstown, Maryland.

Greene, A. Wilson. Executive director, APCWS. Interview, 29 January 1990, Fredericksburg, Virginia, and by Margie Boge, 15 March 1992, Indianapolis, Indiana.

Hall, Clark "Bud." Brandy Station Foundation. Interview, 30 January 1990, Fairfax, Virginia.

Hax, Catherine. Maryland Office of Tourism and Economic Development. Telephone interview, 22 April 1992.

Hazel, Til. Hazel/Peterson Companies. Interview, 23 March 1990, Fair Lakes, Virginia, and telephone interview, 22 April 1992.

Hefter, Philamea. SBC. Telephone interview by Margie Boge, 26 June 1992.

Hertfelder, Eric. Executive director, National Conference of State Historic Preservation Officers. Telephone interview, 30 March 1990.

Iris-Williams, Peter. NPS Mid-Atlantic region. Interview, 24 January 1990, Philadelphia, Pennsylvania.

Kelly, Dennis. Chief historian, Kennesaw Mountain National Battlefield Park. Telephone interview by Margie Boge, 10 February 1992.

Kennedy, Frances. Director, Civil War Battlefield Campaign, Conservation Fund. Interview, 12 January 1990, Arlington, Virginia.

Kimmel, Ross. Capital programs administration, Maryland Department of Natural Resources. Telephone interview, 30 March 1990.

Krick, Robert. NPS chief historian, Fredericksburg-Spotsylvania National Military Park. Telephone interview, 7 March 1990.

Jarvis, Destry. Student Conservation Association. Interview, 2 February 1990, Washington, D.C.

Jeffords, Senator James. Interview, 22 March 1990, Washington, D.C.

Johnson, Eric. Office of Congressman Buddy Darden. Telephone interview, 7 March 1990.

Lawson, Art. Staff attorney, Piedmont Environmental Council. Interview, 31 January 1990, Culpeper, Virginia.

Lawson, Rich. Department of Development Administration, Prince William County, Virginia. Telephone interview by Margie Boge, 4 November 1992.

Lewis, Tom. CCBF. Telephone interview, 30 March 1990.

Mitchell, H. Bryan. Director of preservation programs, Virginia Department of Historic Resources. Interview, 2 February 1990, Washington, D.C.

Mothersead, Chris. Director, Culpeper County Department of Development. Interview, 31 January 1990, Culpeper, Virginia.

Myers, Steven C. NPS ranger, Manassas National Battlefield Park. Interview, 26 November 1989, Manassas, Virginia.

Nagel, Stephen v. B. Assistant general counsel, National Trust for Historic Preservation. Telephone interview, 30 April 1992.

Pohanka, Brian. Editor, *Time-Life* Civil War series. Interview, 30 January 1990, Fairfax, Virginia.

Powell, Walter. Executive director, Gettysburg Battlefield Preservation Association. Interview, 25 January 1990, Gettysburg, Pennsylvania.

Rambur, Richard. NPS superintendent, Antietam National Battlefield.

Interview by Georgie Boge, 25 January 1990, and by Margie Boge, 9 March 1992, Sharpsburg, Maryland.

Robertson, Steve. NPS ranger, Harpers Ferry National Historical Park. Interview, 28 May 1990, Harpers Ferry, West Virginia.

Roulette, Richard. County commissioner, Washington County, Maryland. Interview, 25 January 1990, Hagerstown, Maryland.

Sapp, Frank. Executive director, Adams County Economic Development Corporation. Interview, 25 January 1990, Gettysburg, Pennsylvania.

Schettler, Jennifer. Spokesperson, Saturn Corporation. Telephone interview by Margie Boge, 22 May 1992.

Schmoyer, Dick. Director of planning, Adams County, Pennsylvania, Office of Planning and Development. Interview, 25 January 1990, Gettysburg, Pennsylvania.

Snyder, Annie. SBC. Interview, 30 January 1990, Gainesville, Virginia.

Stokes, Harry. President, Gettysburg Borough Council. Interview, 25 January 1990, Gettysburg, Pennsylvania.

Townsend, Jan. Project director of the Civil War Sites Advisory Commission study, U.S. Department of Interior. Telephone interview, 22 April 1992.

Travers, Jean. Department of Preservation Assistance, NPS. Telephone interview, 1 March 1990.

Walker, Robert. U.S. Department of the Interior. Telephone interview, 28 October 1992.

Wenzel, Ed. CBA. Interview, 30 January 1990, Fairfax, Virginia.

Acknowledgments

This book, a revised senior thesis, would not have been possible without the able assistance and critical comments of a number of individuals and organizations. First and foremost, we wish to express our deepest gratitude to James McPherson, Edwards Professor of History at Princeton University, who has taught all his History 376 students that "the Civil War is the central event in the American historical conscience." For this reason alone, its memory needs to be preserved. Without his enlightened scholarship and inspiration this project would never have materialized. A very special thanks goes also to the faculty and staff of the Woodrow Wilson School of Public and International Affairs for their encouragement, suggestions, and adherence to the idea that students can create public policy.

It is a pleasure to acknowledge the numerous individuals associated with nonprofit organizations committed to battlefield preservation. These exceptional people redirected and updated this manuscript by offering sound advice and endless research material: A. Wilson Greene, Katherine Fishback, and Mark Stephens of the Association for the Preservation of Civil War Sites; Thomas Clemens of the Save Historic Antietam Foundation; Clark "Bud" Hall of the Save Brandy Station Foundation; Frances Kennedy of the Conservation Fund; Robert Dennis, Peggy Maio, and Art Lawson (now in private practice) of the Piedmont Environmental Council; Tom Lewis and Kris Sanders of the Cedar Creek Battlefield Foundation; and Walter Powell of the Gettysburg Battlefield Preservation Association. In addition, we would like to thank the following individuals for providing indispensable research material: Susan Barger of the Marshall-Wythe School of Law at the College of William and Mary, Debra Benton of the Civil War Trust, John Harris of *The Washington Post*, and Steve Thompson of the Illinois Historic Preservation Agency.

We benefited greatly from assistance granted by the many dedicated members of the National Park Service. Aside from offering highly informative battlefield tours and invaluable data, they tirelessly demonstrated their belief in the NPS motto "To preserve and protect": Dennis Frye, chief historian, Harpers Ferry National Historical Park; Richard Rambur, superintendent, Antietam National Battlefield; Robert Krick, chief historian, Fredericksburg-Spotsylvania National Military Park; Ken Apschnikat, superintendent, Manassas National Battlefield Park; John Andrews, visitor center supervisor, Gettysburg National Military Park; Jim Burgess, ranger, Manassas National Battlefield Park; Daniel Brown, superintendent, Chickamauga and Chattanooga National Military Park; Robert Davidson, assistant superintendent, Gettysburg National Military Park; Steven C. Myers, ranger, Manassas National Battlefield Park; Steve Robertson, ranger, Harpers Ferry National Historical Park; James Ogden III, historian, Chickamauga and Chattanooga National Military Park; Dennis Kelly, historian, Kennesaw Mountain National Battlefield; Jean Travers, Department of Preservation Assistance, National Park Service; Maureen Foster, historian, and Marilyn Nickles, staff director, American Battlefield Protection Program; and Jan Townsend, project manager, Civil War Sites Advisory Commission staff.

More than one hundred public servants at all levels of government provided invaluable contributions to this undertaking. Most notably, we would like to thank Senator Dale Bumpers (D-AR); Senator James Jeffords (R-VT); Congressman Michael Andrews (D-TX); Robert D. Bush, executive director, President's Advisory Council on Historic Preservation; Peter Caldwell, Office of U.S. Senator James Jeffords; Howard Coffin, press secretary to James Jeffords; Virginia State Senator Charles Colgan (D-Prince William County); Elizabeth David, heritage resource branch, Office of Comprehensive Planning, Fairfax County, Virginia; Erik Nelson, Office of Planning and Community Development, Fredericksburg, Virginia; Harry Stokes, president, Gettysburg Borough Council; and Stefan v. B. Nagel, assistant general counsel, National Trust for Historic Preservation.

We are especially indebted to those reviewers who painstakingly saw this project through to its fruition: H. Bryan Mitchell, deputy director and deputy state historic preservation officer, Virginia Department of Historic Resources, and Bruce Craig, cultural resources coordinator, National Parks and Conservation Association.

Special recognition and gratitude must be given to Tersh Boasberg for his leadership in the field of preservation law as well as for his helpful doses of reality; to Annie Snyder, the archetypal preservationist whose disquieting observations on endangered parks, battlefields, and wilderness areas make us all want to fight for "the soul of America"; to Brian Pohanka, whose writings on the Civil War strike a visceral chord to a moving legacy; to Ed Wenzel, whose grassroots approach to battlefield preservation set a standard to be emulated; and to Til Hazel, who taught us to challenge every assertion, to distinguish between fact and hyperbole, and to always stand by your beliefs.

We also wish to provide well-deserved recognition to Edwin Bearss, chief historian, National Park Service, and to Peter Iris-Williams, NPS mid-Atlantic regional office, who offered sound advice and useful suggestions after reading every word of the manuscript.

We owe a great deal of credit to our editors Deborah Estes and Joe Ingram, who waited patiently for the final draft and who perhaps have learned that students are not always terribly responsive to deadlines. Their faith in this project is deeply appreciated.

And finally, we wish to extend a special thanks to Honie Boge for her skilled typing of nearly illegible drafts; to Georgie's roommates at Oxford and Princeton for their patience, support, and diversions; to Tom Barron for his encouragement; and to our dear friend Marsha Adler, who was always there in a moment of need. Her loyalty will not be forgotten.

Generous funding for the initial stages of this project was provided by the Princeton University Class of 1934 Special Assistance Fund, the Fred Fox Class of 1939 Fund, the Jerry Horton 1942 Fund, the Dean of the College Roundtable Fund, and the Woodrow Wilson School of Public and International Affairs William DuBose Sheldon Memorial Prize Scholarship.

Index

Project Director and Head of Publications, NMAI:
   Terence Winch
Photo and Research Editor, NMAI: Lou Stancari
Editor, NMAI: Cheryl Wilson
Executive Editor, Abbeville: Nancy Grubb
Designer, Abbeville: Molly Shields
Production Editor, Abbeville: Meredith Wolf Schizer
Production Manager, Abbeville: Lou Bilka

For information about the National Museum of the American
Indian, visit the NMAI Website at www.si.edu/nmai.

Thanks to Citizen Potawatomi Nation Website
(www.potawatomi.org) for information about the Potawatomi.

PHOTOGRAPHY CREDITS
Courtesy Tom and Doug Coffin: p. 31 top left; Pam Dewey:
p. 28 top; David Heald: p. 28 bottom and p. 30 left; Janine
Sarna Jones: p. 30 top right; Fred R. Meyer: p. 29 bottom;
Courtesy Marty Kreipe de Montaño: p. 31 top right.

First edition
10 9 8 7 6 5 4 3 2 1

Library of Congress Cataloging-in-Publication Data
De Montaño, Marty Kreipe
   Coyote in love with a star : tales of the people / story by
Marty Kreipe de Montaño ; illustrations by Tom Coffin. — 1st ed.
      p.   cm.
   "National Museum of the American Indian, Smithsonian
Institution, Washington, D.C. and New York."
   ISBN 0-7892-0162-3
   1. Potawatomi Indians—Folklore. 2. Coyote (Legendary
character)—Legends. I. Title.
E99.P8D4 1998
398.2'089'973—DC21   98-5313

The National Museum of the American Indian, Smithsonian Institution, is dedicated to working in collaboration with the indigenous peoples of the Americas to protect and foster Native cultures throughout the Western Hemisphere. The museum's publishing program seeks to augment awareness of Native American beliefs and lifeways, and to educate the public about the history and significance of Native cultures.

The museum's George Gustav Heye Center in Manhattan opened in 1994; its Cultural Resources Center opens in Suitland, Maryland, in 1998; in 2002, the museum will open its primary facility on the National Mall in Washington.